ADVANCE PRAISE FOR **Shut Up and Listen**

"Voice is the offspring of vision. If the ability to speak isn't fully cultivated, then human capacity to dream envelops into the unexpressed nightmare. If heaven is to express, then we have condemned a generation of American youth to hell…harness the voice of a child and you feel the world of the oppression of itself. Now, *Shut Up and Listen*."

—LeAlan Jones,
Youth Advocate, Writer, and Author of
Our America: Life on the Southside of Chicago (1997)

"If our educators and our politicians truly want to stop the so called 'achievement gap,' they need to understand what Christopher Knaus articulates in this book—that all of us 'educators' must truly shut up and listen to our youth, to their pain, to their truth, to their experience, to what they need in order to make school meaningful. His message here is real, raw, and needed. Knaus moves beyond the safety of theoretical discussion to model what relevant education looks like, and how it can empower our students to be critical, creative, constructive thinkers who will have the tools to make democracy work, and who will be able to live peacefully and respectfully in a very diverse, multicultural, multilingual world. Everyone who works with urban youth should read this book to be reminded that all of us must be held accountable for the welfare of our young people—from the classroom teacher to the counselor, principal, janitor, and school nurse."

—Deborah Cochrane,
Director, Portland Teacher's Program

Shut Up and Listen

Rochelle Brock and Richard Greggory Johnson III
Executive Editors

Vol. 7

The Black Studies and Critical Thinking series
is part of the Peter Lang Education list.
Every volume is peer reviewed and meets
the highest quality standards for content and production.

PETER LANG
New York • Washington, D.C./Baltimore • Bern
Frankfurt • Berlin • Brussels • Vienna • Oxford

Christopher Knaus

Shut Up and Listen

Teaching Writing that Counts in Urban Schools

PETER LANG
New York • Washington, D.C./Baltimore • Bern
Frankfurt • Berlin • Brussels • Vienna • Oxford

Library of Congress Cataloging-in-Publication Data

Knaus, Christopher Bodenheimer.
Shut up and listen: teaching writing that counts in urban schools /
Chris Knaus.
p. cm. — (Black studies and critical thinking; v. 7)
Includes bibliographical references and index.
1. Education, Urban—United States. 2. Urban schools—United States.
3. English language—Composition and exercises—Study and teaching—
United States. 4. Teachers—Training of—United States.
5. Teaching—Social aspects—United States. 6. African Americans—
Education—United States. 7. Urban youth—Education—United States.
8. African American students—Social conditions.
9. Urban youth—United States—Social conditions. I. Title.
LC5119.8.K63 428.0071—dc23 2011019215
ISBN 978-1-4331-1123-5 (hardcover)
ISBN 978-1-4331-1121-1 (paperback)
ISSN 1947-5985

Bibliographic information published by **Die Deutsche Nationalbibliothek**
Die Deutsche Nationalbibliothek lists this publication in the "Deutsche
Nationalbibliografie"; detailed bibliographic data is available
on the Internet at http://dnb.d-nb.de/.

Cover design by Zoë Yi

The paper in this book meets the guidelines for permanence and durability
of the Committee on Production Guidelines for Book Longevity
of the Council of Library Resources.

29 Broadway, 18th floor, New York, NY 10006
www.peterlang.com

Printed in the United States of America

To the students
I was never able to reach

TABLE OF CONTENTS

ACKNOWLEDGMENTS

This book is the result of dozens of educators, writers, scholars, and most importantly, youth who have developed faith in their own words, helped me develop as an educator, and kept reminding me to listen. And I would never have begun to develop the courage to be myself in front of students without the guidance, support, and goofy trash-talking from the late Dr. Kipchoge Kirkland. Thanks for helping me recognize my own voice.

I am honored to include writings from Emma Crane Shaw and Rasheedah Woodard. Emma has modeled well how to move in this world as a young scholar activist, dedicated to developing voice in others. Rasheedah, since first bulldogging her way into my writing class, has modeled how to fight for what you need and never took me too seriously.

Thank you also to Victor Diaz, who allowed me free space to teach and work with students, and who modeled engaging with families. Thank you to Sara Rosell, Jordan Gonzales, Ron Williams, Pedro 'Tony' Cuevas, and a host of others who have helped me teach, help me think through how I teach, and provided examples of how to balance writing with teaching writing.

Dr. Ifoema Amah and Dr. Dimpal Jain both provided inspiration and a sounding board for my capturing of school-wide structures, and helped me think about the links to educational leadership. I was able to talk through several ideas with Dr. Howard Crumpton, who helped me turn those ideas into chapters, and who continually provides a critical sounding board for understanding why students disengage from school.

Dr. Kimberley Mayfield Lynch and Dr. Kitty Epstein have been advocating for voice-centered work at the policy level, and continually develop educators who are urban student centered. Dr. Rachelle Rogers-Ard has been a powerful colleague, friend, and mentor, always reminding me to share this work. I could not have completed this work without her support, encouragement, and affirmation. Rachelle's powerful voice demonstrates the impact of this work, and models the passion educators need to transform.

Dr. Geneva Gay served as a model for this work, and I continually use her books to guide my efforts, and her voice lingers in my head: "Push on," and "share your voice" are two of her quotes that keep me moving.

A big acknowledgment to Dr. Tyson Marsh for his reminders that its okay to piss people off in our writing, and for providing powerful critiques of the entire book. Vivian Hsieh also read the entire book, and provided invaluable, critical editing, helping to ensure relevance to classroom teachers. Thanks especially to Dr. Marcos Pizarro, a mentor and writing partner since the inception of this book, who helped frame my ideas and the way I teach.

Thank you to the Peter Lang crew for editorial assistance, formatting support, and general troubleshooting. Sophie Appel and Chris Myers, in particular, helped this book become what you hold in your hands. I'd also like to thank Zoë Yi, a 9th grade graphic artist at Oakland School for the Arts, for expressing her own voice in creating the cover design.

And especially warm gratitude to Dr. Rochelle Brock, whose work guides me, and who serves as a mentor, colleague, and solid reminder that no matter how isolated we get, we push on. Thank you, Rochelle, for your faith in my work, and for ever consistent lessons on how essential our voices are.

I particularly want to thank Tahtanerriah, who began a class with me by suggesting that we write a book. Tahty, your book is next. Malaysia Smith-Wheaton, Sinque Jackson, and Mark Willis have demonstrated determination beyond belief; after losing family members, mentors, and friends, you three have kept your writing and passionate belief that you can teach the adults who do not yet value you.

And to the many hundreds of students I have had the honor of working with, from high schools to colleges to prisons; you have taught me much more than I ever could teach you.

Particularly extra-special recognition and love goes out to Dr. Cyndy Snyder, who gave me the space to write after long hours of working my "day job," provided me with continual hot cups of tea, helped with formatting, bought me a computer when mine crashed, and patiently listened to me read sections aloud (while she finished her dissertation). Thank you for letting me prioritize students, honey. This book is as much yours as it is mine.

Despite the incredible people who have helped me deepen my thinking, clarify my philosophies and approaches, and edit these pages, this book still contains faults in writing and thought. I am fully responsible for all omissions, errors, incorrect assumptions, and any ill-conceived ideas put forth in these pages.

FOREWORD

Shut Up and Listen makes a compelling case for the therapeutic and liberatory capabilities of writing for students in trauma. It focuses more on these attributes than the more conventional views of writing as an essential part of literacy. Undoubtedly, the students who are led to and facilitated through writing learn valuable technical skills in the process but this is not the primary concern of the author. Instead, he encourages students of color who are victims of racism, poverty, and violence to write about their experience to recovery, to heal, to transcend the atrocities foisted upon them by vicious families, friends, schools, and societies. Thus, writing is presented as a means to achieve psycho-emotional well-being and personal empowerment. The specific medium for the delivery of these messages is what Knaus calls "voice-centered" teaching in which African American and Latino American high school students in urban schools speak their experiences with racism, violence, and poverty in writing.

Chris Knaus is not the first author to give credence to the importance of voice in teaching underachieving, marginalized students. But, he does so in ways that are unusual and exceptional for three important reasons. First, he provides detailed and operational descriptions of voice. In other words, he explains what it means in behavioral terms, thus moving voice from the realm of theoretical and analogical abstractions into the arena of instructional action. Other scholars who write about voice tend to be vague and somewhat illusive in defining the concept. They speak about the importance of activating and accessing the voice of silenced individuals, groups, and communities without clearly articulating what it is, or how it can be actually cultivated and facilitated in classroom instruction. Knaus also shifts the center of the discussion of voice from it being a goal or a precursor of academic engagement. As a fundamental feature of personal understanding and emancipation, voice is a precondition for the academic participation of the students profiled in this volume. Even more so, it becomes a lifeline for many of the individuals introduced, most of whom are challenged students, disenchanted with schools, with poor records of attendance and academic performance. Yet, the same students are highly motivated achievers in the voice-centered writing classes taught by Knaus. These explanations of what voice means conceptually and operationally, and its redemptive effects on students make this book a much-needed and valuable contribution to the scholarship on making education more relevant for marginalized students of color.

A second feature of the discussion on voice that makes it exceptional is the author sharing his own story about how he came into his own voice after years of violence and poverty. This is a bold and courageous step, especially since it defies many conventions of educational scholarship. While narrative is growing as a respective source of knowledge and an instructional technique, few authors have been as graphic in telling their own stories as Knaus. There are no holds barred; nor any attempts to soften the ugliness and intensity of the physical, emotional, psychological, and educational abuse and neglect he suffered. This narrative is not presented for shock effect, or as a model of how the author successfully broke the bonds of silence for others to emulate. It demonstrates, powerfully, that voice is liberating, and it is a statement about allegiance and identity with the students, whom the author wants to help access and express their own voices. It conveys an authentic insider's perspective that convinces the reader that Knaus knows what he is talking about from personal and up-close encounters with poverty and violence at home and in school. It establishes credibility and places him within the community of students whom he writes about and whom he teaches how to survive adversities and go beyond them. The personal and professional are unified in analyses of silence and its antidote, voice. This union begins in the opening chapter with the author's personal story and continues throughout the rest of the book as various students are introduced and their struggles with trying to give form and substance to their voices are described.

A third reason why the portraits of voice in this book are exceptional is because they are not presented as panaceas for all the complex problems poor students of color encounter in homes, schools, and societies. Few of the students Knaus writes about are successful in school according to conventional standards. Nor do they automatically become good school citizens, high academic achievers, and good writers (in a technical sense) as a result of the voice-centered interventions Knaus introduces. But, they are resilient survivors, they have much that needs to be said, and they develop means to speak their thoughts and feelings. Being able to finally speak clearly and cogently gives these students a sense of dignity, command over their own destiny, and a deep understanding of self that they have never known before. These accomplishments are imperative to comprehensive human developmentand are too often neglected or overlooked in the haste of schools to teach academic content and raise standardized test scores.

Knaus is unequivocal about the importance of these kinds of skills, and associated attitudes and values, and his commitment to helping abused students actualize them. He sees no need to dim their luminance by periodically reminding his readers that "academics are important, too." This distinguishes him from some other scholars who take unconventional and radical positions on educational issues, who feel that they must temper these somewhat by reminding readers that what they do not include in their advocacy is important as well. Chris feels no need to do this. While he is adamant in his advocacy of voice for African American and Latino American urban students, he is not apologetic, arbitrary, or arrogant about it. Rather, his advocacy is deeply grounded in knowledge, experience, passion and compassion, thoughtfulness, and critical reflection.

No one can READ this book without being deeply affected in some way or another, probably many and varied ways. And, rightfully so, for it is a compelling presentation of traumatized youth and the potential of genuine education to redirect the course of their lives. Some readers will resonate with the poignancy of the life experiences described, while others may be repulsed by the brutality of the situations and the rawness of the language that is sometimes used. Some readers will experiences feelings of helplessness by the magnitude of the challenge of teaching students like those included here, but others will be energized by the idea of and strategies offered for voice-centered teaching. Some will see themselves or someone they know mired in oppressive situations similar to those of the students profiled, while others will know or be a teacher like Chris who demonstrates caring, compassion, conviction, and activism in helping youth in schools who need assistance the most. And, many readers will know students who have compelling feelings, thoughts, and experiences about poverty, racism, and abuse that need to be said but do not receive any opportunities and assistance in saying them; who are silenced by the mere act of oversight by educational programs and personnel if not by deliberate intent. Despite the ugliness of the brutality that is a central feature of this book, not for dramatic effect, but because it is a fact of life of the students presented, an undercurrent of hopefulness (without fantasy or naïveté) runs throughout this book. It is conveyed through the message that even the most troubled and underachieving students have potential and promise that innovative, dedicated, and competent teachers can cultivate.

In addition to offering slices of genuine life lived by many students, this book provides a wealth of examples for how many prized general educational principles are actualized in practice. These include relevance, scaffolding, critical thinking, caring, communities of practice, cooperative and collaborative learning, prior knowledge, peer coaching, high expectations, trust, and reciprocity between students and teachers. Several principles of culturally responsive teaching also are apparent throughout the scenarios of living, the interpretative commentaries, and the instructional strategies provided for students to work through their social and emotional dilemmas. Among them are using multiple means to achieve common learning outcomes, teaching students through who they are, and social experiences and cultural funds of knowledge as resources for teaching academic skills to ethnically diverse students. The author demonstrates how teachers should not be judgmental about students' lived experiences even when they are personally undesirable and unacceptable. All of these ideas and related actions are grounded in beliefs that schools need to provide opportunities and assistance for poor racial minority student to look critically and analytically at their lived experiences as symptomatic of dysfunctional families as well as larger histories and systems of economic exploitation and insidious racism. The case studies throughout this book exemplify the power of storytelling, and transparent and caring teaching, along with the importance of knowing students as a precondition for designing effective instruction for them, and empowering them through the development of their voice in written and oral forms. Therefore, voice in *Shut Up and Listen* is a means of personal liberation and political activism for oppressed and marginalized students of color. As such it is another critical, but often overlooked, dimension of school achievement.

Geneva Gay
University of Washington, Seattle

Introduction

I was fascinated by book and music stores in South Africa. The range of offerings, the shelves of books and CDs by authors and musicians from across Africa was what I had been looking for in American stores for years. But in America, with all our wealth and access to everything that exists anywhere in the world, we simply do not have much access to Black authors, and particularly not from outside our borders. With the exception of a few Black-owned bookstores, I simply could not have stumbled across *Coconut*, by Kopano Matlwa (2007) in the States. I cannot think of a more appropriate introduction to my own book about voice than a book I stumbled across 15,000 miles from home. Because people around the world talk about voice, use words like preserving, maintaining, sustaining, and developing as they sing songs in indigenous languages, and write books, even in English, that call attention to the silencing power of colonization, imperialism, racism, and schools. Listen:

> *They laugh nastily, Lord. You cannot hear it, but you can see it in their eyes. You feel the coldness of it in the air that you breathe. We are afraid, Lord, that if we think non-analytical, imprecise, unsystematic, disorderly thoughts, they will shackle us further, until our hearts are unable to beat under the heavy chains. So we dare not use our minds.*
>
> *We dare not eat with our naked fingertips, walk in generous groups, speak merrily in booming voices and laugh our mqombothi laughs. They will scold us if we dare, not with their lips, Lord, because the laws prevent them from doing so, but with their eyes. They will shout, "Stop acting black!" "Stop acting black!" is what they will shout. And we will pause, perplexed, unsure of what that means, for are we not black, Father? No, not in the malls, Lord. We may not be black in restaurants, in suburbs and in schools. Oh, how it nauseates them if we even fantasise about being black, truly black. The old rules remain and the sentiments are unchanged. We know, Lord, because those disapproving eyes scold us still; that crisp air of hatred and disgust crawls into our wide-open nostrils still. (p. 31–32)*

In this book, I take Matlwa's sentiment captured here in so few words, spread it across chapters, and try to clarify how educators can transform our schools from the silencing, oppressive places they are and into places that foster voices to capture exactly what that *air of hatred and disgust* is made of in order to overthrow it finally, permanently. While Matlwa writes about South African racial oppression, the U.S. mirrors the racial history of Apartheid South Africa. As one of my friends in South Africa clarified as we drank rooibos tea in the shadow of a huge sparkling new stadium erected by indigenous black hands for an almost exclusively White soccer fan audience in time for the 2010 World Cup, *"White people around the world are different, but our racism is the exact same, extracts the exact same toll."* This book is part of my continued attempt to add my voice to a growing list of activists dedicated to educating African American students to be themselves, to know and honor and be proud of who they are, how they are, and why they are.

> *I didn't always have a song. I was very hurt and sad as a child. I had low self-esteem, was always self-conscious, and constantly felt alone and unloved. I could barely see the point in living if it was going to be such misery. I never talked to anyone about how I felt, and that eventually led to the development of a stomach ulcer. At that point, I knew I had to find some way to express my voice. Therefore, as a young girl, I started writing songs and singing them to myself whenever I felt like my emotions would just swallow me up. They would be slow, sad songs that were just a way for me to wallow in the depths of my despair, but I kept on writing, and I kept on singing. —Regina*

Regina, a Black undergraduate student in my African American Studies writing course, had never thought of herself as a writer. She came into my college writing class with trepidation and fear; she had long since believed what her previous teachers had taught her: her voice should remain silent as she was not a good writer and not a good thinker. In our class, I intended to directly confront previous negating experiences with academics through reminding students of how racism and sexism frame education, frame what we think of as "good" writing, and frame the way we think about what counts as "knowledge." And through such a class, Regina was encouraged to remember that expression was not *her* problem, but instead was framed *by her schools and educators* as her problem. As a high school student, she was told she was too personal and too emotional in her writing. Yet as Regina began making sense of how she was silenced by schools, she began to sharpen her voice, and her writing came alive.

Several years past her collegiate graduation, she now teaches math in urban schools, trying to engage students who disengage from school for many of the same reasons she did. Regina is a warm, engaging presence in the classroom, where students circle around her, laugh, giggle, and yet still struggle through math lessons. Her classroom feels fun, and students are continually at work, often helping one another through a particularly difficult problem. And now, as the only African American teacher in a school that serves an entirely Latino, African American, and Southeast Asian student body, she is reminded that her voice-centered approach to teaching is not collaborative and not based on the standards. Not supported by her principal, who seems to see her as less effective than other teachers who often kick their African American students out of class, Regina is labeled non-collaborative. From my vantage point, however, Regina allows students to be themselves, and provides opportunities for students to talk about who they are outside of the classroom. In essence, she allows students to be themselves, and is told by other educators that she would be more effective if she structured classroom time to limit such discussion. Yet it is her very approach that results in students being more at home with her, and students reach out to her in ways they simply do not (and will not) with other teachers that focus on teaching to the standards, while ignoring issues that might be going on at home.

While Regina has relearned how to sing on the page, and has developed a capacity to capture and express her voice, full of emotion, rage, love, and the details she most strongly values, she still faces silencing pressures. Her foundation in voice and her belief in herself, are precisely what led her to teach, and have helped her build up a teaching practice that centers student experience as a way of ensuring students *can* engage in math lessons. Her approach is unique at her school, and reflects culturally responsive approaches that many of her White and Asian teacher colleagues are neither familiar with nor have been trained in. Yet her approach directly reflects her commitment to exploring, developing, and expressing her own voice; as an educator, she realizes that many urban students live in violent, racist, poverty-stricken communities, and this context directly impacts capacity to engage in academics. Voice, for Regina and her students, is a means of developing a sense of self, and while not directly related to math standards, is directly related to students' capacity to be present during math (and any other) class.

This book is about students and educators like Regina, students who want to express themselves powerfully, but who are repeatedly punished throughout their educational experiences when they try to do so. While not all students end up being teachers, Regina serves as an example of what can happen when voice is fostered; as young people grow up, the more supported they are in expressing who they are, the more they can foster this in others. In this book, I focus on African American students developing voice, because these are often the students I work most closely with, and because there is an intimate historical connection between African Americans and expression of soulful, artful, culturally rooted voice that sharply captures how racism serves as a foundation for global society. This connection, I believe, is systematically and purposefully silenced in schools, and yet has paradoxically become stronger because many African American students consciously resist educational silencing through maintaining a voice that reflects cultural values and forms of expression. I am interested in the purposeful sharpening of such voice, and argue that schools should specifically focus on developing culturally rooted voice. A similar focus could and should be conducted with Latino, Pacific Islander, Southeast Asian, and indigenous students. My focus here, however, remains with Black youth because of the unique historical role of education in strongly alienating and punishing Black people who try to learn what they need in order to survive in a racist society that schools teach does not exist.

While most schools in the United States result in the systemic silencing of students who do not fit mainstream notions, not all students remain silent, and not all educators silence all students. Indeed, in many urban schools, developing culturally rooted voice has been an increasing focus for the past few decades, and many urban high schools have poetry classes or spoken-word programs that center conversations about how to express oneself in culturally affirming, critical ways. While there are often unspoken shared teaching tenets that many urban poetry-focused educators share, perhaps the most important is that reinventing the wheel is exactly what developing voice is all about. Students must come to develop their voice on their own, and as educators, our responsibility is to create the conditions through which voice can thrive; be critiqued, edited, and refined; and ultimately reflect exactly what each student lives, sees, feels, and knows.

This book is an attempt to clarify the ways I center student voice, partially because there are few examples of White educators who use student-centered, race-conscious approaches that directly center cultural expression, rather than, for example, centering on their own whiteness. Yet I am able to develop student voice because I do a tremendous amount of work preparing myself to listen to my students, working through my own internalized oppression and my internalized privilege that promotes arrogance and ignorance. If White educators are to be successful in teaching African American students in ways that arm students to resist the continued racism perpetuated in every aspect of society and schools, then efforts have to remain in deeply rooted understandings of race, racism, and African American expression. In short, White educators have to continually engage in self-critical analysis of the impact of racism on people of color and ourselves; this cannot be done in isolation from African American colleagues, communities, or sharp, critical, antiracist Black voices. That means additional work must be undertaken to prepare and sustain White educators for effective teaching of any students of color, and in particular, African American students, because educator preparation programs do not prepare educators to recognize racism, much less to counteract how these forces shape us.

Why Voice?

The purpose of this book is to clarify how I work with urban African American students to develop voice. I believe firmly that democracy is based upon the critical expression of those most oppressed in a society. Particularly at a time when the United States is led by the first African American president, when many school teachers remind Black students that anyone can now be president, and when many mainstream corporate media outlets declare that President Obama's election somehow ushered in an end to racism. As President Obama leads the charge for a nationally aligned educational structure wherein children in Ohio and Alaska and California and Mississippi are tested on the same core curriculum, the U.S. further embraces a one-size-fits-all educational approach. This national school system is structured upon standards-based curricula developed by corporations and sold to school districts across the country.

As celebrations of the first Black president recede, educators are increasingly held accountable to test score increases (at the threat of job loss), and schools continue to silence students who speak multiple languages. We live in a world of schools that are increasingly standardized, where the rule is the more easily measured, the more it guides curriculum and teaching practices. This fetish with numbers, with statistics that claim to measure academic success and intelligence directly correlates with a collective unwillingness to listen to student voices, which most often challenge these numbers and statistics. As the focus on alignment to standards increases, so too does the drop-out rate for African Americans, Latinos, Native Americans, and Pacific Islander students. The realities behind dropout numbers are scary: nationally 50% of urban students do not graduate (Stillwell, 2010). These are not coincidences; the more irrelevant, scripted, and standardized the curricula are, the more students of color will choose to not learn the material their teachers are being held accountable for. This is because urban students have more pressing concerns to contend with, such as navigating poverty, violence, drug use, and high unemployment rates.

In this context, with a nation obsessed with measuring irrelevance and assessing meaningless statistics on knowledge of trivial information and test-taking skill sets, poverty continues to increase in African American communities. The focus on standards and assessment completely avoids the reality that students of color do not live in the same world as many of their teachers, and certainly not the same world as the policy makers who shape the purpose of school. In today's world, students communicate in milliseconds on hand-held devices yet still go home to empty refrigerators. Students do not e-mail or type on keyboards, they text on phones the size of a small calculator, record videos of police brutality and gang rapes, and know exactly when an on-campus fistfight is about to begin. Students use the Internet for video games and porn while their parents Google Yelp ratings, Facebook third grade friends, and search for 80's videos on YouTube. This is what our world looks like, and this is the world our schools ignore.

In such a world, a focus on developing voice, on ensuring that students are critical, aware of themselves, their cultural context, the historical and continued oppression of people just like themselves, is more needed than ever. If our schools do not begin to develop voice, do not begin to arm students with tools to navigate the society they live in, we will continue to live in a country that imprisons African American and Latino men at offensive rates. And while arguments have been made that the purpose of education is to expand a low-wage labor pool, the rates of poverty amongst communities of color reveal obvious racism. Impoverished communities, teaching irrelevant curriculum, will continue to push students away, and many of those students, with few options to challenge poverty, will resort to violence.

Mike, a 56-year-old African American man I met through letters while volunteering for a prison abolitionist group called Critical Resistance, captured the potential and need of voice. "I'm in prison for life. If I don't develop a way to let out my feelings, they'll sit inside me for decades like cancer. And that shit is exactly what got me in prison in the first place." Mike asked me to co-facilitate a writing workshop at the prison in northern California where he has been incarcerated for the past twenty years. He recruited a dozen young Black and Latino men who had been convicted of violent felonies, and had anywhere between two and five years left in prison. Many were incarcerated when they were 18, and most could not read and write more than a paragraph-long letter. All were angry, and when we went around the barren institutional room, all clarified that they had no way to express anger other than weights and fists. After our first session, Mike told me why he had wanted to teach writing: "I was these kids 36 years ago—lots of energy and rage. And no one sat me down, gave me a gift of writing, showed me how to spell out why I was so upset." Over the course of a month, we taught these young men how to write why they were so angry, and at the end, many of these thick, burly, scar-encrusted men were in tears; they were afraid they would not be able to continue this work. One of the men came up to me afterwards and gave me a note they had all signed. The last line was, "We promise we will keep writing to let the anger out on paper not people."

This, for me, is the point of schools, not prisons. While education may not directly transform the economic reliance upon cheap labor (that will take societal transformation), schools can teach students the capacity to express themselves creatively in ways that release the anger and frustration that racism, sexism, violence, and oppression cause. If students were taught to address the racism they face rather than told they cannot write because they do not write standardized English the way they envision wealthy White people talking, then they might remain in school, oriented towards society, rather than against it. Developing a populace with a healthy capacity for social critique, and with a diminished chance to end up in prison; is this not a purpose of schooling in a democratic society? And the process of developing voice helps students begin to think about who they are and what they have to say; this is personally useful, but it is also an academic imperative. Students who do not see themselves in the curriculum, who read histories from the perspectives of the colonizers, who are told to take their emotion and voice out of their writing and talking and thinking do not typically engage. And despite that we blame them and label them "at risk" and "drop outs," (and sometimes "lazy"), these students are making concrete decisions that demonstrate their capacity to survive despite racist schooling.

Developing voice is a complicated notion; the very words I use are steeped in the oppressive histories of the English language. So while I use terms like "developing" "nurturing" and "clarifying" voice, I recognize these terms reflect imperialistic meaning. When talking about developing student voice, I do not imply that urban students need developing in the same vein that third world countries are forced to "develop" in order to be more "civilized" according to countries that define themselves as already developed. All people need to continually develop voice precisely because we are taught to not be multilingual in our writing, to not be multicultural, to not be overly emotional. Developing voice, as I use in this book, refers to the continual commitment to conveying cultures, languages, and experiences through multiple perspectives, to a wide range of listeners. And this process requires recognition that many of our words reflect colonial histories of oppression; the process of developing voice entails also creating new words to more adequately reflect the experiences of being oppressed.

Aside from the usefulness of developing such voice in helping students navigate their immediate survival, developing and writing with voice is also academically vibrant, rich. The work of developing voice offers a unique opportunity to measure the impact of student-centered approaches, but sounds the alarm: if educators do not document increased student engagement (through such indicators as attendance and graduation rates, grades, writing sophistication and clarity, greater social involvement, and other local generated measurements) then the focus on voice will not be allowed. The focus on voice in schools cannot happen separate from efforts to measure the impact. Thus, the need for documenting student growth in meaningful, accessible ways is ever more important.

The role of education and the purpose of schools in a democracy should be to prepare students to navigate personal and structural levels of oppression; in many ways, this happens in graduate school. But such navigation should be an outcome of public K–12 education. This purpose requires developing voice, and developing voice requires making sense of the oppression we each live. Teaching for voice provides a forum for students to think about who they are, and then examine how they fit within larger oppressive conditions. This provides a foundation for students to examine the strategies they take to ensure they are mentally, physically, and emotionally okay. Expressing such experiences and survival strategies, in clear, coherent artistically creative ways then allows for the creation of public, voice-filled forums to engage a range of parents, families, and community members in the academic work of students. And when students begin to express such voice in public, they often begin to see themselves for the first time. Such forums also allow students to be seen, by communities and educators, who can then respond to student effort. This process is what I loosely consider developing and expressing voice, and while this book clarifies the process, the focus on voice comes directly out of my childhood.

Why I Needed Voice

As I grew up, I was silenced, from fatherly beatings, to teachers' chastising my responses, to low grades for any attempt at creativity in writing. I was told to shut up and was threatened by my father, my teachers, social workers, soccer and baseball coaches, my principal, police officers, and my probation officers. I lived in poverty, spent hours of humility in welfare lines and owned no pants without holes in the knees for much of my life. These experiences are not unique and like the rare few who navigate poverty through to college, I carried the shame I developed as a child with me. I am not the only writer who received a C- in creative writing class during college, nor do I believe I am unique in having professors tell me in no uncertain terms that I was not a writer. One writing professor directly challenged me, behind the closed door of her office: "Are you retarded? Or do you just not know how to write?" Another professor, years later in graduate school, asked me to close the office door behind me, and as I nervously settled into his chair, he leaned towards me and told me, "You need to get help with your writing. You write like an undergrad." I didn't challenge these professors, and internalized the messages they were sending: I was clearly not a good writer, and my voice, I thought, was rightfully timid, soft, and irrelevant. Most interactions with dismissive adults increased my self-doubt, and ultimately, my rage.

Despite low grades, obviously worded cautions that I have no business writing, and despite no encouragement to write at all, I kept writing, kept trying to get better at writing. I wrote furiously into journals that my father would burn with the trash. As the pages slowly disintegrated into their fiery deaths, I would silently seethe, knowing that keeping the words became a luxury I might never have. The process of writing became the point for me at an early age. I often wrote about my experiences, the poverty and violence that shaped me, and the continual silencing from my teachers. What I wrote was almost always angry, almost always captured the rage I felt, and almost always helped me feel better afterwards. As the blood would pool in my fingertips, I would scribble words of hate onto pages I never showed anyone, and I firmly believe that I survived because I wrote. Otherwise, where would that rage, hurt, pain have gone? All of this silencing is what directly led me to writing and eventually, teaching, and specifically forced me to think of teaching as something that had to extend beyond the strict White confines of traditional public classrooms in order to soften the rage that was a direct outcome of being a poor child in the U.S.

Re-envisioning Critical Race Theory

Rather than provide an overview of critical race theory that begins by listing its key assumptions or tenets, I argue that the most effective use of theory is simply to use it. Theorists and academics too often argue and clarify theory instead of doing the work and having our efforts justify the roles we play as educators. Critical race theory, while touted as "of the people" is framed in exclusive conferences by elite academics who speak in monotone voices. Many academics proselytize about the permanence of racialized exclusion under a hegemonic worldview that shapes schooling into a comprehensive self-perpetuating oppressive system. While I do not disagree, the Black and Latino high school students I work with have no idea what that previous sentence means. They do know, however, that racism sucks. While they may not be familiar with the policy context of White liberalism that continues to limit their educational opportunity while proclaiming equity, they do know exactly how racism shapes their daily lives.

While the arrest of Professor Henry Louis Gates, renowned Harvard African American Studies scholar, who was arrested for breaking into his own home, might shock many academics (including Dr. Gates), his arrest is so normal for the urban Black students I work with that they laugh at how meaningless it was. One student at a high school I worked at during the time joked after I presented an overview of the case: "No bullets were fired and no Black man was killed? What the hell are people upset about? Racism?" His point is that racism happens all the time in his neighborhood, and results in young people like Oscar Grant being killed by a police officer. While academics like Professor Gates may have an impressive theoretical understanding of how racism shapes policies in the U.S., what is often missing in theoretical academic conversations are the day-to-day details of racism that urban students of color intimately understand.

While my work is based in critical race theory, I am not a theoretician—we have enough of those. Instead, I am in classrooms, listening. I hang out with urban children, ask them how their day has been. I work with students 10 years after they leave my classrooms. I talk with homeless people on streets across this planet. This is what informs what I do in classrooms and how I approach my own teaching. Don't get me wrong; theory can be exciting, can be liberating for someone entrenched in academia. But for everyday people on the street, theory is a privilege and luxury, an academic exercise, irrelevant, elite, highbrow, colonial, and imperial. As one homeless Vietnam Vet, Robert, whom I have come to know argues, "all dat theory and I still aint got no home." Theory does not feed Robert, and while I agree with critical race theory's foundational claim that "racism is normal, not aberrant in American society" (Delgado, 1995, p. xvi), I have to translate that to my own definition when I talk with "normal" people. I tell urban students that racism is everywhere and all the time, but the reality is that most "normal" people do not need critical race theory or any theory to know this because their experiences show how prevalent racism is already.

If we care enough about low-income people of color to alter the way we live in this world, the way we see ourselves and each other, then we have to be informed by something other than traditional mainstream academic theory or even the revolutionary theories that respond to the status quo. If we want to stop our hierarchical framing of every university and school district and most schools (which teach students that someone should have more power than someone else, and that voices at "the top" are always more important than the voices of custodians), if we want all this to change, then we have to listen to those who are not promoting this hierarchy of oppression. If we want this world to change, then we have to share our voices, not just our thoughts but why we think as we do, the literal experiences that have shaped our reactions to oppression. But we also have to promote other voices, those not privileged enough to publish books, articles, poems, films, or blogs. And if we want to understand oppression, then all of us have to listen to sharp, critical, enlightening, and even the sometimes difficult-to-hear voices. This means having the patience to hear voice that challenges the mainstream ideology of the U.S., and that comes forth in storytelling formats, in non-linear ways that challenge White and Western superiority of thought.

Overview of the Book

The purpose of this book is to demonstrate the power of developing urban youth voice through writing courses and school-wide structures that reflect urban student realities. The book provides guidelines and frameworks for teachers interested in centering student voice as a way of shifting to culturally responsive teaching and curricula that reflect an urban student context. In addition, this book is for new teachers wrestling with the academic and social needs of urban students. While developing student voice increases academic engagement, writing capacity, and youth empowerment, the real reason I focus on voice is to help urban students become how they want to be.

In Chapter One, I demonstrate my voice, clarifying how the processes that silenced me helped develop a knowledge base that colleges and universities do not address. This foundation of living in intense violence and poverty eventually, once I was able to build self-confidence, allowed me to connect with African American urban youth who live very differently than I. As I began to write and express myself aloud, I realized that different forms of silencing and pain impacts poor children in similar ways. And the processes for overcoming silencing, violence, abuse, racism, and poverty require a staunch commitment to listen and respond to students. Chapter One captures concrete stories that shaped me, and offers explicit demonstration of what voice is, how I developed mine, and highlights what educators could have done to teach me.

In Chapter Two, I define voice and clarify the role of developing voice in ensuring a society operates democratically. I provide an overview of what I mean by voice, and how the process of developing voice helps students learn to be themselves, to build up pride in expressing themselves powerfully. I clarify how U.S. schools have intentionally silenced African American voice, both throughout history and in schools today. I conclude by framing a process of developing voice, through centering urban student experience in classrooms designed to engage students of color.

In Chapter Three, I outline classroom-based strategies to engage urban African American youth. I demonstrate how I structure classrooms, how I get to know students, and model how classroom dynamics can facilitate students getting to know their teachers. I argue that students should be framed as living reporters, as young people who can capture their reality more powerfully than can anyone who does not live in their communities. I demonstrate how I center racism in everything I teach, and show how editing helps students negotiate the silencing influences they have been forced to learn. I conclude by discussing the role of expression in completing the cycle of developing voice, and provide student writings and sample assignments throughout the chapter.

In Chapter Four, I center personal trauma, and add the strong caveat that in order to expect African American students to be vulnerable in classrooms, educators have to frame safety in clear, coherent ways to encourage students to develop and express voice. This chapter centers on developing trust and modeling how to be okay in the midst of intense trauma, approaches that educators are not trained in and can be punished for. In addition to addressing how students are often punished for sharing trauma that impacts their capacity to engage in school, I provide basic classroom management techniques to identify and respond to student needs.

Chapter Five concludes the book by clarifying school structures that integrate voice-centered work into the curriculum. I provide examples of how to transform parent, family, and community involvement into an inclusive, real-world feedback loop centered in public forums for expressing voice, wherein students share their work with a larger public as part of the function of school. I show how voice-centered work directly informs youth participatory action research, and guides student-led professional development opportunities for schools and districts. All of this work depends on school leadership structures that validate voice, that provide space for students to be themselves and to express themselves publically. This demands school-wide educator buy-in. This chapter provides a framework for developing such buy-in through student-led efforts.

A Note on Research, Names, and Schools

This book is based on a compilation of interrelated research studies, courses at multiple schools, interviews with students and educators, and author reflections. I pull from my personal journals, observation notes, and in-class writings conducted during my classroom teaching; most of the details from stories are taken directly from these sources. While the majority of quotations are word-for-word, several student quotes are based on notes I took immediately after talking with the student. I often spent twenty minutes or more in my car after class, jotting down notes about conversations and off-hand comments that occurred outside the classroom. These quotes are my attempts to capture the essence of the conversation, including the tone and diction, but because I did not audio-record anything, quotations that are based outside the classroom are not word for word.

While examples and stories are based on my teaching at seven high schools, UC Berkeley, several jails and prisons, and a juvenile facility, the vast majority of this work is based on courses taught at three high schools in California's bay area.[1] Additional context, insight, and examples come from interviews with teachers, high school students, counselors, social workers, school leaders, and parents at these schools in 2004–2009. All names of schools and educators have been changed to protect the anonymity of specific schools, students, and educators. The vast majority of students chose pseudonyms and all gave full permission to include their work. Slight details have been altered to further protect the individuals whom I consulted throughout my studies. I solicited extended writings from several student-educators who had been exposed to multiple levels of my teaching; their work is listed clearly as their own.

These urban students, African American, multiracial, and Latino, paint an overwhelmingly negative portrayal of schools. Their world is a painful struggle of racism, violence, abuse, and oppression dynamically exacerbated by schools. Yet these students have also convinced me that our only hope in transforming society rests with getting educators, policy makers, professors, and the so-called "experts" that shape our schools, almost all of whose knowledge base is rooted in elite universities that sharply limit access to urban students of color, to shut up and listen.

CHAPTER 1

Breaking with Silence

Dulled by school

I relearned to speak

tasted my strength

My voice shatters chains broken...

—Taisha

My first memory is of my father sitting down. He's holding a large wrench, facing the toilet, legs straddling the porcelain, feet flat up against the back wall. I was very little; probably two years old, one of the rare memories of the short time my parents lived together. My older sister and brother were nowhere to be found and my little sister might not have been born yet. I do not remember what house we were in, but we must have been in Fortuna, just south of Eureka, California. What I remember is this: my father was working on the toilet, his face a mixture of contorted rage and frustration. His fingers curled tightly around the red handle, matching the red of his enlarged knuckles. The head of the wrench was slightly rusted, and his lips snarled into a grimace, his brow furrowed as his gaze narrowed inside the base of the toilet. The smell of shit and piss wafted into his nostrils, forcing him to occasionally gag. After a brief cough and gag fit, his snarl returned, and he reached back around the toilet, one hand groping for the pipe; when he grasped it, the other hand instinctively closed in. The wrench fit perfectly over the oversized screw connecting the two pipes, and he expertly twisted his wrist, tightening the clamp around the pipe. Confidence built back up from the success of the wrench, my father let out a slight smile.

But something went wrong. The wrench got stuck; the pipe lurched forward, rattled against the porcelain, the torque slammed my father's right forearm against the bathtub. I still remember how much that must have hurt, still remember the indent left in the porcelain, but my father does not show pain; instead, he quickly scooted backwards as a stream of water shot upwards from the toilet bowl. The steady stream almost hit the ceiling, and then collapsed onto my defeated father. He pulled his soaked legs up, looking over at me as he rose to his feet. Our eyes met and I cringed in fear.

But I was irrelevant, his rage focused elsewhere, and he strode above and over me, headed outside, presumably to turn off the water. I sat in silence, looking at the bathroom floor, covered in two inches of water, and noticed the now-broken pipe bubbling forth more water. I remember crying; remember the wetness of my face as I stood in the doorway, mouth agape. And I remember being pushed aside as my father rushed back into the bathroom. I remember crumpling into the wall, my face smashing against the chipped paint wall. And just like that, on my back staring upwards while my tears were joined by blood from my two-year-old nose, my memory ends.

I do not know how much of my first memory is "true." I do not know why my mother is invisible in my memory or why my father pushed me face-first into the wall. My mother does not remember this happening, and I have not spoken with my father since I was in high school. With no way to validate the truth of my first memory on this planet, I have come to recognize that the reality of facts is simply irrelevant. What I remember, regardless of accuracy, is what shapes my life. And so while therapy and writing have helped me to refine my memory, inaccuracies always exist, and just as importantly, are not the point. Whether or not something happened as I remember it does not alter the reality that I am shaped by what I remember.

In the *Evidence of Things Not Seen*, James Baldwin (1985a) clarified a similar point. He argued that we do not commit to memory many experiences that horribly impact us. Yet it is precisely what we do not remember that "controls the human being" (p. xii). Even when our details are incorrect, our memories are rarely wrong. The key is that, as Baldwin argued, "my memory stammers: but my soul is a witness" (p. xiii). His point is that even if we do not remember, cannot accurately recall situations in our lives, that does not mean that they did not happen or that we are not dramatically impacted by what we cannot remember. So too are we impacted by what we do remember, accurate or not.

What we remember may be altered unconsciously by what we block out to protect ourselves when we are young. We develop memories by taking into consideration experiences that we may not be able to recall, adding in context that we may be unaware of. Our memories fill in details, remind us that while we may not be able to recall why we tremble when a particular aunt comes near us, or why we shrink in fear or sometimes snap into unprovoked rage-filled rants, we do so because somewhere, a part of us is recalling trauma. And so I no longer ask myself "did this really happen?" I no longer ask students I work with "what *really* happened." My point in all of this is to help me, help you recall what we can, to wrestle not with details, but with what we remember feeling, to understand how we have been treated in this world so that we can understand why we are how we are. The process of developing voice, for me, is about each of us coming to understand how we have become who we are, and then diving into what that means for us now, as people striving to be grown.

I share my stories not just for cathartic reasons, though expressing voice has the potential to help release the pain caused by growing up. I tell these stories so that readers understand the complexities of growing up. I tell these stories so that educators recognize how we do not value many children who struggle to live, to simply arrive at school. Growing up, I struggled with a lack of control over my life, and much of my day-to-day issues in schools were results of my attempts to gain whatever control I could, through violence, apathy, trash talking, and through drugs and alcohol. But these stories are not just mine, and my point is not to focus on how hard life was for me. Indeed, my point is that educators do not value students that live in complicated realities of struggle, where poverty, racism, violence, abuse, neglect, and the willful ignorance of all of these runs our schools. I tell my stories to demonstrate the power voice has in helping us all realize what growing up is like, and how schools must address that the silencing I lived shapes academic failure for students of color, poor students, and a host of other oppressed students.

Becoming Christopher

I was born Christopher Stephen Knaus, the third child to David Jeffrey Knaus and Andrea Jennifer Davis.[1] My father was born in Chicago, and raised in Whittier, California, by his two parents. I have no memory of his father, my paternal grandfather, who I have been told was a raging, violent, racist alcoholic. His mother, my paternal grandmother, is still alive, though I have never had a relationship with her. My mother was born in New Jersey, and raised in Downey, California, by her two parents, before they divorced. Her mother, my maternal grandmother, whom we called Oma growing up, fled Nazi Germany with her family, and eventually became a social worker in Watts. In part because of the state-enforced trauma she experienced as a Jewish child in 1930s Germany, Oma dedicated her life to children who grew up with violence and abuse. Yet despite her professional commitment to working with abused children, she was unaware or in denial of my grandfather's sexual abuse of my mother.

My mother was eager to leave the house of her abusive father. She met my father and was forced out of school after eighth grade: pregnancies were not rewarded with continued access to schools in the late sixties. Once pregnant, my parents felt they had no choice, leaving southern California to head north, eventually settling where their car broke down: Humboldt County. I was raised, along with my older sister, older brother, and younger sister, in Fortuna and Eureka, California. We were poor and that was exacerbated by my parents' divorce when I was five. Because my mother did not have enough money to raise all four children, my brother and I lived with my father, and my sisters lived with my mother. But these details only provide the geography of my family; the information social workers operate from, letting readers know how I became eligible for state aid and that according to the statistics, I should have been destined for academic failure.

While I grew up poor, White, and with abuse, these labels ignore and oversimplify the details that shape who I am. Without my voice, demographic information does not convey the depth of what I live, or how I was specifically shaped to become an educator. And yet in the standardized assessment-focused educational world, demographic information becomes linked to test scores and indicators of academic performance become the only sources of "data." Yet without voice, "data" exists outside of its context and meaning. Voice is concrete data, and lets readers know how someone lived, what they struggled through, and what is important to them, from their perspective, full of nuance, emotion, and language. When educators narrowly conceive of data, voice is discounted as "story-telling" or "anecdotal," rather than the rich accounts that demonstrate exactly what is happening in schools and to students. My insistence on voice thus benefits the youth who learn to express their world but also the educators who expand their notions of "data" to include voice. If educators want to know what is happening in schools, asking students is a start. But if educators want to transform schooling to fully engage urban students, then developing voice is the most direct way.

This chapter clarifies how the way I grew up led me to develop my voice despite my schools, which continued to treat me like the stereotype teachers believed I was. In creating my portrait, I demonstrate what voice can do, and, through capturing my experiences, lay out opportunities for growth that teachers missed, ignored, or just were not prepared or committed to address. Who I am is the summation of my experiences, and I had hundreds of "aha" moments; clear, concise memories that I can point to now as concrete examples of the racism, classism, sexism, and heterosexism I saw growing up. These memories of negative treatment sat in my mind throughout childhood and I continually searched for something to help make sense of what I was seeing all around me. I eventually learned to call these memories examples of oppression, but growing up, I was just confused.

Because of my unique (and conversely, all-too-common) school and home experiences, I have dedicated my life to transforming schools, the one public place where adults could have made sense of what I was witnessing. I tell stories to capture who I am, breaking my own silence because transparency about why educators do what we do is key to engaging urban students and communities. As such, this chapter is organized around the stereotypes I have been framed by. I begin by capturing memories of growing up poor, then share how I grew up in a context of violence and cycles of abuse. I then capture how I came to see myself as White within a racist family and racist schools. After each set of stories, I briefly highlight what educators could have done. I conclude this chapter with a focus on how I developed as an educator. Throughout, I write in a personal voice that I have continually been told is not academic, not valid, and not relevant to educators. This chapter is another small attempt to resist feedback from publishers, university colleagues, and practitioners, who tell me that "who I am is not relevant" to the work I do. But this is also my attempt to contextualize how I grew up and to demonstrate the inadequacies of my educators, who often exacerbated the complexities I barely struggled through.

Growing Up Poor—6th and 7th Grade

Growing up sucked. I was constantly reminded of what I did not have, and woke up as I went to bed: hungry, cold, tired, bitter. At home I was continually in search of food, my belly a constant aching, rumbling reminder. At school, I was embarrassed by that hunger. The only thing that seemed worse than the hunger was my fear of others knowing exactly how hungry I was. In my neighborhood, when I couldn't hide my poverty, I adopted an attitude of fierceness, despite my puny size and cozy nature. But that never made me less hungry. At home we gobbled down whatever was in the donated food bank bags, and my father's cooking consisted of burnt hamburgers, prepackaged meals, and frozen dinners. Bowls of generic yellow-boxed cereal flakes were nasty enough with water and honey drizzled on top, but I was terrified of anyone else finding out I ate those mushy flakes without milk. And no matter where I went, I could not escape my poverty; people would notice my dirty clothes, the holes in my pants, could hear my belly growl, would notice how quickly I ate, or might notice the holes in my shoes. Teachers and friends would often ask if I was cold, if I needed a coat, but I would shake my head no, deny my shivering, frail body, and tell them I was cold blooded, and always hot. Despite my vain attempts, something I could not control always gave me away.

To take my mind away from what I did not have, I'd think about ditching school to join my friends, who would be in the midst of a dirt-clod war, aiming makeshift spears at each other, or jumping stolen dirt bikes off exposed redwood tree roots. My father chopped down those giant trees during the days, worked lumber mills during the nights, and I was often left to run wild in those old growth forests. Occasionally, I'd corral other kids together and we'd slip off the junior high school campus just after lunch, diving into the wilderness that was our backyard. There no one could notice my stench because in the forest, we all smelled of fresh dirt and redwood cones.

The lingering dirt from a well-aimed dirt-clod also hid that my clothes hadn't been washed in weeks. With less fear of being found out, I would finally relax, and dive fully into our little wars, reminded of my poverty only when someone pulled out a granola bar, a piece of fruit, or a sandwich.

I loved when we were caught ditching school, because since my dad never came to school meetings to discuss my punishment, I always wound up suspended. Without the need to go to school for the day, I'd steal a bike, fly across the neighborhood, head along my favorite forest trail, catch and release a few snakes, and come home just before my brother got out of that same school. These days were my hidden gems: my dad off to work early, my brother off to school, and me alone with no homework, no teachers, no parents, no neighbors, no one to mess with me. On those days, I'd be starving, since my dad wouldn't leave any food for me at the house, but the blackberries I'd pick along the way and home run pies I stole from the local mini-mart kept the hunger at bay. I loved those forced "vacations" and while hungry, found safety in being alone.

But I never wanted to be home. Home reminded me that I smelled like dirty clothes. My dad saved on soap, used a third of a cup in an overloaded washing machine at one of three rundown Laundromats we'd go to. In the Laundromats, I'd watch my father flirt with someone's mother, while my brother and I would race circles around the folding tables, searching frantically for lost quarters and those small one-shot boxes of detergent, hoping they might have leftover crumbs of soap. I remember staring into the huge dryers, trying to identify my shorts, this shirt, or that jacket as it spiraled across the heat. School was where I tried to hide that we went to Laundromats. And I hated school for exposing that we didn't have enough soap and never any new clothes.

I hated my own smell, too. I avoided showers; afraid of potato bugs the size of my dad's big toe that would crawl up our drain. I also avoided using the toilet as much as possible—that disgusting cesspool of shit and piss my brother and I cleaned by dumping bleach all around and leaving it to magically self-clean. Later my dad, gagging on the bleach, would yell at us to clean up, and we'd wipe up with the same permanently stained towel I'd use after showers. Our trips to the Laundromat always waited until a few days past my last clean underwear, way past my last clean shirt, and since I only had two pairs of pants, well, no matter how much I showered, I was destined to stink.

I added to the problem as I avoided taking a dump until I got to school. But sometimes, they wouldn't let me out of class. Every day, I'd go to the bathroom at least once per class. I must have appeared as if I just wanted to meander the halls, but in walking I was actually trying to loosen my stools, trying to buy me time so I could go to the bathroom. I always asked if I could go, but the teachers just thought I was trying to get out of class. I don't know if I blame them; most seventh graders just didn't have bowel problems and everyone was always trying to get out of class. I asked once, but the teacher said, "No, you go every day. Go before or after class." I responded with a quiet, "but I have to go poo!" The class erupted in laughter, and the teacher giggled out: "after class," not taking me seriously. I sat through class embarrassed and hoping the pain would go away.

PE was my favorite class because I was the fastest kid in the school. I'd race around the soccer field, steal home while the pitcher was admiring his wind up, and run circles around the pebble-strewn lap. It wasn't until my bowel problem got out of control that I stopped running. Unable to shit at home and not allowed to shit at school, I occasionally could not hold it any longer, and a small Hershey's Kiss would ease out, settle into the bottom of my tighty-whities. On those days, I'd just sit in the back of the gym, hoping the teacher wouldn't notice me. He would occasionally approach me, but after seeing my legs tightened up against the wall, he'd back off, laughing aloud and shaking his head in disbelief. The other students were less merciful. They'd see me trying to hide in the locker room, the smell of fresh shit wafting across the tiny concrete and metal room. "Take a fucking shower," they'd chant, and I'd just stare at them, red-faced and deathly afraid someone would find out that I actually had shit my pants.

I was often kept awake, tossing and turning, with a belly full of pain. Hearing me ache and moan, my father would storm into the room I shared with my brother, slap me upside the head, and tell me to "be a man," because "it don't hurt that much." I knew he didn't want to take me to the emergency room or the doctor's office; we rarely had health insurance, and my dad did not want to miss out on a day's pay at work no matter how much I hurt. I knew he was embarrassed by my bowel problems, but he also had no tolerance for what he saw as my inability to endure pain. One time I broke my foot playing soccer, and when he came to pick me up after the game, the coach told him I should go to the emergency room. My dad told the coach to "fuck off" and I never was allowed to rejoin that team (nor go to the doctor's). So I learned well to hide the pain and act like I didn't hurt, even when I limped around for a month or more, even when I felt my insides ready to explode. While my broken bones often soon healed, my bowel problem did not, and led to serious health issues that impact me today. Once my mother moved me away from my father's, I began to go to the doctor's office regularly, but despite these later attempts to address my health issues, I still endure regular undiagnosed stomach pains.

Because my dad did not worry about whether or not we would eat when he was out of the house, I grew up eating sporadically, and what I ate was often just edible. This exacerbated my bowel problem. After school, I'd have a voracious appetite and an empty fridge. I'd join in the mini-throng of neighborhood kids and we'd either terrorize someone whose parents might have food in their kitchen, or we'd split into pairs and raid the local mini-marts, stuffing home run pies, ice cream bars, and anything sweet that would fit down our pants. Depending on the day, I'd have to be home early, cleaning up the house, washing dishes, sweeping the dirt from one side of the house to the other, or, if my dad had been good on bills, I could ride a stolen bike to baseball or soccer practice. But if I was lucky enough to have found food, my belly full of sugar left me almost exhausted by the end of practice. What I did look forward to were soccer games, because my teammates' parents would bring sliced oranges for us to eat during halftime. I remember well the look of shock when I would grab two handfuls, eating those thin slices as if I hadn't eaten all day (which I hadn't). Those parents and my coaches did not seem to figure out that those orange slices ensured I didn't pass out during the games.

Despite my mom threatening to report my father to the health department, our houses were always disgusting. We never had our trash collected while in our two-bedroom house off Excelsior Street, where we lived for at least two years. At first, we'd burn trash in our burn barrel out back, making everything in our house smell like burnt mold, a smell our infrequent laundry trips could do nothing about. But after a citation from the fire department, we began tossing trash bags into the room my dad had been sleeping in. He moved into the living room, and the back room became our trash room. We'd throw bags of trash into that room until it eventually overflowed with bags leaking black and green ooze. When my brother and I left our homework in the living room or kitchen, my dad would scoop them into a trash bag and toss them on the heap in the other room. Not wanting to get in more trouble for not turning in homework, I'd search through bags of leaking trash, riffling through to find my homework, pencils, and used trapper keeper folders. Several times I found my backpack squashed into a bag, my pencils broken, my folders useless. Getting new school supplies was out of the question, so when possible, I'd wipe the trash off my folders, and put them back in my torn backpack, hopeful peers at school wouldn't notice the smell or make fun of my soggy, dog-eared folders.

I also hated having to wake up at 4:30 in the frigid morning, walk the three blocks towards the newspaper drop spot with my brother, and trudge back home with our 40-pound bundles. In the moldy garage, we'd set up packing crates, plop down, and begin folding papers. Our frozen little hands would turn black from the fresh ink, but the biggest danger was rubber bands that would break when stretched too tightly, snapping at our icy fingers, stinging for hours. At school, I'd nurse those welts, struggle to stay awake in boring classes, and hope that my father would forget to wake us the next morning as we headed out in his car, tossing our folded newspapers onto porches of the nice houses that surrounded our dump-filled home. I want to remember laughing at our poverty, or the bonds I made with other poor children, but my memories of being poor are of pain, hunger, embarrassment, self-loathing, and shit.

What Educators Could Have Done

This first selection of stories intends to highlight some of the intense complications that arise when children grow up in poverty. At ten years old, I worked early mornings, had untreated bowel problems, came to school hungry, tired, and often unable to do anything but stare ahead. My attempts to control reality came in the form of doing something to keep me awake, and those things often got me into trouble. Because I was poor, I faced a constant barrage of peers making fun of me. Yet educators intentionally ignored those taunts. What they could have done, however, seemed as obvious to me then as it does now. Educators should have inquired into my family life, and once they figured out that I had a caring mother, should have talked to child protective services to remove me from my father. If adequate protection were promised to ensure my father would not come after my mother or me I would have jumped at the chance to leave him. Educators could have looked into providing public health care options for me, could have offered to take me to a health clinic, and could have offered to take me (and my brother) to a church that offered free clothes. My continued health issues are a direct result of educators ignoring me, and reflect the excuses I hear in schools today about how teachers have too much to do to care about children.

At the very least, my experiences challenge educators to reconsider punishing children for not completing homework. While certainly not every poor or violent family creates barriers to children completing homework, my father did, and teachers embarrassed me in front of the class every time I did not have my homework completed. My grades suffered because I could not turn in homework, but I was also learning less than other students who had the support to work at home. Yet these issues were beyond my control, and a teacher wouldn't have had to do much to learn that. Without making me feel like I was a problem, educators could have helped address the most obvious signs of my poverty, and could have done so for a number of children at the school so I wouldn't have felt even more isolated and targeted. My poverty and the homework barriers created by my father were probably the easiest part to address, yet were continually avoided by my teachers and principals.

Growing Up with Violence—4th through 7th Grade

By ten, I had been punched by my father, my brother, neighborhood kids, kids at school, random adults I did not know, and had been shoved around by two different teachers. I knew that violence was normal, and knew that everyone around me was, and probably should be, violent. I had seen my dad beat my mom, my brother, my older sister, other children, adults, and anyone who got in his way. He seemed to reserve most of his violence for my brother and I, who faced his punches almost every day. I had seen my mom accept his violence, and had seen others take the abuse they received (from my father or from some other adult). In short, before I had reached puberty, I was convinced that, unless I could defend myself, I would continue to be beaten, by adults and other children. I learned to try to avoid adults; there was not much I could do to avoid getting hit by them. And as one of the smallest kids in school, I realized that unless I hit other kids first, I would probably have no chance. So I learned to talk shit, to trash talk potential opponents. If they'd respond to my trash talking, I'd smash their faces in, hit them as hard as I could, and hope to stop them from being able to hit me back. And I realized early on in my life that violence was a way to get people to respect me. I grew up knowing that I was going to hurt, and probably hurt more than the other people who hit me. So if I could hide the pain of being hurt, then I would probably be okay, or at least scare others away enough to stop the punches.

Coming home was a war zone, as I navigated streets trying to avoid neighborhood kids often much older and much bigger than I. On most days, my nemesis was Mike Barkley, who lived two blocks past me. He tormented many of the kids in our neighborhood; he wasn't that much bigger, he just hit harder. One day I saw him across the street walking with a girl and started yelling at him about how his food stamp ass got beat by his father. As I took off down the street, she shrunk away from him, leaving him no other option but to chase me. He didn't catch me that time, but I had enough bloody noses from him to learn to stop agitating him. I just didn't care though, pain was already normalized in my life, and his punches didn't hurt nearly as much as my dad's. So I learned to torment him verbally, always in public, and even on the occasional days when we'd play together, I'd still embarrass him by reminding him we lived the same way. To his credit, Mike never exposed my poverty or family violence—he just hit me real hard when I did it to him.

When my dad got home, if—and this did not happen often—he was in a good mood, he'd fry up burgers, top them with slices of food bank yellow cheese, and let us polish off a half-gallon of ice milk. But normally, we'd gobble up mac'ncheese (with hotdogs!), watch our huge screen TV, and hope to avoid the unavoidable. At some point in the brief time it'd take to finish the clumpy yellow-orange noodles, my father would snap at something that, in his mind, told him that my brother or I did not fear enough. He'd reel back his thick lumberjack arms, and clock us one, without reason and without any warning, save for his quick cocked-back fist. No matter how quickly I saw that fist coming, I never could stop it. If I put my arms up, they'd be bruised. If I tried to dodge, he'd reel back again, hitting even harder this time.

"Dad, can I have paper for a report due next week?"

"Dad, can I have $12 for our field trip?"

"Dad, can you sign the school lunch forms so I can eat this quarter?"

The answer always came swift—either a slap to the side of my head, or if I was standing directly in front of him, a quick blow to my forehead or mouth. And then the inevitable: my nose would start bleeding and he'd punch me again for being a "fag." I'd end up upside down on my bed, holding my shirt to my nose, listening to my brother in the other room, erasing thoughts about homework, forms, and whatever field trip I wouldn't get to go on.

The same lack of turning in forms led to my limited capacity to play sports, despite that I kept making teams during tryouts. But tryouts were free; once a team offered me a spot, I had to either ask my dad for the league fees, or had to show proof of health insurance. I rarely could do either, and the exceptions were when my mother found the money to pay (and the coaches allowed me to keep forgetting the health forms). But even when my fees were paid, my time on sports teams was limited. I initially wanted to play baseball and football because those were the only activities Dad considered "sports," and he'd even give us rides and watch us play. But once at our games, he'd shout at the referees and umpires, trash talk to other coaches, and hit on other players' moms. But the worst was when the coach wouldn't play my brother and me. If kids missed practice during the week, they couldn't play in the weekend games. Inevitably, my father would come home late from work (usually after going out with some woman we'd never meet) and my brother and I would miss practice. If we brought it up to him, he'd punch us, so we just stayed quiet. But when we went to the game, the coaches remembered, and would bench us both. That angered my father; "Why come to the game if you wont play my sons?" The coaches would try to explain their rules, but my father had no patience, and I was kicked off of three baseball and two football teams because my dad assaulted the coaches because we missed practice.

When I realized that my father thought soccer was for "fags," I soon decided that soccer was my sport. I figured out how to get rides, found out there were low-income subsidies, and then began playing soccer exclusively. My dad came to one game, but when he got bored, he yelled at me to come out of the game so he could take me home. But he left, and another father offered to give me a ride. Embarrassed, I accepted, and this parent gave me rides the rest of the year. Eventually, I learned to swallow my pride and ask for rides, recognizing that soccer was one of my only outlets, and my father, I knew, would never again come to ruin it for me.

On the field, though, I was a mess. I would slide tackle other kids, trying to break their legs, smash their faces into the dirt, and hurt them in any way I could. I'd get red cards, and would then yell at the referees. With my dad not at the games, no one knew what to do. They had simply never seen such a violent kid on the field. Yet because I was always the fastest player, I was tolerated despite my rage. My use of soccer as an outlet continued throughout high school, as did my frustration. Every time I began to be seen as successful in soccer, a coach would ask me if I wanted to play on a traveling team or the school team. But those teams cost a lot more money, and there were no subsidies, so I always had to make up an excuse as to why I couldn't play. That just made me even more upset, and I took it out on other children's bodies.

At school, I was constantly in trouble but the red cards were replaced with detentions and suspensions. Yet I still looked forward to being at school because that meant not being at home. School meant hiding in the back of a classroom, hoping to never be called on. School meant serving as a human punching bag to one or more of the other children who expressed themselves regularly through violence. I often hung around the other poor neighborhood kids until my mouth got me into trouble. Then they'd wait patiently until the next day at school, corner me behind some lockers, and the barrage of fists would remind me of home, only some adult would occasionally stop the punches from landing. I'd spend the rest of the day in the principal's office trying to stop the heaving sobs from broadcasting how easily I cried. No one ever asked why I started fights with kids twice my size. I can't even remember being sat down and talked to about fighting, though I remember being sat down and told to be quiet.

I was always in the principal's office, constantly in trouble. I must have been there twice a week for a year, yet we never talked, and I do not remember him ever making eye contact with me. Once in his office, he'd yell at me to stop being a disturbance, and then give me a packet of worksheets for classes I was not enrolled in. When I would say anything he'd dismiss me or threaten to slap me for talking back to him. I was required to meet weekly with interchangeable school counselors "because I was angry," and my required counselors gave me articles to read; I'd later turn those into spitballs. Multiple counselors pleaded for me to calm down, but no one ever asked if I was being beat by my father. None of my educators gave me the space to talk about what I was reacting to. Instead, they gave me articles with titles like "Anger Management" and "Why Kids Fight," and chastised me when I hadn't read them. I was disciplined for living in a violent, poverty-stricken home, and was told to not react to my home life during school.

One particular incident with a teacher sticks out, a memory that helped me learn to not put faith in educators. My head felt cotton candy light as I gasped for air. I could feel his all too lengthy fingernails digging small imprints into my scrawny neck as my feet dangled beneath me, the classroom full of fearful eyes. I wanted my eyes to pierce through my lids: I wanted to see what they saw. Could they see the tears welling up? The sheer force of his fingertips held my sobs in. Were they afraid this would happen to them? Were they angry at my humiliation, dangling in front of them? Were they imagining their own bodies held limp by my seventh grade science teacher's hand? I remember desperately searching for friendly eyes, for someone to rise up and bowl over Mr. Goodwin's incredibly strong, but frail looking old body. I wanted someone to get out of their seats and save me by grabbing something, anything, and smashing it over Mr. Goodwin's shiny baldhead. But no one even blinked. He held me at eye level, fingers around my neck as my legs dangled below me, as he belted out: "Chris! You Will Never Amount To Anything, You Worthless Piece of Shit!"

I knew most teachers thought this way, but a teacher being violent with me was too much. Not surprisingly, I flunked out of seventh grade; after Mr. Goodwin's continued harassment, after the principal's total ignoring what was happening to me, I was done. That summer, I was forced to take English, Biology, and History. I failed all three, and my mouth got me into numerous fights after those short summer school days, usually taking more of a beating than I gave. One day, a friend of one of the several women my father was dating told me my dad was "an asshole," so I told him we'd fight after school. The word must have gotten around, because there was a small circle waiting for me once I got out. He was being pushed around in the circle, but they stopped when I arrived. He was much bigger than me; must have weighed 100 more pounds than I, so folks were excited to see this. I attacked him, punching him in his belly (which was about all I could reach), until he sort of flopped on top of me. I was stuck beneath his girth until the other students pulled him off of me. I hit him a few more times, and then gave up, walked away; my rage was gone. The rest of the students piled on top of him, pounded him into the ground. Cops showed up at my house that night asking me if I started the fight. I said "Hell No!" but wound up on probation anyway, without any legal proceedings, a hearing, nothing.

My mom moved me to Davis shortly after summer school ended, sensing what would happen if I remained under my dad's influence. In a new suburban context, my life dramatically shifted, and the daily violence around me faded, replaced by high school dances, egging people's houses, and peers with fears of not getting into Ivy League colleges. I don't think the teachers were better, but the violence I lived, for the most part, dissipated, and without a daily barrage of punches, I was able to start anew.

What Educators Could Have Done

These sets of stories capture several themes that relate to educators. The intensity of the violence I enacted on others should have been a warning sign and someone should have talked to me about why I fought so much. Instead, I was punished with detentions and suspensions, which I wore as a badge of pride, comparing with other "bad" kids to see who had the most. Educators formally responded to my violence by disciplining me rather than talking to me, investigating the causes of my violence, or by even talking to my father (though that would have gotten me even more beatings, but I like to imagine an educator anticipating this). Educators are legally required to contact child protective services exactly because of children like me, yet my educators seemed to purposefully ignore any sort of responsibility by denying the violence I enacted on others, and by denying the bruises I came to school with.

Many of the boys I grew up with who did exactly what I did are no longer alive, victims of violence, drug and/or alcohol related deaths. These youth were also shunned by my teachers, and like me, they made their way in the world as they could. Our teachers' inactions condoned the violence we lived through, and exacerbated the rage we were building up inside. What educators should have done is provide a space for me to admit that I was being beat, and that would have required building up trust, which would have required caring enough to reach out. Instead, I was punished repeatedly so that I never would trust any educators. I needed a counselor to spend the time with me, to check in on me throughout the day, who might even occasionally visit home to see how I was doing with my father. I needed someone to talk to about the violence I faced from teachers and other adults. Instead, the only counselors that responded tried to solve my problems through useless articles and brochures. Yet teachers could have created the space; it would have taken time, but it would have meant that I had someone to trust. In order to engage in school, I needed someone to care. And throughout my entire K–12 experience, no teacher cared enough to talk to me about violence or the many obvious signs of my physical abuse.

Extending Trauma—10th Grade

I joined my two sisters in Davis, and began eighth grade. While my brother was still living with my father in Eureka, my life took on new meaning. I was immersed in a world of wealth, but kept firmly outside the door. Everyone around me had two cars, two story houses, two parents and a seemingly endless supply of new, brand-named clothes. Everyone seemed happy; I didn't see parents beating their children, and there were no longer neighborhood threats that I had to escape on my way home. I continued playing soccer, continued my violent ways on the field, but did not have to fight my way out of my own house anymore. Free from having to continually look over my shoulder, I allowed myself to breathe, and in my first few years in Davis, only had a couple of pushing matches with kids in school. Outside of that, all I had to face was other students calling me "gay" or a "fag" or avoiding me because I was clearly not rich or popular. But that was tolerable, and with no teachers threatening me with suspensions, I soon realized that I could talk trash as I had always done, but did not need to worry about repercussions because most teachers just ignored me. Plus, I no longer smelled of poverty; my mother spent her loan money wisely, ensuring we had clean clothes and food on the table.

The next year my mother was able to take out enough financial aid loans to move my brother out from my father's house as well. With all four siblings at home, and my mother almost never home, fights were inevitable. Her absence, while she completed college and began law school, meant that the rage my brother and I carried had nowhere to go but towards each other. In my tenth grade year, we exploded into each other, and I soon faced an impossible choice. I remember being on the phone, talking to my girlfriend, one of the few other low-income students in the school. My brother came into our shared room and told me to get off the phone so he could use it. I told him I would later; but he snatched the phone from me, hung up on my girlfriend, and stood menacingly over my bed. As soon as I got to my feet, we got into a pushing match, shouting obscenities at each other. He left our room, but I was enraged and tired of my brother getting in my face. I went over to the only thing in our house worth anything. I knew the way to get to my brother was to smash what he had worked his ass off to buy: a brand new stereo system. With all of my might, I kicked it in. Bits of tape player, plastic covers, knobs, and shards of glass sprayed across our bedroom room. My brother rushed in as I rushed out; I left the house and went to my girlfriend's house, her mother letting me crash overnight.

The next day, I returned to home to grab my uniform so I could get to work (I was working as a waiter in a retirement home). After grabbing my clothes, my brother confronted me. At that point my rage had subsided, and I was just trying to get to work. But as I turned from him, he charged, swinging at the back of my head as I walked away. I turned around to face him and he backed off. We kept at this cycle: as I turned to walk out of the house, he would start swinging. We did this violent dance a few times, while my mother screamed at my sister to call the police on me. My younger sister froze, her sobs swamping her ability to rise and grab the phone. I remember telling them all I just wanted to leave, but my brother confronted me one last time. This time, he stepped up to my face. I grabbed at his neck, pushed him to the floor, and held him there, my fingers grasped tightly around his neck. His life, I felt, was in my hands. This was a perverse version of the control I had been fighting for, and as I looked down at my brother, I remember being calm, scarily reflective, thinking that this was not the type of control I needed. Disgusted, enraged, and confused as to why my mother was calling the police on me (instead of my brother, who continued to escalate when I was trying to leave), I left him lying on the floor, grabbed my bike, and pedaled as fast as I could to my girlfriend's house. As soon as I rode into her yard, a police car arrived, sirens blaring. My girlfriend's uncle came out of the house to my fifteen-year-old face being smashed against the police car by the officer.

Against the rising protests by my girlfriend's family, who had since rushed out of their house, I was handcuffed and shoved into the back of the car. I was arrested for vandalism, brought down to the police station, and forced to sit in a jail cell. I was never read my rights, not allowed a phone call, nor provided any food, water, anything. The police asked me to write down my version of the events, and I wrote: 'my brother attacked me as I was trying to leave.' They didn't like that, but I was pissed off. I didn't understand why I was being arrested in the first place. I didn't want to write for them, didn't want to think about why my mother was pressing charges against her son when my brother had started the fight. In just a few years, mother went from saving me from my father to sending me to jail. My mind racing, I decided to go mute and stopped responding to the officers questioning me. That made them even more upset and they began to ignore me.

Four or five hours later, I heard an officer I hadn't seen yet offer to drive me from the jail holding cell to juvenile hall. He was the first decent person I interacted with; and before putting me in the back of the car, he offered to take off my handcuffs. Another officer quickly chastised him, telling him I was dangerous. But on the long drive, he apologized for how I was being treated. He told me he had spoken with my brother and my mother, and didn't understand why I was being sent to juvenile hall. I seemed like a decent guy, and he didn't trust any parents who'd arrest their children. He told me to hold my own in juvenile hall, told me to avoid fights when I could. "Whatever you do, whatever you feel, do not let them see you cry," he warned me. "The kids and the guards take advantage of that shit."

But as soon as we arrived, he left me at the end of a chain link-lined corridor; handcuffed arms held behind me by a 6'5" guard who made my father seem small. He held my wrists in one hand, and the other held a folder of information given to him by the officer who drove me. My life was in that thin folder and I remember thinking I needed to keep that folder thin. He barked me through the entry process, made me take off my clothes, hosed me down, forced me to put on someone else's whitie-tighties, an oversized white t-shirt, loose-fitting thin-cloth grey pants, dirty white socks, and forced my 10½-inch feet into blue size-8 slip-ons. The words "OFFICIAL PROPERTY OF YOLO COUNTY CORRECTIONAL DIVISION" were imprinted on my pants and shirt.

I was sat in the office by the hulking guard, who told me to 'Sit the fuck down and shut the fuck up." I shivered and waited, seething, for what seemed like an hour, until a woman and man came in together, sitting down across from me. "Don't ask questions and don't speak until spoken to," the man barked at me. "You hungry?" I replied: "Yeah," but before I could even finish he was out of his chair, 6 inches from my face: "Yes what?" he asked. "Yes I am hungry," I eked out, but again, before I could finish, he moved;

this time, his hand slapped hard against my cold cheek. "'Yes Sir!' is how you answer me. You hear me?"

With a weak "Yes Sir!" in response, he led me to my room, my face red from his palm. The woman had given me a ratty blanket, soiled pillow, small bar of soap, and an inch-thick stack of toilet paper, which I was instructed to lay on the concrete slab that apparently was my bed. I was slapped again for tossing the items on the bed, made to lay them down gently, told to stand up straight, and then led into what they called the "diner." I stopped in my tracks as soon as I entered the room; 8–10 bolted-down tables were surrounded by four similarly bolted-down stools, many of which were already inhabited by an inmate who was dressed like me. Everyone was staring at me. Most of the inmates were already chanting "Newbie, Newbie, Newbie," though some just looked at me maliciously.

A guard I hadn't seen barked at me to get in the food line, in which four other inmates were still waiting for their food. I shuffled in behind the last person, at which point the guard told the last table without food to line up behind the "Newbie's ass." When I got to the front, I leaned on the counter, exhausted, confused, scared. The man behind the counter yelled at me to "get the fuck back." He continued, screaming: "What the fuck you think this is, a god-damned restaurant? Don't touch this counter and don't look at me if you want anything from me." I stared in shock, somehow pulled my hands back up just in time to see a fist flying at me out of the corner of my eye. I was down immediately, looking up at what must have been the four inmates who were told to get in line behind me. They were above me, raining kicks all over my body, but before I had time to curl into a ball, one kid after another was being pulled off of me. Someone told me to "Get up! Get up!" and as I got to my feet I saw a kid I knew as Brian, from Eureka. We had gone to junior high school together; and he had pulled the kids off me. "Get your food," he instructed me, and I grabbed my tray, careful not to touch the counter as I lifted it up, following Brian.

I sat down at his table, looked at the guard who had set me up to get jumped, and looked down at my food: something like hamburger helper with macaroni, two pieces of white bread, slices of brown, soggy apple, and pale carrot sticks. I gobbled down the tasteless food, talked with Brian and the other two kids at the table, then was told to get in line to go to our cells. After lying on the thin mattress, staring angrily at the ceiling, I was startled awake by the cell door opening abruptly. I was told I had a call, and told to follow the guard. I entered an office, waited a few minutes, then was handed the receiver. It was my mother. I did all I could to hold back the sobs, but when my mom asked if I wanted out, I lost it. Of course I wanted out, and would do anything I could to get out. She hung up, telling me we'd talk about it tomorrow.

The blank walls stared back at me throughout that long, sleepless night in the cold cell. After breakfast, I was told to go to math class, where I soon realized I had been in school much longer than had these other inmates. After the third or fourth grade math class, I was told I had a visitor. My mother, the woman who admitted me, and another man who I had not seen before were sitting down waiting for me; the two of them were laughing at some joke, but my mother's face was angry. My mom had a proposition; I could stay in juvenile hall, or live with a friend of one of her friends. I had no option: I did not want to live with him, but couldn't stay in juvenile hall.

The next week, I moved into Bob's house, where I had to pay rent negotiated by my mother. He was a single man, had adopted a son about four years younger than I, and lived about half a mile from my mom. I needed to work a lot more hours to pay for rent, food, clothes, anything I'd need to spend money on. So I quit my soccer team, and had to live in a side room, with no door, very limited privacy, and rules partially set by my mother: school, then work, then home. I was threatened with severe punishment if I broke any rules; I would immediately be placed back in juvenile hall for up to six months. Those were the terms of my probation.

And Bob took advantage of my vulnerability from the first night I stayed with him. He began his almost nightly practice of saying goodnight to me and his son and then slipping into the bed he told my mom he'd provide for me. I was trapped; disgusted by him, but unwilling to go back to juvenile hall. I tried to bring it up to my mother, but she told me she didn't want to talk about "my situation." She was more worried about what she framed as my anger problem than any issues I might have at Bob's. After about six months of Bob molesting me, and after my girlfriend had threatened to break up with me because she thought me being molested was similar to cheating on her, I told him to stop. Shocked, he got out of bed with me, and when I came home the next night after work, my mother was sitting at the dinner table with him. Bob had told her he thought I was ready to come back home, and my mom was ready to let me come home.

Eager to get out of his house and with no other options, I moved back into my mom's. I avoided my brother as much as I could, started playing soccer again, and cut work back to 25 hours a week. I had barely passed my classes in 10th grade and had all but tuned school out. But coming back to my mother's house sharpened my focus; I knew that school could be a way out. I wanted to use college as an excuse to not have to interact with our family, just like my mom did. So I dove into school, began to do my homework, and generally became numb to life around me, ignoring students who glared at me, ignoring my brother, sisters, and mother as much as possible. I began to see rewards; my junior year I earned a 4.0, and saw an immediate difference in the way teachers treated me. Some things, I realized, were under my control.

But what I also learned was that I could never fully escape the impact poverty, violence, and sexual abuse would have on me. Leaving the physical place of my childhood trauma did not help me avoid trauma later in life; and just as my father's violence shaped in me a rage that will never leave, so too did my mother's role in putting me into an abusive situation that I was powerless to avoid. How I grew up squashed me in many ways, but also, eventually, gave me the insight to understand oppression, to understand what I needed. And I realized that if my parents could not provide what I needed, my teachers certainly did not care enough to provide anything either. I would, in essence, need to learn to grow up on my own, and learn to take care of myself, both in terms of physical and emotional safety, but also in terms of trying to learn anything in school.

What Educators Could Have Done

I tell these stories to caution educators to not celebrate "successes" too soon, and to remind them that without efforts to protect students from immediate harm, and to help prepare students to navigate traumatic situations on their own, educators fail to adequately educate students. Tenth grade was a huge turning point in my life, but it also could have been the end of the world as I knew it. I had a choice to make, and despite everything telling me to either do serious harm to Bob (and risk jail) or my brother (and risk being impossibly, permanently self-tortured for seriously injuring someone I loved), I decided to tolerate my situation. But most children in similar situations do what their survival instincts tell them, and that is fight or flight. I tolerated abuse, but I recognize many children will not. And they will be punished for not tolerating their abuse, particularly if educators are not aware of such abuse.

I made adult decisions to survive without knowing if I would live beyond my teen years. I did all of this without any support from teachers. What educators could have done was provide an outlet. I needed a teacher who cared, who created the space for me to talk, to release all the rage I was building up, and to give me a space to admit that my life was not okay. I needed serious support around being molested. I needed serious support around my rage. Even an academic focus would have helped, but at that point in my life, no teachers offered engaging curriculum, and no educator helped me figure out how to continue playing soccer (the only outlet I had). Educators could have recognized the trauma I was going through, created outlets for that to come out, or provided some space for survivors of abuse (without having to publicly acknowledge such). At this point in my life, I had every reason to drop out of school, and I still do not think any of my teachers would have done anything to stop it. My educators, in short, did not care enough to reach out to me, and did not stop me from doing serious damage to others. And while in the end I navigated school, I recognize that this was largely due to my decision to tolerate my teachers' ignorance, standardized curriculum, and school's total irrelevance to life.

Growing up White—7th through 11th Grade

I share these stories to show glimpses into how my personal context shapes why I approach education in the ways I do. But I have also omitted race-based conversations, partially to show the reader how I thought as a young White child. I was unaware of racism, and did not know the history of violence and imperialism against people of color, though I was aware of my father's racism. I knew he hated people of color, and would yell racist slurs during the only time he interacted with them: football or baseball games on TV. My father's face would curl into what I have since attributed to a snarl only White racists seem to embody anytime an athlete of color did something great from another team, or made a mistake on my father's teams (San Francisco Giants or the 49ers). Then, he'd stand up quickly as hateful words sneered out of his angry mouth about a "Goddamned cornerback slave" or a "Fucking monkey man can't catch a fucking ball." Even as I write this now I cringe at the violent racist memories, reminded of how hurtful his words were and how he taught me to be racist from my earliest memories. And even now, when I attend professional sports, I cringe in anticipation, waiting for the inevitable drunk White fan to scream out similar racism.

For much of my early life, my friends were a mixed group of poor Whites, and the few African Americans, Latinos, and Asian kids in the neighborhood. My dad hated that. But I don't remember him directly saying anything until seventh grade, when I first invited Shawn Jones into our house. I usually never invited people into our house because I was ashamed of living in disgusting houses. While on the outside, the house just looked ratty and rundown, on the inside, there would be no snacks, no Kool-Aid, no hand towels in the bathroom, nothing but the always present moldy stench. People would know exactly how poor I was if they saw the emptiness of our rusty yellow refrigerator or our bare cupboards. And I knew that I could not hide the ever present, pinkeye-inducing mildew.

But Shawn was different. He made me feel comfortable, did not make jokes about my holey pants, smelly clothes, or school days without lunches. After months of hanging out at his house, the time came for me to invite him in; I simply ran out of excuses. So Shawn came in and as we settled onto the couch, what I feared came through the door: My father never came home early. But he did this afternoon, and his rage-filled voice filled the room faster than the front door could swing open:

"What The Fuck Is That Nigger Doing In Our House?" He screamed, and smashed his fist through the wall, just a foot from my own head. Shawn and I bounced up, shaking. I ducked beneath my father's forearm as he nursed his already swollen hand, and we darted out the door, scared for our lives. We sprinted down the block, forgetting our bikes, and while we eventually slowed to a jog, we got as far away from my house as we could. We ended up miles away at Shawn's house, and by then, our fear was diminished by our exhaustion. We ate dinner with his father, hid out in his room, and never again acknowledged what happened. I was terrified of thinking about my father's violent racism, and hoped Shawn would never raise the issue; I was less concerned about the impact on Shawn and more worried about Shawn finding out how my dad abused me. Shawn likely also did not want to relive that violence, and a powerful opportunity to put a name to what I was witnessing slid away.

I probably could have figured out that students of color were treated worse than I was in situations just like this. But no one ever asked me, and when I brought up such ideas in school, teachers ignored me or treated me as if I were joking. I continually searched for something in school to make sense of how my father reacted to people of color, and specifically to Shawn. But I did not ask about race. I simply did not see an opportunity since it was not part of the curriculum; indeed, we were taught that racism had ended with the civil rights movement. I slowly began to ask questions about income and poverty in any class I could, but my questions resulted in after-school detentions. My teachers simply did not take me seriously, dismissing me when I'd ask what causes poverty or how poverty was related to racism. I also had plenty of life happening around me to keep me focused on my own issues with abuse and poverty. My home life and the way my teachers completely denied racism taught me to ignore racism and all forms of oppression. But in ignoring racism and classism, I was specifically being taught to not make connections between structural poverty and the connections to race.

Yet ironically, because my teachers ignored racism in what they taught and denied the differential negative treatment of students of color around me,

I actually began to learn about racism. Prior to high school, most of my teachers seemed to really dislike me. They did not like touching me, they would not look me in the eye (with the exception of Mr. Cesaretti), and they generally just tolerated my presence, jumping at chances to remove me from class or gloss over anything I had done. While my teachers tolerated me, I noticed that, for the most part, they did not tolerate the kids of color. I could not but help notice the few students of color being treated as harshly as I was, but there remained one huge difference in my eyes: They were not poor. I justified my negative treatment because I was poor; because I had no money, I understood why people treated me with disdain. I had low self-esteem, my father beat me, I had bowel problems. I didn't want to be like me, and I knew others didn't either. I understood that; I was an asshole as a kid.

What I did not understand was why Shawn Jones was treated as what I would have described as poor. He was African American. I knew that. But he was "proper." He did not talk back. He was well dressed. He was nice. His family had what seemed to me to be a lot of money. He lived on the other side of town, near the Zoo, in a middle-class area of Eureka, with huge trees in his front yard. He had a yard! And it was always freshly mowed! And a two story, split level home? I couldn't understand why he wasn't hanging out with the rich White kids. Yet here he was, raising his hand and never being acknowledged, just like me. Despite how schools taught me to ignore that the issues I was seeing were larger than me, larger than Shawn, and larger than what I could notice, I began to watch how others were treated. As a child I thought people of color and poor people were treated like we were not valuable because we were not as valuable. Better people were White, wealthy, and, like the people we read about in history classes, tended to colonize others so that we became like them. And so while I knew firsthand about classism and was witnessing racism against my friends, school kept me from connecting my experiences to larger societal structures.

Fast forward to my tenth-grade world civilization class at Davis High School, taught by an ogre-like teacher who grumbled and barked to the class. She'd sit us in rows, chastise us for talking, and ramble on about "world history" taken directly from our boring textbook. Each class began with her asking random questions about the readings, and the first one to raise their hand and answer correctly got a real Hershey's Kiss speared toward them. I remember one time being the only one who raised a hand to a ridiculously unimportant question about how many elephants survived some ancient leader's crossing of a mountain range. A trivial question, I knew then, but I also remembered that the book said only one. I raised my hand and answered, to the shock of the class and the teacher, who had already dismissed me because I never raised my hand and preferred to talk to my friends rather than respond to her banal questions. And why would I? While I did read, it was all useless dates and insignificant facts. As she taught us dates without meaning, I read books about World War II, examining military strategies and trying to understand what started the war. That led me to World War I, and after a few years of interest, I had read every book in the school library about World War I, World War II, and the Vietnam War. I began to answer random questions correctly, but still wondered why the wars began, and kept asking silently: what about Jews and what about Japanese Internment and where did all the Nazis go and why did the U.S. care about Vietnam but not Cambodia and why was there an "African Front" during World War II? But there was simply no one to ask.

My growing discontent with what I was being taught, combined with how I was largely ignored when I asked critical questions, led me to think of school as a bad joke. I increasingly became aware of my friends of color being treated poorly by teachers. I saw how my non-Asian friends of color were rarely called on in class, how African American and Latino students were in trouble for fighting regardless of who threw the first punch, and disciplinary procedures were always significantly more harsh for students of color. I saw counselors provide White students with information about elite colleges, laying the foundations for support for admissions processes in tenth and eleventh grade. I saw students of color being told, while we waited in the college advising office, that they were not "college material." I knew that I was reading biased books and that the library offered the same types of books that my teachers used. But I did not know then that this was racism, that the total denial of what was happening around me and denied by my textbooks was racism. Not until my eleventh grade Black History course did anything seem to make sense about my increasing confusion around racism and classism.

My Black History course provided some context to what was racing around my head. Mr. Calhoun, the only teacher I still remember fondly, stood out from the middle-class whiteness of the rest of the teaching staff. Mr. Calhoun, in his faux suede jump suits, had style. That his style was 20 years behind the times was irrelevant to me: he had pride and he showed this in how he walked, in how he talked, and in what he taught. He was not a "good" teacher: students would meander into class 30 minutes late, the smell of a joint fresh on their heels. Students would giggle and chat and throw spit wads and sleep in his class; Mr. Calhoun appeared clueless. Yet staunch memories remain: an African American guest speaker who had been abused by the Davis police department; a film capturing the slaughtering of a pig, which Mr. Calhoun used to remind us how Black people used to be treated as a matter of policy in the U.S.; a lively debate on affirmative action, which, for all our opinions, none of us knew anything about. For the first time in school, I was exposed to discussions and readings on racism. And Mr. Calhoun was nice to me, was respectful, and continually told me to take myself more seriously. While I was not yet ready to digest and understand James Baldwin, Mr. Calhoun did what he could to make me aware that I could learn on my own, and if I wanted to learn about race and racism in high school, doing it on my own was the only option.

What Educators Could Have Done

Throughout my entire school experience, I was looking for something to engage me, for something to take me from my poverty and abuse and neglect. I grew up ignorant to the complexities of racism and classism, despite that I had firsthand experiences, tons of observations, and lots of interest in learning. In high school, I was taught to be ignorant and to not question; despite that, I was deeply invested in learning about the world. Yet racism and classism were clearly content areas that would have engaged me, but both were entirely absent from the curriculum, and entirely absent from the teaching styles of my mostly White teachers. This is entirely the issue today; K–12 curriculum is still almost entirely devoid of any serious conversation or critical analysis of historical racism and how that racism shapes current issues today. I was not being taught a multicultural curriculum that clarified the multiple levels of oppression, and lessons instead reflected the sheltered, self-segregated reality of my White teachers and White suburban peers. I would have exploded with academic potential had my teachers allowed me to self-direct my own learning around race, class, and history, as long as they provided guidance and expertise. I would have came to school ready had my teachers offered any sort of relevance in the curriculum, in writing assignments or book reports. My teachers could have integrated local histories, could have facilitated race-based dialogues amongst peers, could have committed to hiring a diverse staff with experience teaching in culturally responsive ways and about whiteness and White privilege, and they could have argued for professional development if they did not know how to do this work.

My teachers failed to prepare me to live in an integrated, racially diverse, multilingual world. And I do not believe I was different than the vast majority of White students I went to school with; the difference was that I kept choosing to try to learn about racism, kept trying to understand how my poverty was related to what I was seeing in how people of color were being treated. That choice was made despite my teachers, just as many poor Whites chose to not dedicate themselves to learning something they are strongly discouraged from by these same teachers. Teachers who reached out, who helped me navigate and make sense of poverty and violence would have made my choice much easier, and would have made the choice for other poor White students more apparent. It was (and is) educator responsibility to learn how to prepare White students so that we do not replicate racism, so that we use the ways we are oppressed to help us understand other forms of oppression. If educators do not know how to do this, then it is their responsibility to learn how. That is what it means to be an educator; we have to learn what our students need to learn. Educators are responsible to teach about what racism is, how it operates, and how to address it. My teachers never did this, and as a result, I grew up angry with my schools for teaching me lies.

Developing as an Educator

As I grew older, I slowly became aware that what my teachers were teaching and how they were teaching was actually why I did not engage in school. And I began to sit in the back of class, talk trash to my teachers, make my peers laugh and at least enjoy school. I also began to imagine what teachers could have done differently. When a student would come in late, I would think of alternative ways to welcome a student into class. My teachers would always chastise, embarrass, or ignore a late student, but I would imagine them doing what I thought they should: welcome the student in by making them laugh, or sometimes, just acknowledge them with a nod and keep on with the lesson. When a teacher would present some historical lesson about China in a boring way, I'd imagine the teacher bringing in people from the region, having them talk to us about how they lived, and imagined us eating the food they ate, breathing in the smells they smelled. I knew people from all the areas we studied lived in California; why were we not learning from them directly? I'd never ask such questions aloud, but instead would imagine guest speakers talking about how difficult being a Chinese immigrant was, how similar their experience was to slavery, perhaps highlighting the Chinese Exclusion Act or other policies that show exactly how the U.S. has structured racism. I'd conjure up panels where recent immigrants from Mexico, El Salvador, and Ethiopia would share experiences with the Black families that just moved to California from New Orleans. I imagined the teacher facilitating conversations about what our home lives were like, what sorts of trauma we lived through, how we all were able to be in class despite the tremendous burdens we faced before and after school. But I never said anything, just sat back, slowly tuned out of class, thinking up ways to do school differently.

In my thirteen years of school, though, I did learn what happened when teachers and schools did not meet basic educational needs. I watched as I tuned out, watched my peers tune out, and watched anyone who seemed to have any home problems slowly disengage from school, until the only students on a college track were the ones who did not appear to face severe home lives. I knew that was not random; I knew that students were children first, and when we were being molested or beat or raising siblings or working 40 hours a week to pay rent, eat, and clothe ourselves, school was not going to be a priority. Particularly when we had to suffer through demeaning lessons and racist teachers and homophobic peers; boring lessons couldn't get through the emotional walls we had to build to survive. And so I learned that there are areas that educators must address, must provide for, so that all students can engage. I learned that students like me need caring adults, need our basic needs met, and need an engaging and relevant curriculum. Without these needs met, students will do what I did: tune out.

Even the teachers who used creative approaches in classes, or who appeared to care the most still had me creating sugar cube missions, recreating the very building structures that were used to colonize, rape, and molest young brown children. I questioned why we were taught about architecture and not the wars that were only mentioned as dates to remember. But my teachers ignored me, which seemed impossible to do: I was always one of the loudest children, always talking back to the teacher, always showing up late to school, and often leaving school early. I was always stealing food from the cafeteria when my lunch was in turn stolen from me, or when my father forgot to go shopping for bread, lunchmeat, apples. I was always in fights, always instigating others. And yet I do not remember a teacher noticing my hunger, my torn clothes, or my stench. I do not remember any lessons about other hungry, poor, smelly children, even though the occasions to teach about poverty came up often. On a required fourth-grade overnight trip, I shared my breakfast with a student; apparently the staff had undercounted and ran out of Pop-Tarts. My teacher noticed me sharing, and made me stand up while the rest of the school clapped for me. But I was seething; no one had ever shared their lunch with me before, and the school was not doing anything to keep me fed; instead they used one of the poorest students in the school as an example of sharing.

Despite dozens of memories of teachers exacerbating my poverty, one teacher sticks out as particularly caring. Mr. Cesaretti, my seventh-grade math teacher, was practically blind, old, sweet. Though his class was often the rowdiest, he never yelled, never even raised his voice. Perhaps that was why we took advantage of him; we shot spit wads through straws over the limits of his tunnel vision, crumpling paper filled with unfinished algebra equations, excusing ourselves outside to the water fountain, returning to the classroom to smack some unsuspecting student in the back of the head with the now soaking paper missile. I hated math, never paid attention, focused instead on dodging the missiles our teacher could not see. I remember staring up at the ceiling: we had a contest to see who could count all the paper wads stuck to the ceiling while avoiding the missiles streaming across the room at whose ever neck was straining above, counting.

Mr. Cesaretti would often take me outside the classroom, seemingly oblivious to the pandemonium the rest of the class would erupt into. "Chris," he'd urge into me, "you are a beautiful young man." His words stuck with me; I used to replay them at home, when my dad would call me ugly or stupid or punch me for handing him the wrong wrench. I'd be swallowing tears, and Mr. Cesaretti would remind me that I was relevant. "You make the class excited," he'd tell me, "you tell others what to do." I was without tools to hear him, though. I simply could not understand that others followed what I would do; that made no sense in a day where I might have my lunch stolen, might bust a smaller kid's mouth open, might get my own mouth smashed for calling an eighth grader a "fat honky," and might get sent to the principal's office for telling another teacher that, "yes, I do think I am better" than she.

Mr. Cesaretti began talking to me regularly, began reminding me that I mattered to him, that I was important to others, that I should care more about how I am in the world. But he was too ineffective, our outside-the-classroom chats too infrequent, too vague to equip me with actual confidence. I was entirely overwhelmed by a childhood with an absent mother, an abusive father, neighborhood bullies, and poverty, all leading to my lack of having anything of worth. I did not realize that the fights I instigated made up the vast majority of my fights. I did not realize that many of my problems were ones I created, though clearly many were not of my doing. Mr. Cesaretti tried to at least get me to take control of what I could, and that is why I remember him still. But I did not have the tools to hear the affirmation in his messages; I needed more than he could give, and he needed to give more than he did. I needed more than one caring educator, and more than 15 minute "chats" after class. If his lessons had been integrated into the curriculum, if our curriculum had focused on violence, exclusion, silencing, oppression, or had given any hint as to why I lived in the world I did and how I could more effectively navigate life, then, perhaps, he would have had an impact.

But Mr. Cesaretti's message was also inconsistent with that of other teachers. I would leave Mr. Cesaretti's class only to slip into Mr. Goodwin's class. He was the science teacher who held me up by my neck. On a good day, I'd last 15 minutes in his class. On a bad day, I'd walk into class; he'd look up at me, grimacing, shaking his head in disgust. I'd tell him to "fuck off," and he'd point to the door. Most days, I simply walked back out and into the woods for the rest of the class, brought out only by the school bell. When I tolerated his personal attacks on me, I noticed his teaching. He crafted lessons after student errors, reminding everyone who messed up why it was a travesty. After I failed a written test in his class, we spent the entire class on the spelling of e-n-v-i-r-o-n-m-e-n-t, a word I have never since spelled wrong. But other than that, I was not paying enough attention to come close to passing his class, and grew to hate him and science, and ignored what Mr. Cesaretti was trying to tell me.

School has always set me up to fail, left me ignorant to the world, ignorant to my own personal power and privilege, and ignorant of oppression. I needed to dig beneath my anger, to uncover who I was beneath the cover of my poor White skin in order to make sense of and no longer blame my teachers, my father, and society. And when I stopped blaming my teachers for what they did not do for me, when I stopped blaming my father for my rage, for my ignorance, for my racial confusion, for my poverty, for my broken fingers and lifetime bruises, I became an educator. And for me, becoming an educator meant becoming a White person who actively challenges whiteness, who actively challenges the investment in whiteness that our schools are based upon.

I am often asked how I came to be "culturally competent" or how I "actually learned about racism." Most folks asking tend to assume that there was some obvious incident that occurred, some bolt of lightning that fried critical awareness into my soul. But the reality is that I learned most of what I know from simply listening to people of color around me and watching how they were treated (Knaus, 2006). During my two graduate programs, I took courses focused on race, gender, and sexuality. But those courses were most often taught in the same ways as my K–12 courses, with one educator in the front of the room telling the rest of us their thoughts as if that were truth. My formal preparation as an educator was through a host of courses in Education, Social Work, Women's Studies, Communication, and Sociology. I should have been taught how to make sense of my previous experiences as a student, and how to develop a vision of how I wanted to be as an educator. But even my multicultural education courses did not prepare me as such; instead we read academic articles by researchers, rarely examining how, for example, I could be a positive White influence. I did find educators to model and support me, and those mentors challenged my privilege, my weaknesses, and served as continual reminders of my incapacity to understand life as a person of color. But that work was on my own, outside the boundaries of graduate school and educator preparation. And for me, that is the point: I have come to identify as a White educator challenging racism because that is what being White means to me. There is simply no other way for me to be, no other way for me to use the lessons I have been taught through oppression, violence, and poverty. And to not spend my life challenging the racism our schools promotes for me is to accept White privilege and the racial order that silences the world around me. That is not the world I want to live in.

Conclusion

Despite my privileges and passions as an adult, I often try to remind myself how growing up demonstrates the ways poverty shapes a fear of being "found out," a fear of being illegitimate, and a continual comparison to others who have resources that were never available to me, and the billions like me around the world. My life demonstrates how violence is silenced by the adults who beat children, and by the general apathy that schools promote. My life demonstrates how racism limited what I was taught, the curriculum I was exposed to, and my experiences frame how I was taught to funnel my rage against other people. And what I try to do in my teaching is demonstrate that the silencing of this oppression is the problem of schools. What is done in schools normalizes the conversation away from the reality of violence, from the presence of racism and poverty in the lives of youth, and because of this disjoint, students of color, gay students, poor students, students with disabilities, and a host of other students choose to leave schools in often failed attempts to protect themselves.

Instead, what oppressed students need from teachers and educators is a personal and academic recognition of both the reality we live and how that reality is not the way things should be. Educators must provide support for impoverished children, and can do so through providing basic services during school; otherwise, student capacity to be at school is severely limited. Educators must be a warm, welcoming supportive presence in the lives of students, and students must feel cared for. Educators must be able to identify and respond to violence in the lives of students, and should have plans for doing so prior to teaching. Educators must also know how to integrate race and racism as content into the curriculum, and should prepare youth to successfully navigate in a racially hostile world. My life demonstrates the intense complications of growing up, and teachers must be able to safely provide space for such complications in all students. Like many urban students, I needed someone to tell me that I was okay, that most of what I was living was not my fault. I also needed a relevant curriculum, disciplinary procedures that reflected my reality, and space to heal. I never had a teacher give me what I needed, and this is the case for the vast majority of students of color in urban schools.

Transforming schools into places where students do not need to leave in order to be safe begins with transparent educators who are clear about why we do what we do. If educators do not understand what students need in order to come to school, then we cannot expect to engage students. As I have been honest with students about how angry I was at school, at my parents, at my teachers, at my peers, at my curriculum, I have built up a way of relating with them. The urban youth I work with are often enraged, do not get to know why their educators are in their classrooms, nor how that relates to the racism, poverty, and violence that shapes our world. Yet bonding with my students over the rage we share is key; in aiming to help students develop tools to make sense of the impossible realities they navigate, I demonstrate that I, too, live in a world that is similar to theirs. My point is not to claim their world; they live a drastically different reality than I. Instead, I urge students to capture the world they see, to identify in details the specifics that anger them, the very concrete details that indicate to them what marks a teacher as racist, the details that evoke rage outside of their school lives. As students identify exactly how the curriculum ignores who they are, they begin to reclaim their identities, which it must be remembered, are stolen. That has been the purpose of education: to forcibly, legally, enforce the standards of whiteness upon people of color. That is the colonizing legacy of education in the U.S.; and the result is an educational system that invalidates identities that differ from what is "normalized" in standardized curriculum.

In order to shift this silencing, educators must be transparent with our students, faculty, and communities in order to provide a context for the work we do. And being transparent in my teaching is difficult. I take risks, sharing pieces of my soul with my students. Trusting that high school students will not take advantage of my vulnerability. Trusting that graduate students will stay engaged and not dismiss my experiences as irrelevant to graduate studies, as just anecdotal evidence that demonstrates that poor people can "make it" if we try. I take risks in sharing my stories, trusting students of all ages with the kind of teaching I never had as a K–12 student, and only very rarely had as a college student. I aim to be myself in the classroom, knowing that at best, my university colleagues will find me odd, if not downright anti-academic. I try to transform by being transparent, by listening, by continually bringing racism, sexism, and reminders of the violence many of us live into faculty meetings, into curriculum conversations, into my scholarship. And I am punished for this still; while I no longer am forced into detentions, articles are not published, programs are not approved, school district leaders wary of change shy away from my impassioned presence, and faculty decry my efforts as "only about racism." Resistance to change follows me everywhere, and resistance to my insistence on addressing racism is a permanent battle. At best, no matter how pedigreed I have become, I am still barely tolerated by most educators. And yet, I move forward knowing that I have been prepared for this work, led by the apathy of my educators, the real pain from growing up poor, White, abused, and the voices of students of color.

CHAPTER 2

You Are the Ones Who Need to Hear Us

The Role of Urban Youth Voice in a Democracy

The purpose of schools is to shut us up.

—Pedro (11th Grader)

Much of my professional life is spent convincing White educators that the depth of racism shaping the lives of African American, Latino, and indigenous American students is real. I speak to disbelieving suburban and urban educators, to teachers, principals, district staff, and university faculty around the country, and in almost every conversation where there are more than a few White people, eyebrows roll, my words are dismissed, and the reality of racism is denied. And yet almost every single high school dropout I have talked with, almost every young African American and Latino man who has been locked up in juvenile hall or in prison can clarify powerfully what that racism looks like. How can so many people who have been failed by schools go on and on about the details of racism while the vast majority of White educators who have successfully navigated K–12 schools and college are unable to explain how racism operates on a daily basis? The same is also true for a number of educators of color. Tyrone Howard (2008) clarifies that this is partially because, "as a country, and as a community of researchers we have yet to engage one another in an authentic, honest, and sustained dialogue about race and racism" (p. 954). Yet our children learn from our collective avoidance of these real issues, and while educators read books about how to have "courageous conversations," few efforts entail systemic analysis of the historical roots of racism, how those roots inform schools today, and how our students live through the racism many of the adults paid to educate them collectively deny (Singleton & Linton, 2005).

Yet if educators and scholars cannot have authentic conversations about the racial realities we live, that we force upon our children, then how can we expect younger generations to learn to transform our segregated society into the integrated, multilingual, multi-social democracy that schools prematurely celebrate? I am less concerned with questions of fault, because most young African American students already know the skin tones of the educators who limit their capacity to be themselves. Instead, I am concerned with action; how do educators recognize the silencing, colonial purpose of schools so that we can teach students to be themselves, to become what Paulo Freire (1973) called, "authentic human beings" (p. 20). Such authenticity, where children learn to maintain the languages of their grandparents, but also learn to speak in the dominant language, learn to navigate socially, learn to advocate for resources, all while learning to be themselves, is a requirement for a socially diverse democracy. But transforming into such an affirming purpose of education requires understanding what schools have intended to do, and have successfully achieved, in communities of color.

In what follows, I provide a foundation for how the United States has continued to benefit off of the free and low-wage labor of African Americans, and how education has been structured to maintain such dramatic—and purposeful—inequalities. I argue that schools have justified the usage of African American labor through segregated schools that have been contradictorily written into law through *Brown vs. Board of Education*. After framing the colonial mission of schools, I capture the importance of voice in transforming what we could do in schools to empower multicultural, multilingual communities. I caution that the purpose of schooling has to shift so as to not require Black youth to choose between identity and academic success, and demonstrate how developing voice is key to shifting this false choice. I share stories that show the impact of developing voice on students and educators alike, and clarify two components of voice that emanate from my work with students and from the work of poet educators. I argue that voice cannot be easily defined and in an era of accountability and school efficiency, likely should not be. I conclude by laying out a process to develop urban youth voice, which leads directly into the following chapters, in which I clarify how I develop voice through instructional strategies that create relevant, supportive school structures.

Education and the Silencing of Black Children

While conversation about Black exclusion from the fabric of society is silenced in mainstream representations of the struggles for schooling, racial educational inequalities intentionally abound. On almost every single indicator of educational success, urban students of color lag significantly behind White, Asian, and suburban students (Aud, Hussar, et al., 2010;

Jacobson, Olsen, Rice, Sweetland, & Ralph, 2001; Rampey, Dion, & Donohue, 2009). The foundation of education in the U.S. is deeply conflicted; on one hand, many Native Americans were abducted and forced to attend violent schools with one purpose in mind: assimilation into White norms (Archuleta, Child, & Lomawaima, 2000; Trafzer & Keller, 2006). On the other hand, most enslaved Africans were violently punished for attempts to learn anything not seen as immediately productive for their White imperialistic owners (Williams, 2005; Woodson, 2004). This contradictory educational philosophy resulted in dramatic inequalities that are often referred to as achievement gaps, but these gaps simply reflect mono-cultural White supremacist frameworks of schooling that deny the experiences, languages, cultures, and oppressions facing urban families of color (Apple, 1993; Banks, 1996; Ladson-Billings, 1999). Schools, in effect, have been designed to do different things with different students, and to misrepresent this oppressive purpose as an "achievement gap" denies the role of education in purposefully maintaining a poverty-stricken workforce (Giroux, 2001; Macedo & Bartolomé, 1999). Yet federal policy efforts center almost entirely on the "achievement gap."

The foundations of U.S. schooling remain: White slave owners and many White abolitionists were adamantly against Black people learning to read, write, add, or subtract. Such acts were severely punished by cutting off tongues, whipping, and hanging (Webber, 1978; Woodson, 2004). This is the foundation of anti-educating Black children and adults in the U.S.; many White people wanted Black bodies for labor, and this was directly supported by policy that legislated fear of Black people who were educated (Davis, 1966; Goodell, 2009). And even after emancipation, even after the literal chains were taken off of Black necks, the education of Black children and adults was resisted, by legal policy and the continual threat of White violence (Anderson, 1988; Watkins, 2001; Williams, 2005). The fear of Black people who could communicate to wide masses, who could count, who could develop community, and think on their own ran deep in the minds of many White people. Of course Black people could already think on their own, had been teachers and healers and farmers and leaders before, during, and after they were enslaved, but White America did what it could to convince themselves and the Black people they relied upon that anything Black people already knew was irrelevant. Throughout the history of the U.S., through policies and *de facto* segregation, Black people, as a group, have not been allowed to learn in well-funded schools, and even when individual Black students have been allowed in, the scope of education is framed around navigating White society (Allen, 1990; Ladson-Billings, 1999; Ture &

Hamilton, 1967). Thus ethnic studies and multicultural education are still relegated to the sidelines of academia, under constant threat of closure, and continually underfunded (Ethnic Studies Now, 2007; Forbes, 2008; McCombs, 2007; Santa Cruz, 2010). While ethnic-framed educational approaches are minimalized, students of color and poor whites are pushed out of schools in high numbers to ensure an uneducated workforce.

James Baldwin (Baldwin, 1985b) clarifies the impact of this fear of Black thought in his Talk to Teachers:

> *The point of all this is that black men were brought here as a source of cheap labor. They were indispensable to the economy. In order to justify the fact that men were treated as though they were animals, the white republic had to brainwash itself into believing that they were, indeed, animals and deserved to be treated like animals. Therefore it is almost impossible for any Negro child to discover anything about his actual history. The reason is that this "animal," once he suspects his own worth, once he starts believing that he is a man, has begun to attack the entire power structure. This is why America has spent such a long time keeping the Negro in his place. What I am trying to suggest to you is that it was not an accident, it was not an act of God, it was not done by well-meaning people muddling into something which they didn't understand. It was a deliberate policy hammered into place in order to make money from black flesh. And now, in 1963, because we have never faced this fact, we are in intolerable trouble. (p. 328–329)*

At East Bay High School, I played a song by Antibalas (2004) to one of my high school writing courses, made up entirely of African American and Latino students. Antibalas' message of anti-imperialism is clear in just about every song, and their Afro-beat rhythms are based on the music of Fela Kuti, a Nigerian musician (Coker, 2004). Antibalas, in a lyric from the song "Big Man," captured the corporate nature of employment in the U.S.:

> *What can I do for you?*
> *I beg o, give me job now*
> *Let me work eighty hours a week to make money*
> *So I can give the same money back to you, big man*
> *When I buy your beautiful products.*

After playing the song, students wrote responses that connected the lyrics to their personal experiences. One student, Jasmine, asked, "what's the point of getting a job when all our money has to go back to the people who keep us poor?" The students resonated with Antibalas' framing of "the system," and wanted to learn more about similar artists. These students also wanted to know where they could read about the historical connections to why, as Jasmine questioned, "shit got this way," and she continued that, "my teachers aint never taught me about this, either in history or economics." The class continued, with students expressing frustration with Pedro's quote that opened the chapter: "The purpose of schools is to shut us up." And the students knew *why* they were being made to shut up, demonstrated in Jacinda's argument: "We supposed to work at Taco Bell or Jamba Juice or Target or as day-laborers. We aint supposed to go to college, learn to question so they have to deal with us."

Despite many popular musicians with similar anti-colonial messages,[1] many educators do not teach (and have not been trained to teach) about the historical purpose of enslaving Africans to create a free labor pool, nor the continued reliance upon low-income labor in maintaining a middle-class standard of living. And yet students feel this purpose everyday, when they sit in classrooms that ignore and deny Robert Allen's clear statement about Black power: "In these cities we do not control our resources. We do not control the land, the houses or the stores. These are owned by whites who live outside the community" (Allen, 1990, p. 7). These disparities in power and wealth reflect a larger struggle: the United States has always had a purpose for Black people. This purpose has ensured the continued benefit of middle class White communities at the expense of impoverished African American communities. As sung in "Big Man," immigrant and low-income families often work upwards of two full-time jobs, only to give the money they earn back to White-run corporations that contribute to the very low-wage labor that forces them to work multiple jobs in the first place. This is in exchange for products meant to convey wealth and status (think i-Pods, cell phones, nice clothes, shoes, and fancy cars). The issue Antibalas and Jacinda raise is that low-wage labor continues a cycle of poverty, ensuring communities of color remain poor and in the hands of the corporations upon whom they rely for employment.

Education is often framed as the one way out of this cycle. Yet despite being lured by the promise of success that the world equates with American education, being successful in American schools does not guarantee economic stability. There is no denying the economic benefit that *can* come with educational success, including enhanced income, access to social capital, higher-quality food, produce, health care, and schools that promise (but do not always deliver) continued access for future generations. Increased income *can* allow poor families to move from unhealthy communities, avoiding medical incinerators, toxic ground water, cancerous air quality, and some forms of violence. Thus, education is framed as a gateway towards the safety, security, happiness, and white picket fences that wealth can provide.

Yet almost 50 years after James Baldwin delivered his talk, educators have still not faced the historical or continued colonial nature of the education of Black children, and still have not addressed the stark disparities in health, wealth, and livelihood. In many schools, students are taught about passive slaves, taught that *Plessy vs. Ferguson* was wrong, that separate but equal was well intentioned but did not result in the diverse, equal democracy that we currently live. In short, complicated historical realities are often left out of instruction, perhaps as much a result of standardized assessments guiding curriculum as unintentional racism limiting knowledge of historical reality (Banks, 1995; Barone, 2006; Loewen, 1996). And so *Brown vs. Board of Education* is often taught as the easily remedied solution to America's racism. There is little connection to why the civil rights struggle erupted into riots some 10–15 years after *Brown vs. Board of Education*. Little is taught about the intense struggles and continual threats of violence that led to *Brown vs. Board of Education*. The immediate fierce resistance to implementing anything remotely resembling desegregation, or any other complicated racially historical incident, is also silenced in American curriculum (Apple, 1993; Loewen, 1996; Martinez, 1995). Instead, stories of the Little Rock Nine are highlighted, Rosa Parks is framed as a tired Black woman and not a community advocate, Dr. King and Malcolm X are positioned in opposition to each other, and the reasons why the U.S. decided to legally desegregate is framed as America addressing past wrongs (Bell, 2004; Bigelow, 1995).

Reality is often more complicated than what schools teach. Immediately after *Brown vs. Board of Education*, incarceration rates for African Americans skyrocketed, and this trend has continued (Mauer & King, 2004). This can be directly traced to the closing of woefully under-resourced Black southern community schools that had been educating Black children to successfully navigate White society while maintaining the cultural values and linguistic traditions of the local (and historical) community (Morgan, 1995; Walker, 1996). Most of the Black-organized, -led, and -focused K–12 community schools were closed so that their students would "integrate" White schools. And immediately, these Black students, used to culturally responsive pedagogy, caring teachers, and educators who were active in their neighborhoods, were tracked into segregated classrooms. In addition, some tens of thousands of Black educators were forced out of jobs when these Black community schools were shut down (Futrell, 2004; Morgan, 1995). So while America celebrated its newfound integrationist schools, within those schools, Black children sat with other Black children, had their Black teachers replaced by White ones, and were no longer embraced as equal members of the community. In addition, as Black children enrolled, en masse, in White schools, White students increasingly fled further away, attended newly created, almost entirely White schools (Clark, 1987; Kruse,

2005). This left Black families with minimal choices. Their schools were being shut down; they had no option but to send their children to schools that were legally forced to educate their children, but not legally required to educate in ways that reflected Black culture, community context, or White racism.

Derrick Bell (2004) argued that *Brown vs. Board of Education* became law in part because the interests of Black families to be more adequately educated coincided with White interests to address growing fear of the communist threat. In addition to global critiques of America's Jim Crow system, quite a number of Black soldiers who had helped liberate Europe from Nazi Germany had returned empowered by fighting for justice. But fighting to free European White people only to return home to be considered second-class citizens did not sit well with many of these men, the majority of whom were excluded from the college expansion that followed WWII and from meaningful job opportunities. In part to quell potential unrest, and in part to address the growing criticism from communist countries that the U.S. was itself a two-tiered society, desegregation became a quick solution to multiple growing problems (Bell, 2004).

While the tangible benefits to adhering to and adopting White values are clear, the benefits to the larger community are more suspect. A debate has continued to filter throughout Black educator circles as to whether or not to embrace the values of White mainstream society, and whether or not to attend, prioritize, and support predominantly White institutions. From an individual perspective, it is hard to argue that access to Harvard, Princeton, and elite public institutions like the University of Michigan, UCLA, and UC Berkeley is not beneficial; the doors of opportunity do open for elite graduates. Examination of some forty years of Affirmative Action programs in college admissions shows that the numbers of Black graduates from elite colleges significantly increased (Bowen & Bok, 1998). But these graduates were far too few to decrease segregation, poverty, violence, or the long list of indicators that reflect the dire state of Black America. Indeed, an argument could be made that these educated elite have been taught precisely that the issues facing Black communities are due to individual lack of drive; those who succeed in school are told they are "different" because they work harder and are smarter than other Black students, just as many Black students, particularly males, have been socialized to not be seen as academically successful (DeMeulenaere, 2009; Ferguson, 2001; Fordham & Ogbu, 1986; Ogbu, 1991).

As the number of elite graduates of color increased, the number of Black families living in poverty also increased, just as did the number of incarcerated Black men. Not surprisingly, and despite increased access to elite education, school inequality largely looks the same as it did 50 years ago, and the achievement gap still correlates directly with a wage and wealth gap (Western & Pettit, 2005). While *Brown vs. Board of Education* can be seen as the legal justification for sending Black children to White schools, this argument only works when focused on the individual. Sending children to elite schools has resulted in a larger middle class, but has not diminished racism against Black people, nor begun to address racial inequalities.

Brown vs. Board of Education ultimately cemented in the public imagination that excellent education is White education. Thus, meritorious students are the students who explicitly embrace the values of whiteness and who can demonstrate such on standardized tests. Ensuring Black students are educated by White teachers in White-run schools also contributed to the silencing of cultural norms, the conflicted reality of Black children who are taught to act "White," and a conflating of mainstream White thinking with academic excellence. Desegregation resulted in Black children attending schools taught and organized by White educators uncomfortable with Blackness, with Black children, and with any obvious reminders of the cultural distance Black people might be from whiteness. Thus students operating on a communal basis, concerned about their peers or siblings, socialized to value voice and storytelling, particularly from elders, were (and are) taught to ignore these values, to focus on individual grades and individual notions of success. But this silencing occurred (and occurs) in the curriculum, too, with White European biased curriculum, standardized English only, and "proper" behavior encouraged while "improper" behavior is punished. This leads Black students to adopt survival strategies; those who are quiet are rewarded with success, and those who resist the stereotype often required for Black academic success are punished. Thus desegregation, without meaningful integration to shift White schooling into multicultural, multilingual educational approaches, has led to the purposeful silencing of Blackness.

This silencing creates a tremendous social cost that has been documented by scholars throughout the world (Fordham & Ogbu, 1986; Gibson & Ogbu, 1991; Woodson, 1933; Wright, 1957). In short, children are told to give up who they are in order to become successful in schools, and for Black children, this equates to giving up a lot more of themselves than must White children. And not surprising, many do not wish to give themselves up for a pathway towards the promise of wealth. And many recognize that there are other pathways (that have been illegalized), and that the promise of wealth is nothing more than a fleeting potential. Many youth of color do not graduate high school, and even fewer go on to graduate college, and even fewer of those become economically stable (Aud, Fox, & KewalRamani, 2010; Children's Defense Fund, 2006; Holzman, 2006). In essence, Black wealth is neither permanent nor promised, and the pathways towards education and prestige are purposefully limited. Black children recognize this.

But just as making something taboo encourages its popularity, the very traits Black children have been punished for exhibiting become stereotypical outlets for behavior. Black children have continually been punished for being too loud, too violent, too disregarding of authority, too late, too anything that broke the established norms of whiteness. And just like when alcohol was outlawed and subsequent drinking increased, so too do punishments lead some Black children to adopt stereotypical behaviors, reinforcing societal myths and fears. Black children who are told they are not smart because they choose to adhere to values their families and communities embrace, because they speak languages or colloquiums that reflect those they love or how they grew up often begin to act out. And what other choice are such students given? Consider a six-year-old Black student continually punished for trying to help a peer student on math problems when they are supposed to be working on their own. Or what about a twelve-year-old Black child whose teachers tremble in fear of him? One can imagine such children rejecting the values of their teachers, and such rejection should be seen as responsible choices. But instead, children are encouraged to survive as quietly as possible, to not support their peers, to ignore the fear in their teachers' eyes. There is little middle ground here.

Perhaps the most insidious impact of the legal commitment to require Black children be educated by White society is the internalizing of oppression by many Black children, who are rewarded for embracing societal values that deny their individuality, culture, community, and history. Educators could not have planned this better; Black children learn to prioritize White values above their own, and this has been exemplified year after year in studies documenting Black children preferring White dolls to Black dolls (Clark & Clark, 1947; Davis, 2007; Fegley, Spencer, Gross, Harpalani & Charles, 2008). But this is also demonstrated when Black children really do believe that White children are smarter than they are when they score higher on tests designed for White children to score higher on (Steele & Aronson, 1995). When Black families move out of urban areas, following White flight, fleeing to the suburbs, they do so in part to send their children to better-resourced schools. That these schools are also predominantly White is not coincidental, the hope is that such schools will provide more access to wealth and stability for Black children. The issue, though, is that there is little legal requirement for such schools to teach Black children, which is why dropout rates for Black and Latino students are significantly higher than for White students regardless of attendance at suburban or urban schools (Hauser, Simmons, & Pager, 2004; Rumberger & Thomas, 2000).

Schools directly teach Black children to embrace the values that directly oppose their physical, emotional, spiritual, and economic well-being. An obvious example of this can be seen in the teaching of history from a White European perspective, wherein enslaved Africans are often taught as docile and passive, rather than as a forced collective of community-driven people living under intense, purposeful violence. The complexity of being taught to be like the very people who colonized one's historical family is clarified by James Baldwin (1962) in a letter to his nephew: "There is no reason for you to try to become like White people and there is no basis whatever for their impertinent assumption that they must accept you" (p. 8). And yet there are tangible reasons to become like White people, tangible rewards in the form of access and wealth. The very purpose of education is to force Black children to become like White people, even though, as Richard Wright (1957) argued, the "chances of resembling [White people] are remote, slight" (p. 7). Baldwin (1985a) further clarified that, "to be poor and Black in a country so rich and White is to judge oneself very harshly and it means that one has nothing to lose" (p. 64). Having nothing to lose is hardly justification for applying oneself in school, particularly when schools intend to colonize young Black minds. The impact of imperialism and colonization are magnified when those colonized begin to take on the values of the colonizers, begin to embrace the values that directly deny Blackness.

In all of this, Wright (1957) reminds us that "we are here dealing with values evoked by social systems or colonial regimes which make men feel that they are dominated by powers stronger than they are" (p. 7). His point is that we can shift the internalized oppression we teach our children. Educators can begin to undo the trauma schools impart in students, can begin to arm children with culturally relevant knowledge. But this means refocusing our efforts, becoming student centered to help students see the power of their voices and perspectives. This cannot happen without authentic conversations about the purpose of school, the historical roots of oppression that shape what we do in schools today, and the reality that the United States has yet to meaningfully include Black communities in shaping democracy.

Standards, the Achievement Gap, and Racism

Recognizing that the purpose of schools is to silence Blackness, to ensure young Black people silence their cultural strengths, values, insights, ways of thinking, knowledge, and language in favor of standardized notions of whiteness is key. Because otherwise, educators cannot get our minds around the ever-present and intellectually irrelevant achievement gap, which, as Kitty Kelly Epstein has stated repeatedly, is "nothing more than a wealth or opportunity gap" (Epstein, 2006; Epstein, personal communication, November, 2010). The achievement gap was created by standardized tests that were designed specifically to segregate society; this is well documented (Epstein, 2006; Garrison, 2009; *Larry P. and Lucille P. v. Riles*, 1979; Rees, 2003). And after years of struggle against standardized assessments, the battle has been lost. In schools, districts, and communities across the country, Black educators, parents, and community advocates assess schools in terms of their standardized test scores, despite that these tests have much more to do with family income than intelligence, academic engagement, or student effort.

What the focus on the achievement gap has done is shift meaningful conversation away from the silencing mission of schools. Rather than discuss school reform in terms of transforming the mission of schools, national conversations focus on more efficiently educating children. In practice, this means more efficiently silencing Black children. Reform efforts focus on opening and closing schools, research-based best practices to increase test scores, and hiring new, highly-qualified teachers. But none of this addresses what schools intend to teach, that the teaching force is still mostly White, or that to become a classroom teacher, educators have to successfully navigate exclusive schools that rarely challenge such racist views. In urban communities, that means we have not changed the dynamic of sending Black children into the arms of White educators, who are taught to defend their colonial mission. Many of these White educators do not intend to colonize; they are often disengaged from this conversation because they, too, have never been forced to challenge their own notions of knowledge, academic success, and what it means to develop a multicultural, multilingual democracy.

The achievement gap will continue to exist until educators reframe the purpose of schooling to reflect multiple perspectives and uses. In English Only schools and classes, students are taught that "correct" ways of communicating mirrors Western thinking. Regardless of whether or not funding in schools is equalized, gaps will always remain when students are forced to learn and respond in languages that were not designed to encompass their experiences. Standardized notions of English exclude the vast majority of students who come from homes that might communicate in ways that conflict with how they are taught at school (Gay, 2000; Ladson-Billings, 1994; Valdes, 1996). This disjoint is enhanced by schools that completely deny the existence and value of indigenous knowledge. Linda Tuhiwai Smith

(1999) clarifies: "Having been immersed in the Western academy which claims theory as thoroughly Western, which has constructed all the rules by which the indigenous world has been theorized, indigenous voices have been overwhelmingly silenced" (p. 29). The focus on standardizing language has been increasing with the onslaught of standards-based high-stakes testing, and No Child Left Behind and Race to the Top federal reform efforts only exacerbate such alienating approaches that deny indigenous knowledge and the languages designed to communicate such knowledge. Rochelle Brock (2005) asks the question educators and scholars should be concerned with: "How can I use a language that is more meaningful, but less academically accepted?" (p. 3).

This narrow focus on assessing for standardized adherence to White values creates a double bind for urban educators attempting to empower students of color. Even if educators respond in culturally relevant ways to their students, their effectiveness is still measured by student test scores that measure their facility at expressing White values and White-normed language. Silvera (1983) argued that "the traditional methodological instruments of the academic are inadequate to handle the complexities of recognizing the extent of powerlessness and engaging in the task of empowerment" (p. ix). The tools we use for measuring and defining academic merit are simply not complex enough to capture the nuance of how oppression shapes student thought. Effective teachers, then, often try to develop the capacity for urban students to code-shift; to be able to express themselves in their cultural tongue and still excel at the White-framed language of school. (De Fina, 2007; Perry & Delpit, 1998; Wheeler & Swords, 2006). While this multilingual approach should be taught, the problem is that multiple languages are not valued, and many of the cultural nuances of urban students are not classified as language systems anyhow. So, as happened in Oakland, California, in the mid-nineties, when urban educators tried to teach students to communicate in Ebonics and standardized English, their efforts became a debate over whether or not Ebonics is a *real* language (Epstein, 2006; Perry & Delpit, 1998). The notion of code switching is relegated to the backburner because of intense White racism to efforts that actually validate cultural forms of communication.

And this is what it means to standardize writing: ultimately, as a society, we decide which forms of communication are valid and which are invalid. Gloria Ladson-Billings (1999) clarifies the use of critical race theory in capturing "the official school curriculum as a culturally specific artifact designed to maintain a White supremacist master script" (p. 21). If the purpose of school curriculum is to maintain White supremacy, then it should be no wonder that urban students of color often argue that they must devalue who they are in order to do well academically; that is precisely what the formal school curriculum asks students of color to do. The problem with the way standards have been defined and framed is that they simply are not adequate in framing an understanding of what is happening with students of color in schools, because they are only designed to assess adherence to a *White supremacist master script*. While many have advocated for multiple measures in assessing high school graduation readiness, individual schools, and increasingly individual educators, are being assessed not in terms of multiple measures, but their students' test scores in just a few standardized tests (Darling-Hammond, Rustique-Forrester & Pecheone, 2005). But even multiple measures will not address gaps in knowledge unless the entire way knowledge is seen is democratized (and not uniformly standardized along notions of whiteness). Instead, what is often measured is capacity to express oneself in a passive language that is more readily heard by the largely White mainstream academics who design the tests based on their own cultural values and norms. The processes through which urban students are taught to write in dispassionate, emotionless ways that often directly contradict the cultural context of urban youth of color are demonstrated throughout studies on schools (Delpit, 2006; Fine, 1991; Gay, 2000; hooks, 1994; Macedo & Bartolomé, 1999; Oakes, 1985; Valdes, 1996).

Standardizing language is not a new phenomenon; dictionaries offer historical timelines of the status quo of language in America. Taught to school-aged children as the source to go to for "real" definitions of words, dictionaries provide limiting definitions of words that reflect societal racism, sexism, and oppression (Carr, 1997). When students are taught that the source for "accurate" meaning in words is the biased definitions developed by corporate publishing houses with a vested interest in sustaining their roles as knowledge producers, students are taught that their own cultural context around such words is irrelevant. In a similar vein, much reading, writing, and comprehension is taught with only a White, European-background cultural context behind words (Gay, 2000; Ladson-Billings, 1994). Thus as children of color begin to develop language and vocabulary in schools, they learn to speak words that deny their very existence. Urban students of color are, in many ways, made to forget what is important about who they are when they enter the classroom, but also learn to speak in ways that deny who they are as well.

Standards are the formal way of measuring this process, but instead of framing the process as colonization and racism, standards are framed as a way of measuring intelligence. Adherence to whiteness, then, is a direct equation to the capacity to be defined by our schools as "intelligent," "smart," and, "well-qualified" for admissions into college. My point is not that urban educators should not be evaluating our work, but instead that we need accurate measurement tools that assess culturally relevant knowledge forms as well as a range of academic skill sets. As Duncan-Andrade and Morrell (2008) clarified, "We, as educators and researchers, need to be ready to show how the students are learning everything they need to in the context of undertaking meaningful, life-affirming work. All of this could be accomplished, we believe, without the use of most of the standardized-tests that currently occupy so much of our thinking" (p. 170).

The Importance of Developing Voice in Schools

James Baldwin (1972) clarified the importance of voice as a foundation for the role of educators in a democracy. "If one really wishes to know how justice is administered in a country," Baldwin argued, "one does not question the policemen, the lawyers, the judges, or the protected members of the middle class. One goes to the unprotected — those, precisely, who need the law's protection most! — and listens to their testimony" (p. 149). Black youth have answers to how our nation's schools contribute to societal segregation, poverty, and racial animosity, and it is in the interests of schools to prepare youth to express such voices. Schools should be in the business of developing the skills in youth to identify problems that shape their inequalities, and then to testify about such inequalities. Transforming schools into such proactive roles requires doing something dramatically different; something that we, as a society, have yet to try: empowering and affirming children of color to express themselves, providing forums for such expression, then shutting up and listening. And isn't that exactly what we want from children—active, critical thinkers?

I am certainly not the first to advocate for developing youth voice, nor for student-centered education (Dewey, 1916; Freire, 2004; Krishnamurti, 1953; Power, Higgins & Kohlberg, 1989). Many educators, activists, civil rights leaders, artists, writers, and musicians have advocated for, through multicultural education, Afrocentrism, and culturally relevant and responsive approaches, an arts-integrated, culturally rich curriculum (Asante, 1998; Banks, 1996; Gay, 2000; Greene, 2001; Ladson-Billings, 1994). But these efforts have been decreasing in direct relation to the standards-movement, pushed outside a narrowing curriculum (Knaus, 2007). Public expression has continued on, despite how Black voices have been made illegal throughout historical policy and practice. Yet expression cannot be silenced: despite intense racism, the Harlem Renaissance demonstrated the potential impact of aligning education, youth development, and the arts world with local businesses, churches, and civic organizations. Such periods of vibrant Black communities were built up in in urban cities across the U.S., always on the foundation of artistic expression, always reflecting the soul of the community, with songs clarifying racism, oppression, and resistance (Campbell, 1994; Martin, 1983; McKay, 1930). Pulling on such work, individual schools have maintained a strong focus on the arts, music, dance, or poetry throughout history. The core problem, however, is that most of this work, and certainly the development of skills related to expression, is outside the scope of everyday public education, as exceptions to the rule. My push is to transform schools to center on developing such critical, culturally rooted voice, and help foster student voice so they can express exactly what they see as wrong in the world.

Such testimony is already spray painted on walls throughout urban environments. Urban youth speak their voices, claim what space they can, and do so despite their schools, in part because there is no room for their voice in schools. So urban youth are forced to break laws, to sneak their points in between railroad cars, on delivery trucks, abandoned billboards, and through YouTube videos, blogs, and Tweets. Graffiti is a powerful example of an expression of voice that is systemically silenced and literally painted over. Many urban communities stand out because of graffiti, which to those less familiar, may simply look like random scratches and spray painted names on buildings across a cityscape. But many graffiti artists spend time crafting messages of hope and anti-police brutality, recording the names of young children killed in urban violence. Impromptu and commissioned murals pop up all over urban cities, often only to be silenced by poorly paid maintenance workers, who are made to paint over youthful artwork. While not all graffiti is meaningful or tells a story of resistance to violence, racism, or negativity, most graffiti is an attempt to claim space, to honor the community or the individual artist in culturally responsive ways (Alonso, 1998; Brewer, 1992; Feiner & Klein, 1982). June Jordan, in talking about poetry, argued that she "would hope that folks throughout the U.S.A. would consider the creation of poems as a foundation for true community: a fearless democratic society" (in Muller et al., 1995, p. 3). Graffiti, in many ways, reflects such a democratic society, with freedom of expression taking on a plea for recognition, as young people attempt to tell community stories on the concrete walls that block their view of the world.

Because most schools have not historically taught content that reflects multicultural histories, languages, and resistance to oppression, nor linked such content to contemporary community struggles, much work is needed to reframe schools to provide a foundation for developing such voice. Pihama (1985) argued that: "Maori people struggle to gain a voice, struggle to be heard from the margins, to have our stories heard, to have our descriptions of ourselves validated, to have access to the domain within which we can control and define those images which are held up as reflections of our realities" (p. 241). A voice-centered curriculum cannot operate in isolation from the reality that oppressed voices are silenced systematically throughout the educational system, but also in mainstream mass media. Yet forums for voice, which exist outside the realms of schools, cannot be integrated into education without developing student voice. The two must occur at the same time, as core functions of public schooling.

Thus schools must provide relevant curriculum, encourage students to develop their voices as part of what it means to "be educated," and create forums for youth expression. In the process of coming to see schools as reflecting the inequalities of society, students can begin to create their own ways of expressing themselves based on who they are, what they see, live, and feel in the world around them, and begin to merge the social distance between school and their personal lives. The focus on voice helps prepare urban students to interrogate still-in-place racist, colonial educational structures in ways that will not ultimately lead them to turn away from school. This is entirely the point of teaching for voice; in my courses, students are reminded that they should be themselves, should use their own experiences as ways of informing what they say and write, and should recognize the cultural knowledge they live by so that they can challenge the oppression they live. Centering the cultural context of students in the classroom is needed in order to help students recognize that academic knowledge must include their perspectives and can be useful in helping understand how distinct communities fit within larger social struggles (Banks, 1993; Gordon, 1995).

Multicultural education has long argued for approaches to help students find their voice through inclusive curriculum content (Banks & Banks, 2009; Gay, 2000; Nieto, 1996). Recent efforts have highlighted the need for students to develop their own stories; this allows for comparative analysis of student stories with historical narratives (Duncan-Andrade & Morrell, 2008; Fisher, 2008; Morrell, 2004). Shields, Bishop, and Mazawi (2005) clarify that "A narrative approach argues that we story our lives, and repositioning requires new stories" (p. 147). Multicultural education efforts that lead to more inclusive curriculum lays a foundation for repositioning schooling, but in order to transform the silencing impact of schools, student culture has to be centered in more meaningful ways than adding curriculum content that might mirror student life (Banks, 1995). Developing personal stories empowers youth to begin to document their own history while building a student-generated curriculum that interacts with cultural histories. Such an ongoing process of students generating curriculum also helps ensure educators do not co-opt student ideas and water down student passion into a removed, academic discussion about the main point.

Geneva Gay (2000) argues that "because of the dialectic relationship between knowledge and the knower, interest and motivation, relevance and mastery, Native Americans, Latinos, African Americans, and Asian Americans must be seen as co-originators, co-designers, and co-directors (along with professional educators) of their education" (p. 111). As students become more centrally involved in shaping what they do in the classroom, they tend to become more invested in their education (Ginwright, Noguera, Cammarota, 2006). Unfortunately, most efforts at instituting cultural responsiveness in the classroom fall short of also empowering students to develop curriculum content, much less to analyze the content they are provided (Gay, 2007; Knaus, 2007; Weis & Fine, 2005). While Gay (2000) asserts that inclusive curriculum has to include a wide array of knowledge bases (including mass media, literature, music, personal experience, and research), she ultimately argues that "ethnically diverse students and their cultural heritages must be the sources and centers of educational programs" (p. 111).

Gil Conchas (2006) argues that "one pillar of a strong self-identity for African American students is pride of heritage" (p. 52). What this ultimately means is that schools have to be in the business of building up student consciousness about heritages (theirs and those of their peers). Centering students in the classroom ultimately entails centering the cultural contexts students bring; developing voice allows other students (and teachers) to learn how culture operates on a daily basis in students' lives. The more focused a curriculum and teaching approaches are on developing student voice, the easier centering the cultures of the students will be. Centering students does not always have to be teaching about presumed monolithic identity groups (such as African American or Latino). Indeed, centering culture may mean letting students clarify what growing up as a multiracial African American and Latino person feels like. This is the purpose of voice: to clarify exactly what life is like from the perspective of the speaker, author, poet, playwright, actor, musician, artist, and student. And when developing voice becomes the central purpose of schools, intricate complications such as living multiple realities as a multilingual multiracial African American and Latino young woman become part of the curriculum, and part of how people learn about the boundaries of race, class, gender, sexuality, ability, and identity.

The issue with expressing voice, however, lies in expectation. After reading a poem that took her seven months to craft, edit, and finalize, and after months of tearful work spent trying to work through the trauma captured in the poem, Shantel gave an intense on-stage reading. The audience loved the performance; she brought them to tears, received a standing ovation, and after walking off the stage, was immediately surrounded with affirming hugs. But the next day, Shantel asked to meet with me. As we walked around the neighborhood after school, she expressed her frustration: "So what do I do now? I still need a job, still need to help my mom with rent, and still wake up in fear." Developing voice helps prepare urban students to be more present to their realities, more able to concisely capture the complications that shape their lives, but does not alter those realities.

Linda Tuhiwai Smith (1999) cautioned:

> *Taking apart the story, revealing underlying texts, and giving voice to things that are often known intuitively does not help people to improve their current conditions. It provides words, perhaps, an insight that explains certain experiences—but it does not prevent someone from dying. (p. 4)*

Shantel and Smith remind educators that teaching for voice does not actually remove young people from the oppression they navigate. And while the purpose is to arm urban youth with the tools to navigate and live more healthfully, the reality is that without also eradicating the oppressions they live, teaching for voice is ultimately not going to change society. Developing urban youth voice only prepares students to live more authentically, to develop a facility with language and words that enables and empowers them to speak more forcefully about the world they envision. But voice, as Dave, a Filipino and African American high school junior who had taken two writing classes with me, argued, is also about concrete solutions; voice clarifies what can be done about systemic inequities. "Let us write our own histories, study our own cultures, and examine what happens in our communities." History has to be more than pilgrims and Indians sitting down peacefully to a Thanksgiving dinner, but also has to be more than just victims and perpetrators of genocide; developing voice helps students begin to see themselves in a historical light, with responsibility in what happens around them. Developing voice requires educators to take responsibility for incorporating student knowledge in the curriculum. Students should be empowered to facilitate their own research studies, and educators can support and challenge urban youth to examine what has happened in local communities and what they can do to address local issues. This is what Dave argued is the responsibility of urban youth: "We can figure out solutions, but you gotta let us understand the problems and not keep testing us on White versions, because that doesn't help us with reality."[2]

Dave also pushed against notions of students as disengaged from their schools and communities. Urban students are often depicted as uncaring, and voice directly contradicts this false stereotype. An Oakland teacher who implemented a youth participatory action research process for her students as part of a requirement for an educational leadership course I taught had urban students focus on community trash, particularly in the streets. The neighborhood was dirty; heaps of trash sat on every street corner, and student lunches, bags of Cheetos and Doritos, empty beer bottles, used condoms, and never-attempted homework packets spiraled across lawns, front porches, and every sidewalk. The teacher's assumptions were that these African American and Latino students simply did not care enough about their communities to not litter. After spending time in the community, literally walking the streets with her students, the teacher realized that her assumptions were wrong. Students cared deeply about their communities, but had few trashcans. Overflowing trashcans rarely offer an enticing place to dispose of trash, and nearby apartment dumpsters were equally overfull. Midway through the project, students clarified that the people outside their community, who might have access to lobbying for better trash service, particularly in public areas, did not seem to care about their community. They were also increasingly frustrated by efforts to beautify their community, because those seemed like wasted attempts; they did get several trash cans placed on dirtier street corners, but the city did not regularly empty these (like they did in more affluent areas just a few blocks away).

Angela, a high school senior, expressed this frustration after her teacher lashed out at the class, thinking students were not taking their research projects seriously. "It's not that I don't care, I just don't know what to do. Everything I do is pointless because all my efforts are shot down by other teachers or the city." Angela's point was that efforts to care, to clean up a community, to fix broken realities eventually stop when each effort is met with resistance. "I went to the district office to ask for recycle bins," she continued, "and was told that 'niggas like us won't use them anyways.'" She continued, "And where were my teachers? They told me this was my job to fix this, saying it was 'student advocacy research.' But in order to change this, I need teachers to advocate with me." Angela's experience is not uncommon, and the point is that students cannot be told to fix their problems, but instead must be guided and supported to name problems; to identify causes; and then, in coalition with adults, educators, and others, move to action. Students do care, and yet often grow frustrated, because in most cases, students cannot transform schools or their communities unless they are actively supported well beyond what educators typically do.

Voice (a freewrite by Jacinda)
Voice. My voice is so loud it
can be heard, everywhere. My
voice makes your body hot, N
they stand up, every hair.
My voice rips through the paper,
every tear. But in jail, I never
have a voice when im there.
N at school, you hearin my voice
is Very rare. N when
I voice, sometimes I don't even
think what im sayn, sprayn, I
don't know when I stopped
prayn. That's the big voice, but is
he really there? She? Or maybe
my god is me. But I rarely hear
the voice that is said to be.
Rarely hear the voice that
come from me. Or the voice
that rules the U.S.A. A
collection of people, picking us
off like prey. But the voice
comes back and it's all just
a stage. But it your voice
that keeps everyone, their own
individual, calm, everyday. N
it's funny cuz it's your voice
that let's you do fucked up
shit, N with the help of other
people's voices you know what
it is.

Many democratic theorists argue that young people are the foundation of building and sustaining democracy (Barber, 1992; Gutmann, 1999; Steiner, 1999). Yet in the U.S., with few exceptions, students have very little role in structuring schools, shaping curriculum, or determining what matters in their educational processes (Duncan-Andrade & Morrell, 2008; Ginwright, Noguera, Cammarota, 2006). If urban students are continually limited in their local forms of expression, told to not clean up their neighborhoods, to not write on walls, to not claim local space, and are not allowed to shape any of their school day, what public opportunities do they have to express voice in sanctioned ways that help them sharpen their messages? Instead of promoting the development of and sharpening the impact of voice, educators continually silence expression of voice in urban students, the opposite of what is needed to prepare students for democratic participation. Indeed, as Geneva Gay (2000) argued, "the freedom to be ethnically expressive removes the psychological stress associated with and psychic energy deployed in 'covering up' or 'containing' one's cultural inclinations" (p. 36). Centering voice as the purpose of schooling sets a foundation for youth of color to wrestle with and make sense of the oppression they face while giving them space to be their authentic selves.

The Impact of Voice on Students and Teachers

I tell the following story to demonstrate the impact my focus on developing voice had on one disengaged student and to show the impact students can have on educators. In particular, I share this story to capture how I came to deepen my teaching and how I dedicated myself to teaching for voice because I began to listen to my students. The student, Tony, also provided me with the space to reflect on my purpose as an educator, and reminds teachers of the humility required to continually learn from our students.

"Is there anyway," Tony asked me, "I can get into your class? I know I don't have good grades and can't write and got some issues an' stuff. But I really wanna get into your class." I asked him to write a one-paragraph justification for why I should let him in the class, given that he had been in fights and passed only two courses in the past two years (both in PE). He told me he had never before written a full paragraph, and after clarifying to him that a paragraph is essentially a complete idea in a small set of connected sentences, he left with a grin spread across his scarred, 18-year-old-stubble face. He did not show up to school or my class the following day, confirming my concern that while he wanted in the class, he would not do the work it would take for him to fully engage. Indeed, I thought he had wanted to be in our class because we took fieldtrips, had cool guest visitors (poets, civil rights activists, filmmakers, graffiti artists), and because I was laid back (and he probably thought that meant I was an easy grader). Two days of my assumptions later, however, he gave me a crumpled up note, his scrawny chicken scratch scribbled in diagonal lines tilting downward towards the right; the last line started horizontal midway through the wrinkled sheet and ended exactly perpendicular, landing 2 inches from the bottom right hand corner of the page: what was clear was that he had never written that much in his life.

> *Drear Doc Kris:*
>
> *I wunt to b in ur class. YOU du thang diffrent. I c student b Peeple in ur class. u an them stan taller. N cuz 4 realz kidz in ur class be speakin trufh trufh I aint heard 4. I cant write I cant spell I cant I I cant. I mis class I clean KFC they git me hilth cure an I got baby sis and baby bruh and I don need gwramma I need to learnt to speak me mindz. Will u help Doc Kris? I wanna write I wanna speak.*
>
> *Uno—Toney*[3]

Tony had been continually in and out of juvenile hall; teachers warned me prior to interacting with him that he was "violent," "crazy," "erratic," and "disrespectful." But he had always been very polite with me prior to asking to be in my class. The class was designed for students who excelled at writing; students had to be recommended by another teacher in order to get in. Tony certainly did not meet the stated requirements. "He spelled his own name wrong!" I thought to myself incredulously, as I read over his letter. And yet something was compelling me to push my own practice deeper: could I teach someone with very limited writing skills? Here was Tony, a young multiracial African American and Latino man telling me that he was frustrated by grammar and traditional writing instruction; this was his senior year after all, and his writing suggested that at least he be tested for a learning disability. I wondered if he might have been better served in special education classes, yet I knew that, as a senior, the school would be very reluctant to test him, just as he'd be reluctant to get tested. What would the point be for him? He already hated school.

I kept reading Tony's letter. The clarity he wrote with reminded me that what I was teaching was more about how to express oneself than English, more about how to live in this world than to pass writing tests or develop five-paragraph essays (though all of that, I would eventually learn, improves when students want to write). Tony was more to-the-point than I was: he just wanted in a class that let students be people, where he could be affirmed, and maybe, finally, learn how to write in a way that he wanted to write. Tony's voice showed that while he had not effectively learned how to express himself in standardized English, he could express himself well, and in minimal words. He was concise! Tony's letter captured that he cleaned Kentucky Fried Chicken restaurants so he could have health care to take care of his siblings; that meant he worked full-time while going to high school. Tony's vulnerability clarified precisely what voice is: the capacity to express one's reality, capturing the way we speak as a reflection of the world around us. How could I not let him into the course? Indeed, how could I not let him transform our course to focus entirely on developing voice instead of grammar, punctuation, or the nuances of writing form?

Yet I still feared that I would fail these urban students if I did not teach them basics; and being measured by test scores, I would fail as an educator. Tony's letter haunted me, implored me to rethink my practice. I had taught writing classes in prisons and juvenile halls at this point, but those students knew they would not be tested on Standard English; I was teaching them poetry as a way to release rage. My school-based teaching, in contrast, featured poetry and creative writing within a framework of academic skill sets. I had been using two completely different teaching approaches for two different student populations. When I taught in prison, I dove in deeply, urging incarcerated young men to find their voices. Something was holding me back in schools, though, and Tony made that clear. Shouldn't I be pushing all students to develop their voice, to speak to their realities, to capture what they see and live? Shouldn't I try to engage students before they drop out and end up in the prison classes I see them in later? Wouldn't all students do better if they developed a greater purpose for speaking, for sharing their thoughts on how they navigate and are seen by the world?

I had been thinking about voice for years, but Tony's letter made me realize I had no overarching framework from which to conceive of voice. I had been teaching based on my own experiences, and while I was a popular teacher, I was not nearly as effective as I could be. In hindsight, I was trying to bridge my own development as a writer with the academic success I never had; I had taught myself to write well, and was trying to teach that process to incarcerated youth. But since I did not know how to teach, I tried to do what I saw being done, despite the fact that those efforts did not work with me. And I was perpetuating a false notion that teaching for voice is separate from high-quality teaching, and should just be taught to those already deemed as academic failures. I justified my approaches to myself, but Tony helped me see that I needed to learn how to teach based on who I was, and needed to make school more meaningful for students who had not yet dropped out.

From my first effort to teach others, I had seen the purpose of my teaching as raising awareness about oppression. My first intentional public speaking was as an undergraduate student at a Women Take Back the Night rally, and from there, I began teaching about race and racism, hosting dialogues for high school and college students. Those experiences led me into the high school classroom, and I began teaching week-long seminars on civil rights history and poetry workshops. When I began teaching in my own classroom, I tried to combine my focus on civil rights with poetry, exposing students to stories and poems that expanded notions of privilege and oppression. My classrooms were always dialogue-based, and I rarely lectured. Instead, I posed questions based on the readings and urged students to make connections to their own lives. In these urban schools, my teaching was fairly effective; students were engaged, and students who were typically disengaged from school tended to be much more present in my classes. Because I did not have behavioral issues in my classes, I was never given feedback from a principal or another educator; they instead focused on the teachers who sent children out of their classroom regularly or who struggled with classroom management. So I thought I was doing well, my students appeared to appreciate me, and most continued to write poetry well after our class ended.

Around the same time, I was invited to teach poetry workshops for incarcerated young men. We talked about the purpose, and agreed that I would try to use poetry as a way of helping the young men make sense of and release their rage. I co-taught with an African American woman psychologist, and while she would help frame the writing process, I would push students on poetry and capturing details. From the first day we stepped into the barren concrete-walled room with bolted-down desks, barred windows, and prison guards observing each and every move (students or ours), my teaching began to develop in a parallel but distinct route. In that space, she and I collaborated across race and gender. We urged those young men to release their rage, to capture when they were most frustrated, angry, and emotional, and then to share aloud with the class. Despite the presence of the guards, the men exploded, cursing with angry voices, and afterwards, they'd slump into their desks, spent. After a few weeks, the men started asking for extra journals, and encouraged each other to keep writing, until ultimately, they asked for several journals a month. The guards also began to shift, as they would tell us the young men's behavior began to change; they got in less fights and some of them began breaking up fights.

We kept teaching to similar populations, and I began collaborating with a science teacher who was also in my doctoral program. We began combining our classroom-based approaches with community-based readings, local poets and artists to develop voice, and right about that time, I received Tony's letter. As my educational stars aligned, I began to question my methods of teaching. In my classroom-based efforts, was I preparing students to shape the curriculum, to shape what was happening in their classes? Was I ensuring that all students developed and expressed their voice, in the ways that they wanted to be heard? Was I helping the incarcerated young men develop skill sets to address violence as it happened around them? Was releasing rage enough? Was reading a range of poets writing about civil rights enough? While I did not have immediate answers, I knew that I needed to develop my own skill sets, and most importantly, knew I needed to develop a framework for teaching that blended these arenas.

Tony reminded me that as an educator I must learn from my students; even students not part of our classroom communities can dramatically reshape our purpose. My students were already telling me that they were learning how to navigate their world more effectively, that they were writing daily in journals about how demeaning people in their community were, how offensive television images were, and how difficult growing up in a racist society was. But they were not tapping into the same emotion that the incarcerated men were. They were not capturing concrete details that demonstrated what the racism they survived felt like, looked like, and tasted of. As I began to talk with my students more, I began to develop a more conscious philosophy of teaching. I considered the lessons I was learning from multicultural education experts, considered my multiple student populations, wrestled with my own voice, and rethought the purpose of schooling.

Tony is an example of how essential teaching for voice is for students and educators. Prior to my class, Tony had no reason for being in school. He had been repeatedly labeled by schools and his probation officer as illiterate, yet no one had reached out to him and taught him to write nor recognized how powerfully articulate he was. No one had seen Tony from a lens other than his academic failure, and in response, he rejected school. In our class, Tony began writing and developed a foundation to learn how to read well. I was impressed with his capacity to care, to be vulnerable when he had failed almost ever class over the past two years. I was and am impressed by his purpose: he did not want to learn to write, he wanted to learn to express himself. As unprepared and unsupported as I was, I helped him learn how to be himself, and in the process, learned how to teach. He ended our class with a note to me:

> *And I wanna say this so you stand me. school does evry thing wrong. I don need to learnt sentenences and pawragrafs. I don. I do need to learn to speak my mind. I do need to learn to speak my hart. And I need to speak how I talk, how I am. These are not schools. They are hear to train us to slave us. And I am no slave. I can say dat now.—Tony*

While Tony eventually navigated through to college, his experience and relative success are not the norm. When urban student dropout rates hover around 50%, the urgency to engage students cannot be greater (Alliance for Excellent Education, 2009; Swanson, 2006). Teaching for voice in schools that are organized around invalidating such voice, however, sets up students to be punished for not adhering to academic norms. Tony was able to say what he felt he needed to, but also realized that he could only do that in our classroom; he continued to be standoffish with the rest of his teachers, who did not take the time to know him. Many urban schools also engage in urban poetry movements that have validated, in small subsets of populations, multiple forms of expression and have helped keep students like Tony engaged, at least in one class. But this expression is rarely connected to the standards these schools are measured against, leading many teachers to limit their creative approaches. In addition, critical expression can get these students in trouble. In essence, such efforts are limited because student-centered educators who focus on student voice are not the norm, and students have to learn to navigate the rest of their schooling without a focus on who they are. Julia, a 12th grader at the time, clarified teacher expectations. "They teach me what to say, how to repeat what the teacher wants." The problem, she argued, is that she is punished for developing her own ways of communicating that she sees as valid: "Pero no puedo speak in my native language. I cant say what I want to say, just what the teachers think I need to know. So they penalize me for writing in Español, for speaking en mi language." Julia and Tony both highlight the importance of centering voice as a school-wide strategy, and point out the need to develop voice, to clearly define what voice is, and ultimately require educational structures to be built to support their development.

Defining Voice

The purpose of education, in my mind, is to provide space for students like Tony and Julia to learn to speak their own minds, to understand what society does to urban African American and Latino students, and to feel comfortable hearing their voices challenge such realities. Yet voice is not just documenting personal realities or challenging the purpose of schooling. Voice depends entirely upon the authors' experiences, ways of speaking and thinking, and reflects a complicated, multilingual, multicultural, multiracial, multiethnic world. I often tell my students that "voice is difficult to define concretely, but you know voice when you hear it." June Jordan, who wrote extensively about voice and the purpose of speaking out throughout her career as a writer, poet, and professor, argued that "poetry means taking control of the language of your life" (in Muller et al., 1995, p. 3). Poetry is one of the ways to express voice, but there are infinite ways to take control of our personal language (drawing, cooking, watercolors, building, song, dance, knitting, novels, journals). My focus here is on writing, but I argue that schools should be in the business of promoting all kinds of artistic expression that captures voice, with writing as a foundation.

In what has become a seminal article in defining critical race theory as a framework for educational transformation, Gloria Ladson-Billings (1999) clarifies that "the 'voice' component of CRT provides a way to communicate the experiences and realities of the oppressed, a first step in understanding the complexities of racism…." (p. 16). Voice, seen through the lens of critical race theory, is about "naming one's own reality with stories" and doing so in a way that clarifies oppression (Ladson-Billings, 1999, p. 16). In the poem below, Christina, a first-generation college student who took my classes in high school and again in college, provides her take on voice as a capturing of the details that make up the fabric of her life.[4]

My voice is the sing song lullabies de mi tía screaming from prison walls

Mi voz es the fist rising inside of me, breaking walls I did not know surround me

My voice might stab you with the sharpness of rape from mi molesting tíos

Mi voz might remind you that I sleep hungry and wake with medical bed sores

My voice should make you cry in shame at how little public assistance I survive on

Mi voz es the one thing I have left and yet my teachers teach me silence

I write to figure out what I have to say

And I speak to tell you who listen (which is not enough of you) how wrong the world is

I speak so that you who listen know how I bleed, what causes my pain

So that those of you who care will join me, join us

In speaking listening learning and then shaping a healing world where we can all be

Full of our languages, aware of our histories, writing survival manuals

Teaching others, through our voices, how to keep on when on might get us killed

Mi voz is the air that keeps me mi hermanas y perhaps you también alive

—Christina

As Christina began to document her life through writing, she began to recognize the oppression that plagues her family, severely limiting her family's opportunity. Only through writing was she able to see her own role, as she came to recognize that the violence she grew up in is what gave her insight into the world. "When I started writing, started finding my voice, I realized that I was not alone, that I was just like the authors we read," Christina argued. Writing became a way to create her own living history, and she began to consider ways of disrupting what she saw as "the way things are because we all just tolerate this." For her, the key was in editing her work until her words reflected what she felt, "I realized, in our class, that saying what I want en mi voz es muy dificíl." She continued, "pero, I've been taught to never ever speak my voice, much less learn to speak how I actually talk about the things that make me me." Such work is difficult; Christina had spent years working on developing her writing, on learning to tell stories, and on learning to value writing in *Spanglish*, the conglomerated language she grew up speaking. Yet the importance of voice is that such writing creates stories that contradict mainstream U.S. avoidance of critical voices of people of color and oppressed people in general, but also helps individuals make sense of their own survival (Yosso, 2005).

The key to such voice is in developing a language to express stories that reflect what we live, how we live, and how students feel about both. Rochelle Brock (2005) argues that "language is personal and needs to bring forth the personal stories it is trying to relate to the reader. Words should be shaped and molded to your needs" (p. 3). Voice is a personal attempt to develop a language that makes sense to the author, and captures our stories in our own languages, in our own multicultural rhythms and multilingual words. Without voice, the language of the colonizer is used to explain the experience of being colonized, and those that live racism use the dominant language to try to explain that racism (Smith, 1999; Thiong'o, 1986; Wright, 1957). But the words don't match: such "formal" language frames the experience of the people who develop that language. When students begin to recognize that the English language really does define "black" as negative and dangerous and "White" as positive and beautiful, something happens to their voices. They begin to search for meaning, to develop new words and recognize that they are the ones who must recreate and reclaim language to reflect who they are.

But in the meantime, this language disjoint leaves women searching for language in a world dominated by men, people of color in search of words in languages imposed by White systems of colonization, and people with disabilities striving to recreate a way of speaking, talking, and writing that reflects disabled realities in a presumed able-bodied world. But our language doesn't work: "disabled" lives in opposition to "able-bodied," "Black" in juxtaposition to "White," "woman" in relation to "man." Our binary colonial languages struggle to find words to clarify the continuing marginalization of people who are multiracial, transgendered, multilingual, and multicultural. Thus, voice is resistance to systematic oppression kept firmly in place by our daily language, by academic language, by the very dictionaries that teach us, as we grow up, what words mean, and what part of which people matters more, as if there can be a universal definition of language, oppression, or experience.

Dorothy Allison (2002) speaks to the role of voice in daily survival: "Once in a while, I can make the world I know real on the page...Writing these stories is the only way I know to make sure of my ongoing decision to live, to set moment to moment a small piece of stubbornness against an ocean of ignorance and obliteration" (p. 7). Developing voice is a process of thinking through and documenting both what and how we survive; it is these realities that shape opportunity, awareness, and consciousness. Beth Brant (1994) clarified the responsibility of voice: "As an Indigenous writer, I feel that the gift of writing and the privilege of writing holds a responsibility to be witness to my people...to be witness to the sometimes unbearable circumstances of our lives" (p. 70). Voice is captured through writing that demonstrates exactly what is unbearable in our lives; these are the details that are systemically silenced through mainstream academics, literature, corporate mass media, and schools.

Components of Voice

To capture the nuances of our lives, voice is full of concrete details that show the complexities of our lives and how we fit within oppression and privilege. Jordan clarifies the need for concrete details: "Good poetry requires precision: if you do not attempt to say, accurately, truthfully, what you feel or see or need, then how will you achieve precision?" (in Muller et al., 1995, p. 3). *Jordan here names the first component of voice: a concise capturing of the author's reality, responding to the author's culture(s), language(s), race(s), gender(s), sexuality(ies), ability(ies), religion(s), spirituality(ies), and class-based experiences.* Voice is who we are, all of the silenced parts that make up our identity, the very pieces of us that we have been told to hide. This means, like most artistic endeavors, practice is essential to ensuring our words convey truth that others can feel as we would have them feel. Jordan argued for maximum impact with minimal words, and I teach students and educators alike to repeatedly draft and edit to ensure clarity and purpose. Writing for voice requires continual editing to concisely capture personal context. Stories and experiences come out naturally, but through our schooling we are taught to write in ways that contradict our languages and cultures. Thus continual editing is required to ensure our words and personal contexts blend into our voice, full of our emotion and experience.

After one of my courses culminated in a public poetry reading, several of my students excitedly bounced with energy when they left the stage. Their words shook many in the audience, and they were reflecting the energy from the performance. Two students, Shay and Loni could not contain themselves; they were shaking with nervous energy and excitement. I asked them how they felt, and they couldn't hold back: "I've never felt like anyone really listened to me before because I never really said anything." Loni said, "But now, I made people cry! CRY! Not because I hurt them but because I showed them how I have been hurt." Shay clarified the impact of expressing her voice: "I moved the audience. I did that. I didn't think I could. I didn't think they would care about what I had to say. But they were feeling me!" Loni and Shay were capturing *the second component: voice captures and exudes passion, moving audiences to feel a depth of emotion that reflects the speaker's life.* Musician Oliver Mtukudzi (personal communication, October,

2007), in visiting my voice-centered high school writing class several years ago, clarified that, culturally, in Zimbabwe, "if you are going to speak in public, you have to have something to say." Voice is used to convey something meaningful, and I argue in my classes that if what you have to say is not worth saying, then you do not say it. The very point is that voice reflects the passions of the author; thus teaching for voice means helping students see how they can share their passions. The end result is often shock as students express the beauty of finally having something to say, and at being validated when they say it (instead of being chastised for "incorrect" grammar or spelling). Voice moves people, and voice does this through honest representations of how we see, how we are seen, and how we attempt to be sane in a deeply conflicted, insane world.

Dorothy Allison (2002) clarifies the importance of clarifying her life through writing, arguing that the process is connected to the purpose of living: "I put on the page a third look at what I've seen in life—the condensed and reinvented experience of a cross-eyed, working-class lesbian, addicted to violence, language, and hope, who has made the decision to live, is determined to live, on the page and on the street, for me and mine" (p. 7). Voice is that decision to live, to be more conscious of our daily surroundings, and how the world we live in silences our reactions so effectively we are left searching for words to describe how growing up in violence, poverty, and systematized oppression *feels*. The point of voice is to capture clearly, powerfully, what exactly living as a "cross-eyed, working-class lesbian, addicted to violence, language, and hope" means. Whoever you are, whatever you live, the point is to help develop voice that captures what your own survival means, looks like, and feels. I often use this example with high school students: "I grew up in a fucked up environment" simply does not clarify the depth of what precisely was fucked up. The reality is that one has to search for words that can clarify, in depth, what about us and what about those around us is "fucked up." Developing voice is the process of finding the right words, of learning how to speak those words in a way that conveys to your intended audience exactly what you feel and why you feel this way.

June Jordan taught poetry as a way of helping students make sense of their own lives. Her approach was powerful specifically because she saw the world around us as being committed to what Donaldo Macedo (2006) terms "stupidification," where people see the world around us through the silencing lenses of mass corporate media. Jordan clarified that:

> *Because poetry is the medium for telling the truth, and because a poem is antithetical to lies/evasions and superficiality, anyone who becomes a practicing poet has an excellent chance of becoming somebody real, somebody known, self-defined, and*

> *attuned to and listening and hungering for kindred real voices utterly/articulately different from his or her own voice. (in Muller et al., 1995, p. 8)*

Thus I see the role of education and the purpose of schools as to prepare students to navigate the structural and personal levels of oppression. Such navigation requires developing voice, and developing voice requires making sense of the oppression we live. Thus developing voice is a cycle of healing, where individuals make sense of themselves, make sense of the world around them, and learn to navigate, publically, through self-expression, to create the socially just world they believe in.

Process of Developing Voice

The process I use to develop voice, in my courses, talks to educators, and in work with students and incarcerated men, is based upon five interrelated arenas:

1. *Self-recognition and examination.* Developing voice begins with a thorough examination and critical self-reflection on who I am as a person. This includes an intense focus on learning to see myself as an individual, but also learning to center individual experiences (as I do in Chapter 1). Writings center on what I literally look like, sound like, smell like, and feel, including multiple cultures, races, languages, families, geographies, and communities. This arena focuses entirely on the individual expressing what they see in themselves.
2. *Reflection on Context.* After beginning to wrestle with and document the individual, developing voice then requires an examination of and reflection on personal context. This entails examining social conditions that shape life, including what literally surrounds the author on a daily level (including family, community, school, but also violence, racism, sexism, abuse, drug use, weather, housing). Writings capture concrete details of the world around the author and ensure the author's perspectives are made clear.
3. *Personal Responses to Our Context.* After wrestling with who and where the author is, I urge those developing their voices to begin writing about how they are, given their context. In essence, how do I respond to how I see myself and how others see me? Writings include critical recognition of the ways individuals respond to their personal contexts, and include specific capturing of efforts made to ensure survival. Writings also include tapping into emotional responses, including rage, violence, and addictions, but also love, romantic relationships, and safety.

4. *Translation of Experience into Voice.* As students write about the first three components, they begin to transform these writings to capture emotional power. This requires extensive editing to ensure what is written actually reflects intended content, but also reflects the tone, language, and details that clarify personal nuance. This component is key to ensuring that voice actually develops; what poets often call "work-shopping poems," the focus is on connecting what is being said to the person saying it.
5. *Critical Expression.* After writings are work-shopped to capture the depth of the author, and drive home the intended message, the focus shifts to expressing that voice. With writing, this is most often through spoken word, poetry, or vocal storytelling, though creativity in expression is expected. Thus, many students create films, dance, drawings, photography, graffiti, and silkscreen t-shirts, and express their written voice in a range of artistic methods. The key is that the methods of expression fit with the purpose, tone, and overall feel the author is trying to capture and convey.

Each of these arenas, or areas of academic focus, is centered in the upcoming chapters. In Chapter Three, I capture how I frame classroom dynamics and academic courses, providing concrete examples of how I approach the first three arenas, in terms of assignments, structures, and feedback processes. In Chapter Four, I center activities and processes I use to translate experience into voice, and focus on the role of trauma in shaping the importance of this work. This entails a critical need for educators to be responsive and not push students too quickly, too deeply, unless they have a solid foundation from which to engage. In Chapter Five, I frame school-wide approaches that can foster the first four curricular areas, and provide concrete examples of forums through which voice can be expressed. It is this fifth arena that I argue schools should be structured around, particularly in terms of shifting notions of academic success and measurement to community-based forums. These forums are key to validating student expression, and connect student voice to communities, families, and educators.

Shifting the purpose of schooling to preparing urban youth to shape their local communities begins to shift the historical treatment of urban communities. How schools develop urban student voice reflects how the U.S. prepares youth to lead communities in the future. In a similar vein to Paulo Freire's notion of critical consciousness (*conscientization*), students learn how to develop and express themselves through understanding their world, and then begin to take action about what they see as unequal in their world (Freire, 1973). Teaching critical literacy, which can be expressed through voice, is an essential condition of both a democratic society, and the schools that are the tools for transforming (or perpetuating) the social inequality that the U.S. is known for worldwide (Duncan-Andrade & Morrell, 2008; Shor, 1992). Ultimately, the greatest test of a democratic country is the expression of critical voice on an intimate personal level; how schools help urban youth of color develop and then express who they are, how they live, and the structural limitations to both reflects a commitment (or not) to the work of creating and sustaining democracies. These five steps have become one way in which I have been able to deepen my efforts to develop such student voice, while ensuring an academic foundation that enables students to succeed in the rest of their courses as well.

Conclusion

Shifting classroom practice to center on urban student voice is not enough to transform public schools into communities that culturally affirm student experience and worth. Adding voice as yet another responsibility or requirement for teachers will not shift the dramatic intentional inequities that are reflected in dropout rates and urban teacher turnover. As Ladson-Billings (1999) argued: "If we are serious about solving these [race, racism, and social injustice] problems in school and classrooms, we have to be serious about intense study and careful rethinking of race and education…we will have to expose racism in education *and* propose radical solutions for addressing it" (p. 27). Critical race theory and a focus on centering the development and expression of voice requires a deeper, sustained transformation of public schools to center on a social justice mission to prepare students to shape democracy. This means shifting the purpose of public schools to prepare students to express themselves on the social realities they live (and are shaped by).

This book is a culmination of attempts to develop urban student voice. This work is based on students I have had the honor and privilege of teaching, and includes direct quotes and writing excerpts from students over the past 12 years. These students have been my greatest teachers, and they have directly shaped how I teach, how I research, how I write, and how I move in the world as a White male educator. As I define how central their voices are in transforming schools to address structural racism and inequities, I argue that voice is the foundation for democracy: as schools prepare students and communities to express themselves, as students and communities listen to each other's clarifications of oppressed realities, our collective notion of reality deepens, as does our collective commitment to alter the oppression we perpetuate in schools. If we listen to these students, then we know the urgency cannot be more immediate. Schools cannot be allowed to train students to be silenced or, like Tony, to feel enslaved. Educators cannot allow more students of color to believe that they really are worth less than their White counterparts.

CHAPTER 3

Developing Urban Youth Voice:
A Framework for Culturally Responsive Classrooms

Urban schools are not broken; they are doing exactly what they are designed to do. (Duncan-Andrade & Morrell, 2008, p. 1)

On a cold, rainy Monday morning, I noticed Juan, a student who had all but dropped out of East Bay High, slip over the fence. Through our classroom window, I watched him toss his journal over the 7-foot-tall chain link fence, and then scale, pivot, and in one smooth motion, his feet hit the ground, he scooped up the journal, and within seconds was at our classroom door. He slid into an open desk as I glanced at the clock: 10 minutes left. He immediately began freewriting (the topic from the beginning of the class was still written on the board), and did not move again until after the bell rang. A few students greeted him as they left our room, and as I was packing up our class, putting our stack of journals into the box I used to carry our supplies, he finished his writing and asked me if we could talk. As students began to fill into the classroom (which would be used by its fifth teacher of the day), Juan and I settled onto a bench relatively hidden from others. As soon as his body touched the bench, Juan began:

> *Chris, I'm so sorry I've been missing class. My brother was involved in a gang fight and our family has been forced out of our house. I aint got nowhere to go and I know I'll be kicked out of this school for missing so much class. I know I wasn't a good student before all this. But I want to ask if you will let me keep on writing, even if I am kicked out. I have been writing; I lost this journal a few times, but I keep finding it again, so I know I'm supposed to keep at it.*

We talked for an hour, with Juan clarifying the continual threat of violence and homelessness, wondering what he could do to escape juvenile hall for missing so much school. As we strategized approaches to engage with his probation officer, I realized what Juan was actually asking. He wanted my permission to keep writing, to keep journaling, and he wanted my affirming feedback. Despite not caring about the rest of his education, Juan was learning how to write for himself, and was developing a practice of using reflective writing to help make sense of his impossibly complicated, violent world.

Such intimacy and trust with a teacher has largely been lacking throughout urban student experiences, and yet such closeness is a precondition for instructors learning to respond to their students; if we do not know our students, how can we respond to them? If we do not create conditions for students like Juan to reach out, then we will not engage them. The purpose of this chapter is to clarify how developing voice can lead to classroom communities where students like Juan deepen their approaches to life. I demonstrate how I integrate the process of developing voice into classroom practice, and capture my attempts to model student-centered culturally responsive instructional approaches.

This chapter specifically focuses on how schools can create instructional loops with students, wherein students learn to speak aloud their experiences, listen to their peers, give feedback on each other's work, and begin to educate others about the struggles they live within. As an educator, my role is to co-create the conditions through which students can develop and refine voice, then step back and allow students the space to express themselves as needed. In the classroom, this entails, at a minimum, structures that allow students the space to be themselves, but that are rigid enough to keep students moving forward, with concrete assignments and routines. I use personal at-home and in-class journals, punctuation-free papers, daily freewrites, cycles of editing to workshop writings, and a continual stream of exciting, passionate, relevant intellectual sparks, including poetry, music, novels, short stories, films, documentaries, but also live voice-filled poets, musicians, and artists to incite students to write.

Self-recognition and Examination

Maricella was a student in a high school class that I was co-teaching with an English teacher. Maricella had not turned in the first few assignments, and this troubled my co-teacher, who had thought she would do really well in the class because of her prior academic performance in the school. I met with Maricella a month into the course, and she was shaking with nervousness as we sat down to chat. After a few minutes of small talk, Maricella burst out: "I just don't know who I am. Everything in this class asks me to write about who I am, but I don't know." I remained silent as I listened to Maricella express her frustrations with being seen as a "good" student, but she had always felt she did not know what to say. "I know how to say things, that's what those A's mean. But teachers don't ask me what I think 'cause I'm the good, quiet kid." She continued, her voice trembling: "I never know what to think because I've never been allowed to talk about me." Maricella clarified why she did not want to be seen as talking: "The students who talk—they talk about their problems. And see, they got in trouble. Every time. So why talk? Plus, who is going to listen to a little *Mexicana Negrita*?"[1]

Because she had always done well in school, Maricella told me she never had anyone ask about how she was doing. She never felt like she developed opinions because she just kept quiet and did the assignments she was given. Yet Maricella had witnessed complicated, violent circumstances, like when her cousin was being beat by her uncle. When he said something to a school counselor, he was placed into a group home; she hadn't seen him in the two years since. Her older sister was also arrested as an accomplice to murder when she was trying to explain to her teacher and counselor that she was forced into a gang. Her point was that she had lived through a lot and was only seen as successful because she had been able to hide these experiences from her teachers.

But now, in our class, she struggled because she really wanted to talk about her family, about how teachers silence her, and how few choices she has. "My parents don't have papers, and I have to go to college to get a job and pay for them. I think I've never had a chance to stop and just think about what I want to be." Our class became a chance for Maricella to learn how to speak aloud and develop her thoughts. But she needed support in overcoming her intense reluctance to write or speak. She did not think she had a voice, and she thought the role of school was to reinforce her silence. Maricella reminded us that we had to do a better job of setting the tone, of helping students be honest with themselves and their peers. A focus on self-recognition and self-examination requires students to be comfortable being uncomfortable, as they are being asked to confront personal fears (not just about speaking in public, but about being who they are). This means creating the conditions for students to be themselves, and we then set up space for one-on-one, outside-the-classroom discussions where students like Maricella could open up and talk about fears and frustrations.

> *My Voice (a freewrite by Maricela)*
> I wish my voice was as
> loud as it is in my
> head. I want to explode
> and let my voice go. I'd
> talk until my throat got
> dry and my voice went horse.
> Since I don't speak, no
> one hears my voice and
> I'm left to sink, real
> deep. I have no choice. My
> voice is unheard. You never
> hear me say a word.

Developing voice begins with a thorough examination and critical self-reflection on who the writer is as a person. Such centering on who we are requires, at a personal level, recognition of the pain that shapes how we navigate the world. This requires not only creating a classroom community of trust and respect, but also modeling how, as educators, we live with purpose and grace while also being transparent about the tremendous burdens we carry. Key to developing such trust is developing what bell hooks (1994) argues is a commitment to "insist that everyone's presence is acknowledged" (p. 8). In my classrooms, I try to create an environment where all students are valued for who they are, and that means that students have a responsibility to express their languages, cultures, and insights. Such expression is particularly important in an anti-immigrant, anti-ethnic studies political environment, where students of color face a barrage of English-only laws, and mandatory reporting that limits capacity to trust educators with intimate details. Such a context of oppressing children of color led me to encourage Maricella, and it was precisely my insistence on recognizing her that led to her realization that because societal pressures wanted her silent, she had a responsibility to speak. She soon wanted other students to develop voice, and reached out to reluctant peers helping, as she told them, "to free yourselves from the racism we are taught." A few weeks after our chat, she read her paper to our class and invited three additional students into our class, all of whom were identified by Maricella as "silenced."

While I create opportunities for students to write about how they experience the world, the point is to also get students to write with passion, to undo the damage from previous educators who have silenced through White, English-Only educational notions. That means letting students free in their words, and encouraging them to capture pieces of who they are that have often been silenced. In addition, educators must help undo the damage previous English teachers might have enforced, such as a focus on structures without ensuring students develop something to say; students of color often internalize their failure rather than question that the way they are being taught might be the problem (DeMeulenaere, 2009; Fordham & Ogbu, 1986; Gibson & Ogbu, 1991; Steele & Aronson, 1995). A central aspect of developing voice is affirming in students that what they actually think is valid, and our role is to help them say what they think more clearly, and to push on depth of thought. Because this work is intensely personal, I do not require students to share aloud everything they write, but I do require all students to write, and all students are expected to share their voices at some point. I also set the tone for students, modeling that while writing about our pain is difficult, speaking aloud this pain in public is even more difficult. I am clear to students: speaking voice aloud is partially what enables us to learn how to feel and walk with more dignity in the world.

Setting the Context: Instructor Modeling

All of this framing requires that I be present to what has shaped me, to the very things that have silenced my own voice. I cannot do this work without developing trust throughout the modeling process, and this includes showing students how I examine my own context, edit my work, and learn to express myself. I am intentionally transparent about my personal work to learn about who I am and where I teach. I begin classes by sharing my own critical voice and what led me to teach that particular course, in that particular school, and in that particular community. I continually process my upbringing, my educational experiences, my pain, and the details from my life that have taught me to be an educator. And this very personal work is exactly what teacher education programs do not teach, is exactly what brings me closest to my students; this is what educators are taught to not share with our students. Without having the support of educational institutions, educators have to learn to process who we are and how we have come to be with others. And we have to demonstrate to students that we have developed a sustained community of people around us. This is difficult work, not seen as relevant to teaching, and yet is exactly what fuels my capacity to teach in student-centered ways. In short, if I do not know myself, I cannot help students learn to develop voice.

Shared in-class freewrite
Last week we talked of rape and molestation
in academic settings not meant to be meaningful
After class my office filled with women raped molested beat down
always by men and now I think of my father
the only male influence in my life
beating down my mother
16 stitches across her chin
beating down my brother
our baseball football and soccer coaches
public humiliation nothing compared to his fists splattering against
my chest my face my arms
these are the 7 fingers he broke 7 different times
the only thing saving me most days
are the very words you listen to now
and the hope that speaking out up and on
will move each of us to live how we need

I thus come into the classroom with a developed sense of self, in which I try to be both pro-student and deeply anti-oppressive. I write about my experiences as a student, teacher, and faculty member, but also as a violently abused child. I show my students my writings, which they critique and challenge so they can see me as also trying to learn, also trying to shape the realities I live in. Being known is a precursor to knowing students; I cannot expect them to share details of their lives if I do not share who I am. And I do not try to compare my wounds. Instead, I share who I am, what has impacted me, and what I do with my lessons (and subsequent issues). In this way, I do work prior to the class that informs how I think about my life, and this continual work informs what I do in classrooms.

Who I am also frames how much work I need to do to learn about my students *before* planning out a course. Because I am male, I know that I need to build up working knowledge about sexism and how my own male privilege affords me opportunity to speak. Because I am White, I know that I need to build up working knowledge about urban communities, especially the community in which the students I will be teaching live in (Howard, 1999; McIntyre, 1997). Before the class begins, I research the community, gaining a general idea of wealth, employment status, and the educational background of local adults. I look into incarceration rates and examine how prisons might impact students growing up. I look at incidents of police brutality and violence rates against residents in that community. I do background work on local community advocates and try to identify historical figures that played a role in civil rights struggles. Most of this is available online, and all of this I do prior to reaching into local resources.

Armed with basic demographic knowledge of the community, I reach out to local community leaders. I call or stop by local churches and service providers (including social workers, probation officers, HIV counselors), and stop by a local food bank to have an idea of who is being served and what kinds of food they are being served. While some of these interactions lay a foundation for me to later invite experts into the classroom, many simply provide a deeper understanding of the context in which my students live. Such community voices shape content areas that I might prioritize in class, such as a lack of local grocery stores, abnormally high HIV infection rates, and a lack of mental health services. Knowing about communities before teaching builds bridges to local resources that might not be connected to school, all while highlighting community voice for students.

Excerpt from Shantel's letter to me
...This, Chris, is my point:
My previous teachers have molded me into quietness
have smashed my mind to where
everything I think I know is wrong and
everything you told me makes sense but I didn't want to hear you
and was able to shut you out until three weeks ago
when you came to my house and met my grandmother
and brought that social worker
you hafta know that the 12 before her were wack mean punked my grandmother
disrespect you showed me was colonial
and you taught me learning
is the best respect we can give
you taught me that there are more out there
like me like you like the speakers in our class like the poets like the guitarista
there are always people learning and
I want to be one of them
one of us
the ones who know who we are

Then I dive into the school itself, chatting with counselors, teachers, custodial staff, parents, and district personnel, trying to understand what people think of the school, the staff, and the students. Such conversations directly inform my understanding of previous curricula, histories, and recent local politics. This is particularly enlightening in underfunded, low-performing, and/or alternative schools that are designed to serve low-income students of color so that I can identify potential curricular gaps that limit student knowledge and writing preparation (Duncan-Andrade & Morrell, 2008; Knaus, 2007). In short, I invest significant time and energy prior to teaching to prepare myself for the specific school. I research the context of the school in which I am to teach as a way of setting the stage for my curriculum and teaching approaches. This is especially important, as I will be pushing students to document their realities, and they will know if I am unprepared to deal with these realities: thus, I tap into the resources that can support me and students, but also gain an understanding of what living in the community feels like prior to urging students to capture what they feel like.

With a basic understanding of the local neighborhood and resident resources, I tap into a larger community of experts to inform and expand the curriculum. I reach out to other area educators, artists, poets, musicians, comedians, playwrights, and chefs, looking to see who might be available to come and speak to the class during the term. I plan ahead to identify experts I can call on to potentially bring them into my larger framed curriculum. This previous work positions me as a practitioner instructor; when I come into class knowing about the context these students struggle in and the resources they may benefit from, students see how I have prepared. This shows that I am humble enough to still want to learn, that I use what I learn to inform what I do, and that I know a bit about the context within which they live. This is essential; urban students often complain about not having educators who know them, who know their realities and understand some of what they live through (Delpit, 2006; Goldstein, 2007; Wyngaard, 2007. This drive to learn is precisely what I am trying to teach and model for students and precisely what is key to developing voice: being humble is required to continually frame ourselves as learners who reach out because we simply cannot know everything we need to.

The key to setting up classrooms that center students, student voice, and student realities is transparent educators who practice what we preach (Duncan-Andrade & Morrell, 2008; Freire, 1973; hooks, 1994; Krishnamurti, 1953). This means listening to students so that we know enough about them to shift our curriculum and teaching to reflect their needs. My goal is to help students make sense of the power of their voice, and that means I must demonstrate such power. If the goal is to help students tap into their own experiences, to help arm them with personal tools to transform their experiences into power that informs their efforts to shape the world, then educators have to model how to do that. That means making sense of the oppression we have lived (and take part in). In essence, I set up outside-the-classroom structures to help me reflect on how I have grown up on my own, navigating through less-than-stellar K–12 schools, through college, and through emotional trauma and structural silencing. All of this directly informs how I set up my classroom, and informs my work prior to stepping into class on the first day. This is an important clarification: caring, responsive curriculum and teaching approaches are still limited by my own capacity to reflect on and address race, gender, and class-based privileges that shape everything I do within (and outside of) a classroom (hooks, 1994). This is particularly important as a straight White man; I cannot know what life is like as a young person of color, as a queer youth, or even growing up poor in today's world, but I can learn as much as I can, and develop a team to support me.

The First Day of Class at East Bay High School

Prior to students arriving for their first class at East Bay High School, I write "Who Are You?" on the board. I sit in a desk, watch students settle into the same desks as far away from me as possible. A few minutes after the bell rings, students look around a bit bewildered: who is this teacher and why is he not in front of the class? After a few minutes of letting students talk to each other, discomfort begins to show as they glance nervously towards me, waiting for me to begin class. Just as students start to get up and walk around, I stand up. The class becomes quiet, and I ask students if they think I know more than they do about everything. They laugh dismissively. I keep asking until a dialogue begins: some note that I am the teacher and that they have to listen to me in order to pass the class; others say I probably do know more than they. I ask if they think I know more about race and racism than they do, and students emphatically reply "no." "Then why," I counter, "Are you waiting for me to start a writing class in an urban school? And deeper, why are you all sitting in rows of desks facing the front of the class, as if I have all the answers?" A discussion erupts as students talk about their frustrations with school. They talk about how they have to learn to be quiet. One student, Sherise, notes that students are graded by how well they "shut up and listen to the teacher." I tell students that this class will be different if, and only if, students in this class are different. I tell students that if they take themselves and this class seriously, then we can shift the dynamics by designing the class as they wish. I stop the discussion and tell everyone to move desks how they want to be arranged.

At this point, I bring the now-sitting-in-a-circle class' attention to the board, pass out new journals, and lay out freewriting ground rules: continual writing, no worries about grammar, spelling, or getting it "right." I state multiple times that the point is to continually write, so the pen or pencil is always moving. I tell students to push beyond their names, urging them to show us how they think of themselves. "Set a context for how you want this class to be," I urge, before joining students to write for five minutes about the question on the board ("Who are you?"). I continually remind students to write and not talk, not text, not do anything other than write. After five minutes, we share what we wrote as an introduction to the class, and despite initial hesitations and discomfort, everyone shares. Below are three introductions shared aloud that day:

Enrique Intro:

Yo Soy Enrique and I am in este clase porque I hafta be

Jasmine Intro:

Alive today I am Jasmine and
I am here to tell you I matter

I am from Moms and Pops
but Pops passed and Moms is
hardly here and I have two younger
sisters I take care of them and
I think you'll all know me soon enough
because I am here to say
something.

Marco Intro:

I been rappin with style
when others lay tile
I am the ghost of my pahtnas
layin low they been taken
and I still fakin tryin to stay alive
when my body be shakin
gots lots ta say just be listenen
cause I drop truths like home runs to babe ruths

As we shared introductions, the above examples stood out because of their vibrancy, rhythmic flow, and language. While students clapped loudly after Marco's poetic introduction, his content did not tell the class much about who he is, though we can assume he's known friends that were killed. Enrique, though brief, demonstrated that he speaks English and Spanish and was not particularly excited about being in thc class. Jasmine, in contrast, got several quieter claps, despite that she shared several details about her life. But it was only the first day, and students were not yet focused on purpose, meaning, or voice: instead the default purpose is either to make other students laugh or to sound "smooth." Thus, students on the first day save their reactions for peers who read their words with the most energy. Meanwhile, I take notes during student read alouds, recording students who read powerfully, have sharp words, are nervous, are trying to say something meaningful, or who are trying to avoid sharing much, and those who are generating laughter.

Because I work in urban schools with huge ranges in abilities to read and write, there are also corresponding disparities between comfort levels in public speaking. I often work with students who have only a rudimentary foundation of writing, and I strongly encourage them to read aloud to help come to terms with why they have not been taught to read or write very well. Some students have refused to read, and I work one-on-one with them until they are comfortable sharing in front of the class. Most students, at least at the outset, share relatively boring introductions, with several class poets and clowns serving as obvious exceptions. A more typical intro is one by James, written in a juvenile facility in 2008: "I am James, still loct up." In the class at East Bay High, perhaps a third of the students introduced themselves with something similar, stating their name and sharing one additional, not-very-revealing line.

The dynamic of the classroom, shifted slightly by the alteration of the classroom chairs, our discussion of school issues, and students sharing with each other, moves even further when I share my writing last. Students do not expect me to share, but particularly nothing engaging or powerful. While I freewrite a new version for each course, here is the intro I wrote and shared for Jasmine, Marco, and Enrique's class:

Chris' Intro:

Christopher Bodenheimer Knaus I
born into dad's punches
welfare lunches and teacher hunches
everyone assumed I cheated on tests
couldn't be smart this poor white kid
no one knew my grandmother was
a social worker in watts
fled nazi germany at 17
or that my mom was kicked out of
8th grade, 4 kids by 21, divorced and on
her own by 24 and I
told I'd fail every day I
flunked 7th grade
never gave up even as my rage
burned bridges at every turn
and still burning I
fighting so that each of you
stand on your own words
powerful, alone and exactly
what and who and how you and I need to be:
Christopher Bodenheimer Knaus I
honored to be with you all
ready to learn and grow and push and move
and move
and move
and be moved.

As soon as I finish reading, students erupt into excited hoots and hollers, likely exacerbated by their surprise. Students call out: “Teacher can kick!” “Step back, Chris is about to flow” and “Whooo, teacher’s a poet!” I ask students how they feel about this process of starting off the year. “I feel like we could be a family,” one student remarks, while another argues that, “we already shared more in this class than we have all last year in all of our classes.” A few students are notably quiet and have muted responses, and I jot down their names so I can follow up later if they are not more engaged within the next few days. I let the class out on a high note; students are generally excited at the notion of building up a community around sharing their own voices.

On the second day, I lay out the course syllabus. When I first began teaching, I used ground rules from June Jordan’s Poetry for the People, but I have since learned to guide students in the development of their rules. I provide ground rules only for our freewriting process, and then ask the students to develop additional ground rules for ensuring students will feel comfortable reading aloud their work, and will honor what each student says. Students develop a list, write it up creatively on posterboard, and I post these laminated ground rules in front of the class. I remind students that while I will hold each student accountable for the agreed-to rules, it is their responsibility to maintain these rules, and I will also hold them accountable for holding each other accountable. Within a few weeks, students generally begin to take charge of the classroom, stopping someone mid-sentence when they challenge a peer too harshly, or dismiss someone’s attempt at writing.

Ground Rules
(adapted from June Jordan’s Poetry for the People)

1. We consciously respect each other
2. We foster in ourselves and each other an ability to craft our messages for others to contemplate
3. Expression is an art of telling the truth
4. We are the community
5. Writing is how we connect
6. We are responsible for what we say and how we say it just as we are responsible for helping others craft writings through critical feedback

Writing Assignments: Self-recognition and Examination

As we begin the second week, I frame the rest of the major assignments, and focus on the first paper. This paper extends the class intro read aloud. Sample extended prompts have included: "This is how I live Racism," "Capture what your voice sounds like," and "Here I Am, Listen." At East Bay High, the class completed a draft of a "What You Need to Know About Me" paper at the end of the second week. A complete draft was due the following week, and students had to read the three-page paper aloud and turn in at least three sets of peer feedback. I demonstrate how we begin the feedback process later in this chapter, and more extensively in Chapter Four, but these first few weeks focus more on writing than providing feedback. "You have to learn to write before you can learn to edit," I tell my students.

What You Need to Know About Me

This assignment has three purposes:

1. Introduce yourself to the class in a way that dramatically extends beyond your intro read aloud
2. Help develop your capacity to clarify, in public, who you are in a voice that reflects who you are
3. Push beyond your notion of standardized writing to see that you can write powerfully

Thus, there are two rules:

1. This paper is to be written and spoken in your voice
2. No punctuation or standardized writing structures of any kind are allowed

This paper is expected to be the equivalent of approximately 3 pages, and should be well edited to capture your points in vibrant language. Avoid any vague terms (it, good, nice, interesting, etc.), and speak with purpose and passion. As with all assignments in this class, the more effort and energy you put in, the more you will get out. This paper will be read aloud in class. This paper is non-graded; there will be no credit given unless the paper is read aloud, is free from punctuation, and includes three edited drafts from peers.

To help scaffold the "What You Need to Know About Me" assignment, I asked several students to share aloud "Where I Am From" poems (Lyon, 1999), which they had written the previous year in their English class. While students appreciated their flow, there was general consensus that the poems were vague and did not tell nearly as much as did the introductory read alouds. Students were ready to push beyond what is typically written for other courses, but many expressed that they did not know how to do that in creative ways that demonstrated their voice. We continued freewriting with prompts to help stimulate ideas to write about, and I provided a different poem each day that demonstrated voice.[2] In addition, I played several hip-hop and reggae songs, and printed out lyrics so students knew what exactly was being said. The class would respond or engage in found poetry, a process where students listen to a poem or song, and write down any words, phrases, or ideas that come to them as they listen. From there, the class wrote, edited and eventually read aloud their papers, continuing the practice of getting students comfortable sharing their voice in front of the class.

Self-recognition Writing Assignments

1. **Where I Am From**
   A popular assignment used widely in schools, these short poems or essays typically capture a student's personal history and family context.
2. **Describe a Scar on My Body**
   Adapted from an assignment by John Malloy, an educator and community leader, this assignment encourages students to capture, with concrete detail, what a scar on their body looks like, where it came from, and what it might represent.
3. **Letter to Your 10-Year-Old Self**
   This assignment teaches students how to write personal letters, using traditional letter-writing structures, but encourages critical writing as students talk to themselves when they were 10 years old. These letters include self-affirmation, but also require students to use knowledge they know now to ensure mistakes they made are addressed.

Examination Writing Assignments

4. **How You See Me/How I See Myself**
   This comparative assignment asks students to capture a portrait of themselves as others see them, and then contrast that often-stereotypical image to how they see themselves. This assignment encourages students to challenge assumptions about themselves, and requires students to show how they are different from how others see them.
5. **This Is How I Am Beautiful**
   This paper encourages students to develop a list of how they see themselves as beautiful, and then turn that list into a creative writing. Beginning with a list of 20 examples of how the writer is beautiful, the paper requires challenging stereotypes of beauty, but also requires students to convince the audience of their beauty, focusing on persuasive skill sets.
6. **Snap Shot of Grade-Level Navigational Strategies**
   This more advanced-level paper encourages students to identify personal strategies they developed to navigate schooling at each level, and requires evaluation of each strategy's success. Examples include tuning out, becoming a class clown, drugs, alcohol, and violence.

Reflection on Context

After setting ground rules on the second day, we review the syllabus and lay out a bare-bones curriculum. I typically begin a high school class with a no-more-than-two-page syllabus with course expectations, an overview of key assignments, and due dates. This syllabus clarifies two key course goals that can be integrated into other content areas: 1) Students will develop their voice as a tool to capture and make sense of racism and urban life, and 2) Students will express their voice in forums that make sense to them. The point, to which I return throughout the rest of the class, is that students are living reporters: most mainstream news perpetuates urban stereotypes of violence, drugs, gangs, and low test scores, and students know the community better than mass-media reporters, and often their teachers. Their role, as framed by the syllabus, is to become the types of reporters we need, the sort that stay alive because they have to report on what is happening through their unique voices and insights. Thus, students expect that we will shift readings, assignments, and strategies to respond to what comes out of their writings.

Introduction to the Syllabus

1. *Course Overview*

   This course is designed to develop your intellectual and personal voice. Using critical writing, film, and creative expression, we will analyze identity, oppression, and the use of voice as a way of working toward our definitions of social justice. As high school students, our role is to develop our voice, our understanding of who we are, how we fit within society, and our tools of expression, so that we become more articulate about the social issues we care most about. Two core questions that we will return to throughout the course will guide us: *What* do I, personally, have to say? And *How* do I say it?

2. *Course Expectations*

   Every member of our course community is expected to deeply engage, participate, challenge our self and others, learn, critique, express, and ultimately develop our voices. We each come as experts in our own experience, with our own voices, insight, and unique perspectives. Our entire classroom community is expected to be open, supportive, and critical of how we express ourselves and how we assist our peers in expressing themselves.

After spending the first third of the class helping students wrestle with and document the pieces of their identity that make them who they are, I shift focus to examine personal context. I remind students of the point they already made: very little of their schooling is framed on urban realities, and I tell students that in speaking their realities, in the everyday voices they speak and listen to, they honor their communities and begin to document their communities. Capturing and preserving local, cultural, and linguistic knowledge is a skill, I state over and over again, and we are going to practice that skill until we become adept at sharing who we are and where we come from and what moves us with whatever audiences we think need to hear us. This entails guiding student assignments and thoughts around the immediate world in which they live, encouraging them to capture the social conditions that shape their lives, including what literally surrounds them on a daily level (including family, community, school, but also violence, racism, sexism, abuse, drug use, food, housing conditions). When done well, students capture their everyday realities, and with support, learn to see writing as a tool to capture the ugly and beauty of their world, but also as a means of demonstrating who they are, and what they survive. This is how students reclaim their identities and begin to see school as useful. For when students see a purpose in writing, they can tap into what they need to say, and ensure words reflect their lives.

Depending on the course length, I select two to five core texts, which I use as a foundation for discussions around voice, language, and reporting about our personal realities. I have used Sapphire's (1996) *Push*, LeAlan Jones and Lloyd Newman's (1996) *Our America*, James Baldwin's (1962) *The Fire Next Time*, June Jordan's (2000) *Soldier*, and Jamaica Kincaid's (1988) *A Small Place*, among dozens of others. I purposefully choose non-fiction and fiction that offers direct insight into the author while demonstrating voice that reflects the authors' language and personal cultural context. *Our America*, for example, reflects two young African American students talking about what living in low-income urban Chicago looks like. The authors, who spoke their text through voice recorders, capture their daily life, narrating what they see in their neighborhood, complete with interviews of family members, educators, and neighbors. Photos that provide concrete imagery accompany the book. Such texts also show students that people just like them write and publish books.

My America by Shantel
LeAlan and Lloyd tell me what they see on the bus so listen to my never seems to end bus ride because I too have a voice and I too have something that no one seems to want to hear
Mr. Bus Driver pats my ass as I squeeze past
He never seems to care that the 75c I pay mean I am younger than his daughter
I sit down next to an old man with drool on his chin
Clutch my bag and hope I get off this bus
But my stop aint for 25 minutes
35 if cars litter Oakland streets or if these girls act like the bitches the rappers behind me be rappin about
I don't like that the words they say about me come out of my mouth
These girls telling the bus driver this stop this stop even though they never get off
Those open doors just hang empty in the west Oakland wind
Bringing the same cancer my mom died from
I see men my age hangin on the corner with 40's in their hands
Brown sacks don't hide them they should be with me on the way to school
Too cool they just wait for some life to take hold
Instead the police linger two blocks down our bus flies passed
Boarded up homes
Just like the one I live in with my 3 cousins 2 aunties one uncle and way too many "friends" who like to creep into our room or sell us the weed they sell to the addicts on the corner that looks just like the one we ride by almost every morning the police arrest kids my age who should be in school
But at 8 am they head towards another day in jail
I am on the way to school
And Mr. Bus Driver pats my ass as I squeeze past.

Our America contrasts with *A Small Place*, which students appreciated because Kincaid's writing, as Jasmine argued: "helps me see that I can write using standards and still show how fucked up those standards are." Rather than narrated from a personal perspective, Kincaid shows colonization from a national perspective, and uses details often known by those who live in the context of the colonized. Many urban students, quick to dismiss formal writing structures, often find Kincaid's work useful to see that the issue they have is not with formal writing structures. Instead, her work helps students see the racism that shapes how educators uphold formal writing structures. After reading *A Small Place*, Jasmine argued that there should not be "one true correct way to write that just so happens to be the way White people talk." I thus use a combination of books to show that there are multiple types of reporting and reporters, and all can be engaging and well written, while showing how racism works.

The rest of the course is rooted in student perspectives, energy, and decisions. I continually affirm student effort in writing, and just as continually urge students to express themselves more deeply, more in the language they use daily, with friends, and at home. How we communicate about the things we care about becomes the focal point for both the curriculum and my instructional techniques. I center the ways in which students talk and communicate on a daily basis as a way to deepen their writing and to honor the ways they frame ideas (Gay, 2000; Lynch, 2006). I tell students I will hold them accountable, and that they need to hold each other accountable, for what their words literally mean. I then demonstrate how their words can mean something other than they intend, and that they must be responsible for their clarity. We examine offensive terms used to degrade people of color, women, people with disabilities, and dissect our daily language for the historical roots of oppression in words, and students attempt to shape the languages they have previously felt oppressed by. One particularly powerful exercise is a discussion to generate a list of everyday words with oppressive roots (such as "gyped" or "gipped," "red-handed," "ghetto," "peon," but also what many educators refer to as the "N-word," to name but a few). The sheer impact of filling up every whiteboard or chalkboard in the room within just a few minutes reminds students of the powerful negative impact our words have.

In reclaiming affirming language, students begin to take more responsibility for the words they use. But beyond being more purposeful about word choice and what we say, I expect students to shape daily agendas, writing assignments, and classroom dialogue (Knaus, 2009; Stovall, 2006b). My role, which I make clear throughout the course, is to ensure students are continually writing, continually editing, always pushing deeper to communicate what they see and feel, and to ensure they respect each other and themselves in our shared space. In essence, my role becomes a drive to ensure students are getting what they say would bring them to school. Collectively, this means striving to say what we mean with as much passion as we can, and then critiquing to ensure our purpose is conveyed well. In this way, students begin to frame themselves as reporters capturing the reality they live but rarely see reflected in traditional school curriculum.

Freewriting

Perhaps what most marks my voice-focused courses is the daily freewrites; much of our time throughout the year is spent freewriting about our daily context. Sherise talked about my classes like this: "Chris be havin' us writing every-dang-day!" Almost every time I run into a former writing student, the first thing they'll tell me about is how they still freewrite in journals. I recently ran into a former student who was relatively disengaged throughout our course. He had just walked down a block that I had taken his entire class through during a neighborhood freewrite four years earlier. With his memory spured, he purchased a journal so that he could get back into freewriting. Our chance meeting just a few days later reminded him of the imperative to keep on writing, and reminded me how freewriting sticks with students years later. Even with the students who do not write daily during class.

> *Neighborhood freewrite by Jacinda*
> Graffiti, boarded up doors, liquor stores,
> nice new alternative school lock up,
> Mental health services, boarded up
> They serve them
> A field of dew green grass,
> Drugs, street named MLK Jr,
> Cars, more beat up cars,
> the majority of us students isn't white,
> no smoking but some flowers,
> the ones that smell good,
> some nice houses, some not
> stop BUSH signs, bikes,
> purple house that's where the Smoke spot used to be,
> graffiti, stop.

My typical writing courses begin each week by checking in about the previous week's work, and each day begins with 5–10 minutes of freewrite, followed by a chance for volunteers to read aloud what they just wrote. Within a few weeks, most students begin freewriting on their own, writing phrases or topics on the board as a prompt to guide their classmates' writings. I hold fast to my freewriting rules: continual writing about the topic or where ever your mind takes you. Once we begin, the pen is constantly moving and there is no self-editing, no worries about grammar, spelling, or punctuation, and no stopping to think about what you want to say (and what you will not say). I push hard on students who come into class not on task; I continually assert that the five or ten minutes are exclusively for writing. This is when I am most harsh on discipline: there is no talking, no sharing, and no texting; nothing except the quiet scratch of handwriting. The point is to write about what is on your mind, what you are struggling through, or what you need to get out of your system. And I restate this whenever students need reminders.

While there are dozens of examples of potential freewrite ideas available in writing resource books (Behn, 1992; Berdan et al., 2006; Goldberg, 1986; Muller et al., 1995; Tannenbaum & Bush, 2005), the vast majority of writing prompts come from listening to students, having them bring in ideas, and from feedback that sparked further writing. Some days we focus on close writing assignments, with students capturing feelings, items, and experiences in thick, descriptive details (Muller et al., 1995; Tannenbaum & Bush, 2005). Other days students write about a highly charged topic at the forefront of many students' minds (such as recent police brutality or a drug bust that resulted in a student being arrested). Some days I play a short film clip to spark ideas, other times, a song, and occasionally, I'd temporarily place snacks students were eating in the middle of the room to spark topics on texture, taste, and smell. If we had a guest speaker, the speaker might initiate the freewrite. Mostly, however, after the first few weeks, students initiate the bulk of the topics. By the end of the term, many students fill their in-class journals with daily writings, and I provide a new journal for each completed journal. As an additional incentive, I remind students to freewrite about papers they need to develop for other courses.

I occasionally use extended or linked freewrites to help students expand upon previous ideas. One particular musician-centered exercise helped deepen a class notion of how to ensure the flow of writing enhances emotion. I played a song for students to freewrite with, capturing what they hear, feel, see directly in response to the song. This method is commonly known as "found poetry," where students write down words, phrases from a piece and then later edit their own notes into a poetic response to the original piece (Dunning & Stafford, 1992). The song the students wrote to was, *Tozeza,* a soft yet upbeat tune typical of Oliver Mtukudzi and the Black Spirits (2004). The students wrote about how the music took them to the Caribbean, to the beach, and how the song seemed happy, yet was also building up importance as the song went on. They liked the rhythm of the call and response throughout the song. I told them the song was by Mtukudzi, from Zimbabwe, and we talked about how little we know of Africa, which might explain the guesses of Caribbean or how urban youth might correlate African music to being on holiday at the beach.

> *Tuku Response by Marco*
> Baby reggae this song takes me to beachez
> on a sunny day I could sit there watching wavez
> I think its from Jamaica I wonder what he sez
> I think he means something like:
> 'Live life free and resist these chains'
> the music is upbeat this is good roots music
> I like it

The next day, I played a video of the same song (Mtukudzi, 2006). In the video, we see a man hard at work chopping down huge trees. The backdrop is of Mtukudzi singing and dancing, yet somehow somber looking amidst a forest. Meanwhile, the man works tirelessly, his muscles bulging through his sweat soaked skin. The video shifts to a woman the man comes home to; she serves him food, but rejects him when he pulls her towards him. He beats her for rejecting his sexual advances; all the while we see a young child watching from under a table, hiding and afraid. The video transposes to trees being chopped down, and in the final scene, the boy is crying as he watches the woman we assume is his mother being pulled away from him: she is holding a finger in front of her lips, urging him into silence.

The class mirrors this silence and we freewrite for ten minutes. The students barely contain themselves, and when I tell them to stop writing, students burst out that while the song seemed upbeat, it really was not. They are conflicted about the meaning they previously attributed to the song and what they now recognize the song is about. We dive into a discussion about tempo and rhythm, and how to carry a message forward ensuring your words are conveying what you want them to. Several students note that the song seemed hopeful, that in hindsight, the upbeat tempo actually helped them think of the song as hope that the child will end the cycle of violence. Many students excitedly jot down notes about how they can read aloud their work more rhythmically, but also how they can write in ways that capture hope. The conversation about violence against women and children lingers. Students raise this just before the bell rings, and we pick up the conversation the following class when a student writes the words "parent abuse" on the board to kick start the day's freewrite. We spend the next two weeks focusing on family violence, child abuse, and domestic violence, all stemming from freewrites about a song and accompanying video.

Another example of the power of freewriting to engage students in conversation about what they live occurred during a class at Central High School. Several students heard that a fight was going on in front of the school, and word spread immediately to all students; the excitement in the room made editing peer papers impossible. As several students rushed out of the room to watch the fight, the rest of the students looked around confused. While most wanted to watch the fight, they did not want to leave our room, and we had already talked about avoiding violence by not rushing into it. A student stood up, marched up to the board, and wrote, "Capture what you feel right now." The student-initiated freewrite topic was relevant, and tapped directly into the heat of the moment; students began to write furiously. When the students who ran out of the room came back in, they already knew what to do, and despite their heaving breaths, began to write. Many of those freewrites became the foundation for poems that students later read at a district-wide student convening on youth violence.

This is the importance of continual, everyday writing; students develop their craft while engaging in conversation about the very issues they see around them, but often do not have a language to talk about. Providing numerous forums to reflect and then to share with peers allows students to frame a dialogue they have largely been kept from through standardized curriculum. Yet these are the very skills students need to develop if they are to arm themselves with skills to negotiate this increasingly violent world. Continual freewriting helps build up foundations for such conversations, but also helps prepare students for dialogue around issues that are risky to bring up without some sort of structure. Having students write prior to discussing potentially traumatic issues helps ensure students have the time and space to reflect *and then* speak. Freewriting thus becomes the backbone of a voice-centered class, bridging the academic structures that often limit voice with the need for students to make sense of the world around them. Freewriting becomes a tool through which students capture their daily reality, and students begin to freewrite in cafés, on the bus, at parks, on street corners, and in bathroom stalls as they hide away to record their thoughts and emotions.

Writing Assignments: Reflection on Context

Depending on the length of the course, I usually assign two or three assignments to clarify personal experiences with racism, such as a paper based on interviews with local elders or a letter to a newspaper advocating for a local urban issue. Drafts are due in advance of deadlines, and students are required to provide critical feedback to each other (and to turn in feedback they have received and addressed in their final drafts). The course ends with student performances of the final paper and with letters to an adult of the student's choosing. Throughout the course, topics loosely follow themes from the readings, music, film, and guest speakers, adapting according to student writings. I focus on quick writing exercises, capturing details, eliminating passive voice from our vocabulary, and creating the maximum impact with a minimum of words.

In a class at East Bay High School, one assignment designed to encourage students to detail their context, and then reflect on what those details mean was a paper framed around an incident that happened during class. A student at the school was placed into a forced mental health facility because, as one student had said, "she just went ka-razy." Several students in the class were close with the student and asked for help in supporting her while she was detained in the mental health facility. The two-part assignment documented issues that make children "go crazy," including, a bullet point list of up to 50 examples from the local neighborhood, and the second part was an up-close expansion of one of those issues. The lists of examples included police brutality, dismissive teachers and administrators, violence amongst peers, watching parents get beat, and watching parents beat other people, homelessness, lack of quality food, and addictions (to drugs, alcohol, violence, porn, and gambling).

Students were continually checking in with each other about how they experienced most of these painful circumstances firsthand, and then they shared the exact details they expanded upon to ensure others felt they captured enough to make the reader "go crazy." This was one of the students' favorite assignments because they were able to rely upon peers to identify issues, and, as Angela shared, "they got to talk about what hurt in a safe way, with a friend they could trust." She continued: "That was how we got to know each other, and our class was so tight after, cause we *felt* each other."

Assignments to Capture Student Reflection

1. Responsive freewrites:
   a. Neighborhood walks. At least once per week, students walk around the local community, and at random stops, do 5–10 minutes of freewriting to capture local neighborhood details. These help students learn to capture concrete details, while documenting aspects of their communities they often do not notice.
   b. On-spot writing about tense issues. Throughout the class, tense discussions emerge, often about racism, sexism, or other forms of oppression. In the beginning of the year, I often stop students in the midst of a heated conversation, and urge them to freewrite for 5–10 minutes on a perspective that is valid, but not being heard. Within a few weeks or months, students begin to stop conversations on their own for freewriting to help clarify complexities.
   c. Textured Close Observations. Once per week, students freewrite a textured, close detail-filled capturing of a small object or area. Students might be asked to write an entire page about a broken yo-yo, an ice cream cone on the sidewalk, a crack along a wall, or someone's shoe. The point is to narrowly focus on detail to sharpen capturing skills.
2. Longer assignments:
   a. Capture Your Block. This 4–5 page paper, which can also be read aloud in class, provides a comprehensive portrait of every building on the block that the student lives on. The focus remains on concrete details to show the condition of the buildings, the state of repairs, the depth of potholes and the amount and type of plants, trees, cars, and how trash is disposed of.
   b. Where You Buy Food. This 4–5 page paper captures the 3–4 closest stores and marks the distance to the nearest full-service grocery store. Students are required to interview nearby shop owners, assess for fresh produce, and provide an overview of what is primarily sold at each store, including overviews of what sort of food is marketed in which ways to which customers.
   c. Driving Through Your Community: What the Police See. This 5–6 page paper captures the neighborhood through the perspective of local police, and includes either a ride-along with an officer or a drive with a school security or resource officer. The assignment includes interviewing the officer, probing for specific details the officer is trained to notice and respond to, and then an analysis of what the officer was not noticing.

Personal Responses to Our Context

After setting a foundation for student writing that vacillates between capturing who students are, and the world they live within, I urge students to begin writing about concrete survival strategies. This is where students begin to merge the first two sets of exercises, expanding upon previous writings and thinking about who they are and what the world around them looks like. Here I shift writing exercises to guide students to reflect on how they respond to the world, literally prompting students: "Given the racism you already captured, what are your personal strategies for survival? And how is this working?" Writings include critical recognition of the ways individuals respond to their personal contexts, and include concrete capturing of what students do every day to survive. This is where I also focus on capturing emotional responses, including anger, pain, fear, love, and safety. But there is no guarantee that students writing about these issues will be rewarded by other educators.

> *What I have learned is this: No matter how well I speak, my words will be used to show how I am not like my peers. White people will use me to show how I am not like these other niggas. And now I write to show that we are all the same: articulate, powerful, and young. We live in their racist world, so now I have to write because my life, because our lives, depend on my words. Even if they twist our words against us, we must still write. —Shantel*

Shantel names the central problem with developing urban student voice: no matter how well students of color speak, they will often be disregarded because of their fashion, their styles, the tone of their diction, their race, gender, poverty, and youth. And even if Shantel is "heard," she will often be framed as being better than her peers, as an exception to the rule, as articulate despite her surroundings. And because of this reality, because urban students of color are simply not afforded the same opportunities that more privileged students are, I center curriculum around racism so that students of color develop an understanding of and language about the structures of racism that they know intimately. While students capture the intricacies of racism in their daily writings and in their papers, they share such work as a way of informing each other about the realities they live. Focusing on racism so intensely also allows students to detail what they do in response to the racism they capture.

A powerful example of students teaching each other about race and racism came from student assignments that directly capture how students live racism. At Central High, two students who had previously fought each other during what they had called a "race war" in their school came together in our class. I paired them up knowing they had been violent towards each other, and urged them to capture how they are seen individually and collectively by the world. David, a tattoo-covered Latino who had been in and out of juvenile hall for his gang-related activities, wrote about how everyone assumed he was stupid and violent, despite his love of playing the acoustic guitar and his desire to take care of his mother and father. Robert was also in and out of juvenile facilities, a young African American man who never got the chance to play basketball though his 6'4" frame and athleticism likely could have provided him with a college scholarship. He had intense rage at how he saw his family treated by White police and had a thick distrust of White people and teachers. After initial resistance to working together, David and Robert read each other's papers. I set up a meeting with the two of them to talk through feedback, concerned that they did not have the tools to listen to each other, despite what I perceived as similar growing up contexts. Getting them to start talking was difficult, but after they began to share, I became irrelevant, sitting back to take in the beauty of two young men of color who have been taught to hate each other bond over their shared stereotypical treatment. They wrote a powerful collaborative paper about how their White teachers were constantly afraid of them, and four years later, still reach out to me letting me know how they are friends, aligned in their commitment to addressing racism against young African American and Latino gang-affiliated men.

> *Excerpt from You Judge Us by David and Robert*
> You Judge Us
> The way you walk by
> Cant look away
> Afraid to stare
> Eyes peeled
> Will we rob you steal your purse your pride
> But you the ones who stole from us
> Our youth our manhood our identity
> What you take you afraid we take
> but you the ones who stole from us
> setting black and latino against each other
> we suppose to fight each other
> but you the ones who stole from us

Centering racism in the curriculum encourages and allows for the dialogue that David and Robert needed to validate each other, to see each other as human and as being treated in similar ways. Students continually make connections to understanding racism as a system that silences critical challenge and that makes their voices ever so essential. My point in centering racism is to help students of color see that just as their White peers normalize racism, so too do students of color. We do this through our daily writing and sharing, but also through creative assignments: Students show how "normal" racism is through freewrites and sometimes, through creating 4-minute documentaries or through interviews with elders about what today's racism looks like. Creating racism-focused assignments helps students dive into racism while still being able to maintain their own voice (and thoughts) around race. The focus also enables students to illuminate their own survival strategies, enabling them to talk through what they do to navigate racism, and how effective their strategies appear to be.

Students of color often find the purposeful centering of voices of color to be inclusive and empowering, yet White teachers often ask if I am excluding the few White students by doing such. One White student clarified the tension of focusing on racism, and on centering the experiences of people of color: "I always feel welcome in this class, even though I don't have much to say about racism. But its good, I get to learn a lot, and I realize that [White] people like me are never quiet enough to hear what racism is." I encourage such dialogue in the class, and urge students to wrestle with why I chose which readings, and with my focus on prioritizing authors of color who speak clearly about racism. Most White students have had tremendous exposure to White authors; few students of color have been exposed to many authors of color, much less authors that speak directly to the pervasiveness of racism. For most students, this will be the only class they will ever take that only has readings by authors of color. Regardless of who is in the class, and what I might want to assign, the key for me is in acknowledging everyone's presence, being transparent about what sorts of authors I assign, and not allowing the conversation to shift away from racism. Even as I facilitate in such a way to center the racism we all live, I still strive to respond to student needs, no matter how well planned out a curriculum may be.

An opportunity to shift the curriculum and course focus came midway through a high school writing course in 2004, when school-wide rumors spread about several students who had been recently diagnosed with HIV. We were in the midst of creating documentary film shorts about local community leaders when the class erupted into a physical fight; one student had called a student with HIV a "fag." While I had known of this student's HIV status, he had not disclosed it to the class, and now everyone correctly assumed that this was one of the students with HIV through the context of another student's homophobia. The student who initiated the fight was immediately expelled from the district (he had numerous prior offenses), and the rest of the class had a week-long discussion about how we support students who are being marginalized, particularly when it is around something life-threatening like HIV. The class ultimately bonded over the incident, and wanted to increasingly understand both homophobia in the black community and the prevalence of HIV amongst people of color. I asked the class if we should shift our focus to these two issues or maintain our focus on our already-in-progress projects. The class unanimously decided to merge the focus and continued the interviews they had begun, but shifted the focus to homophobia and HIV within the black community. I reorganized the class, identified relevant readings, film clips, and guest speakers, and aligned additional assignments to focus on our new topics. The course concluded with a school-wide forum on HIV within the black community, whereby the students presented the findings from their interviews and brought in guest speakers to educate the school. Student papers documented how their collective response informed their individual strategies to address racism.

Even the student who was expelled was invited back to the classroom to offer an apology. Despite the fact that the student was not allowed back on campus, I was able to negotiate bringing him to campus (with his parole officer, two police officers, and the school principal) for one class period, during which the student broke down, asked for forgiveness, and disclosed that his mother died of AIDS-related complications (which he had not known at the time of the fight he initiated). The class wrote a collective letter to his parole officer, formally accepting his apology and testifying to his growth and humility in a powerful display of forgiveness and recognition of responsibility for peers. While that student has not yet attained his G.E.D., he regularly reaches out to several of the students from the class (they became friends after he was expelled from the school). Despite living as a young adult in poverty, he regularly volunteers at an HIV clinic, and speaks to the importance of a class he was kicked out of.

For me, the importance of that class was the lesson that no matter how invested I am as an instructor in course content, I must remain flexible so that I can support student needs. Student-generated topics should shape the class, and while I might begin with a curriculum framework, I build into the curriculum space for students to guide content, topics, readings, films, and writing assignments. No matter how essential a topic is to me, I do not own the curriculum. I am reminded, when I listen to students, that the purpose of a curriculum is to foster student thought, action, and voice development. So when students speak to a greater, more pressing need, I shift with them, integrating the lessons I was trying to teach with what they ask for. This is based entirely on my capacity to create the conditions for voice, and to step out of the way, facilitating based on what students say, write, or share so that they recognize their experiences are shaping what they learn, how they learn, and what role I take as the formal instructor. And this is precisely how I create the conditions for students to explain their responses to what they see as racism.

Peer Feedback to Focus Voice

Throughout my shifting of the curriculum to reflect student need, I continually center racism through editing. I set a foundation from the first days of the course so that students recognize that part of racism in schools means their work is typically ignored by teachers. This is demonstrated through educators who pass students of color despite the fact that these students might not yet have developed the capacity to read and write (Howerton & Thomas, 2004; Jimerson & Kaufman, 2003).[3] As a way of dealing with this institutional racism, I remind students that they have to help each other develop because schools are not often invested in their intellectual development outside of standardized tests. In addition, while students like Lupe, a multiracial Black, Latino, and White junior at Central High, might state that, "I don't like school because it's racist," I use editing as an opportunity to push her to clarify vague terms like "racism." Most everyone, I argue, is against racism generally. But when students get detailed, capture the concrete feelings that racism creates, and highlight the ways in which racism manifests, they move beyond terms and metaphors to reality. So I push Lupe to clarify what she means by "racist" and she eventually, with help from peers, comes up with this: "My white teachers tell me what learning means. They tell me that to know means to speak like them. And to be successful means to act like them." Lupe continued: "But they don't act 'right,' they act white." Her observation is critical; Lupe sees that how her teachers teach requires her to be what she frames as "White" which would mean denying her Black and Latino heritages.

The importance of students clarifying what racism actually means, looks like, and feels like is essential in schools that do not acknowledge or teach about what critical race scholars term 'racial microaggressions,' the dozens of seemingly minor acts of racism that people of color face throughout the day (Allen, 2010; Pierce, 1974; Solorzano, Ceja, & Yosso, 2000). The notion of racial microaggressions reflects critical race theory's assertion that racism occurs everyday to people of color, and I urge students to identify the racism they face each and every day. Editing becomes the academic lever to help students clarify reality in more concrete terms, and so just after setting up the practice of in-and-outside the classroom freewriting, I set up the notion that writers need to continually refine our words to ensure our voices are heard in the ways we would like to be heard. One component of this clarity is to push beyond blanket terms (such as racism and oppression) that lead to White defensiveness. This requires intense, personal editing to ensure what is written actually reflects what the author intends, including aligning with the tone, language, and details that clarify personality and presence. Julia remarked that when she edits, she does so in order to ensure that "White people cannot tell me what I am saying didn't happen, and if I say it was racism, they get all denial-like. But when I break down racism, and don't even use the word, then they get all mad for me—instead of at me." Julia captures here the process of turning words on the page into "voice," what poets often call "workshoping poems." This editing is the bulk of the "academic" work in my classes, where students learn to spend time crafting their words, learn to ensure they are saying what they want to, in ways that reflect who they are but also maximize the potential to be heard by the intended audience.

Going back to Jasmine, Marco, and Enrique's introductory writings, I frame the second week to push beyond the excitement of voice. By then, as is typical, the class is back in rows, and I ask why students are waiting for me to tell them what they need to know again. Some students grumble, then move desks into a circle so that we facing each other again. The culture of resistance to students taking over the class is something that I confront continually over the first few weeks. Even as students excitedly challenge how most of their schooling has silenced them, they slip back into their roles as subservient students. This becomes my continual push, arguing that students have to take space if they want to shape classrooms, schools, and communities. If students wish to develop their voices, I argue, then they have to claim our classroom dynamics. They have to make this space what they want it to be, despite not having formal training or experience being in classrooms that value their voices or perspectives.

I ask the class to freewrite for five minutes about the first week, and several volunteers read aloud their insights. A few students share their excitement and hope that the class will keep being this real. I make a point to stop the class after each student who describe the class as "interesting," "great," "okay" or even "freakin' fabulous." "These are very vague words," I press, "be clear what is 'interesting,' what specifically is 'great,' and what 'freakin fabulous' actually means to you. Do not assume we know what you feel—show us with your words." Students begin to express frustration at me jumping in, and I argue that clarity of our words about what we think and feel is our collective point, and vague words will not get us there. Vague words, I often say, will not shift society. Eventually, after everyone has read, several students speak up that they appreciate me challenging them because they agree, vague words are everywhere. The class falls into a discussion about how we are taught in English classes, and then reinforced in all other writing assignments, to write passively, to not say anything concretely for fear of being told we are wrong.

I tell students to bring out their introductions from the first day and re-read them in pairs, with each partner asking clarifying questions or responding as appropriate. They do this for ten minutes, and then I ask for a brave volunteer to help deepen our class commitment to voice. Jasmine volunteers and writes her original introduction on the board. I ask her if she is ready to have her work dissected in public, and she reaffirms that she is. In just the second week of class, I begin to demonstrate how our words are often vague, and while a particular set of words might get applause, the words might not mean all that much. Jasmine reads aloud her poem twice; the first time I ask students to listen. The second time I urge Jasmine to slow down, to read in her "normal" voice, and to help us listen to her. I tell the other students to jot down any line that sticks out because it is fabulous or because the line is not working. After students complete their notes, I guide the class in collectively analyzing the poem, going word-by-word and line-by-line.

We start with Jasmine's first line: *Alive today I am Jasmine.* The class loves the line, notes the reference to being alive when so many young people they know are killed. I point out that Jasmine tells us who she is after telling us she's alive, and students reply that being alive is the most important thing given the daily violence they face. Several students appreciate how "today" tells them that she may not expect to be alive tomorrow. That leads perfectly, they argue, into the second line: *I am here to tell you I matter.* I agree with students but ask them to clarify how that line works, and for the first time in the class, there is total silence. One student notes the importance of stating why she is here, and students start talking about what it means to matter. I ask the class to whom Jasmine matters, and they all agree: while she sounded like she meant to herself, they also thought she meant they had to think she mattered, too. Students dissected this line into hearing Jasmine issue a directive, like Marco argued: "Jasmine told me straight up she matters. She didn't give me no option to think she don't."

At this point, the students are engaged in breaking down the meaning of each line, and eagerly shift to the third line without my prompting. *"I am from Moms and Pops*" immediately becomes a problem. The students do not like it and do not have a language to critique without stating that they do not like it. Juan captures the class sentiment: "It just don't do nothing." I push them to clarify why and one student retorts: "Duh, we all from moms and pops." I step us back and note that not all of us know our birth parents, and ask "how many of us were raised by aunts, uncles, and grandparents." A show of hands indicates two thirds of the students were raised by a range of relatives, neighbors, and adoptive parents. They conclude: the line is too vague. I ask them to think about what this line adds and where the line moves us from the previous forceful directive and they agree that the line is not needed. We talk for a few minutes about the importance of having meaning in each word, in each line, and not wasting words. I remind them of June Jordan's (in Muller et al., 1995) notion of maximum impact with minimal words and then students start to resist, complaining that I am too focused on meaning and that I care too much about each word. I have gone too far, they argue, but then a few students jump in, clarifying that we are helping Jasmine's piece get even better. Jasmine agrees that this process is helpful, and urges the class to continue: "Ya'll have no idea! This is helping me think about where to go next. I can write a *whole* paper from all this stuff!" She continues, cautioning: "But can ya'll take it easy on me? Dang! I can't wait to tear your stuff up!" The class erupts into laughter.

Jasmine Original Intro

Alive today I am Jasmine and
I am here to tell you I matter
I am from Moms and Pops
but Pops passed and Moms is
hardly here and I have two younger
sisters I take care of them and
I think you'll all know me soon enough
because I am here to say
something

Jasmine Revised Intro

Alive today I am Jasmine and
I am here to tell you I matter
I am from torn sheets and bullet riddles streets
too much sugar and ribs and 40's and Pops passed
too much wine and diabetes and tricks and Moms is hardly here
and though barely raised I raise two others
6 am I wake Bobbie and Senti, hurry them into the shower
Unfold the clothes I washed last night
pick their day's outfits
I rush quick oats into the microwave into their mouths
I put the homework I made them do last night into their packs
with quick-made sandwiches, apples, granola bars, and cheetos
because I am here to say
even if I don't matter to you
I matter to me
I matter to Bobbie
I matter to Senti
and if I don't matter to you
I am here to say
I should because I am their future
I am you are we are in the same streets
and will only be beautiful together
Alive today I am Jasmine and
I am here to tell you I matter

We continue to examine the next few lines, pushing Jasmine for more detail. We stop again at "*I take care of them*" when students ask specifically what Jasmine does. After a few vague starts ("I clean up, I wash up, I make dinner") students guide Jasmine into creating a quick list, which, after some minor editing, ends up on her revision. The last line splits the class: half of the class likes how Jasmine tells us she is here to say something, but the other half is confused. "Why not just tell us what you want to say," they ask Jasmine. She ultimately agrees, and in her revision, tells more about who she is and how she lives. And that is the point in writing with voice: saying what you want to say in a voice so clearly, so powerfully that your intended audience can hear and feel your point. Jasmine's example is typical; most students revise their intros to say more about who they are, and excitedly share details about their lives that they do not share with most of their friends.

The second week ends with students presenting their revised intro read alouds, after spending a few days providing feedback to each other in pairs. When pairs get stuck, they come up to the front of the class, write the troublesome lines on the board and lead the class in soliciting feedback. The point is to get used to starting the class with freewrites, to provide and receive feedback, to ask for individual and collective help from peers, and to get into the practice of continually editing. This helps everyone become more comfortable expressing oneself in public. A shift begins at this point, when students start to share their work in public, and become responsible for honest feedback to each other. They've never done this before, and while it feels scary at first, within a few days, most students are eager to get feedback from peers. There are always exceptions; the impact of being silenced by peers, teachers, and other adults has shut down many students and some need additional support to open up. I meet one-on-one with those who are most uncomfortable and resistant, and usually after a short discussion or my offer to provide feedback prior to sharing with the rest of the class, students dive in.

Writing Assignments: Personal Responses to Student Context

There are countless examples of assignments that help students examine how they respond to the context of racism they live within. I often have students respond directly to a poem, song, or short video clip that demonstrates racism in a quick, concise way. I have used dozens of poets, including Audre Lorde, Ai, Chrystos, June Jordan, Sherman Alexie, Aurora Levins Morales and Rosario Morales, Patricia Spears Jones, Rita Dove, Assoto Saint, Ana Castillo, Jimmy Santiago Baca, Justin Chin, Haunani-Kay Trask, augmented by a dozen poetry compilations. I also use books and writing excerpts from James Baldwin, Richard Wright, June Jordan,

Sherman Alexie, Derrick Bell, Jonathan Kozol, Sapphire, Jamaica Kincaid, Sara Lawrence-Lightfoot, Danzy Senna, Dorothy Allison, Wallace Shawn, Ngugi wa Thiong'o, Edwidge Danticat, and Junot Diaz, to name a few. In addition to writing texts, I use songs by Oliver Mtukudzi, Zap Mama, Thandiswa, Asa, Gigi, Gil Scott-Heron, Sade, Nneka, Roots, Ice Cube, Midnite, Damian Marley, Clinton Fearon, Annie Humphrey, Immortal Technique, Blue Scholars, Ise-Lyfe, and artists that students bring in to share. To stimulate using visual media, I encourage students to identify YouTube clips that offer particularly concrete or creative examples of racism, and augment these student-initiated sources with clips from films such as *Not One Less* (Guangxi Film Studio & Yimou, 1999), *Life and Debt* (Black & Kincaid, 2001), *The Business of Fancydancing* (Alexie, Bond, & Benear, 2003), *The Matrix* (Silver, Wachowski & Wachowski, 1999), and other films that are popular at the moment. These sources challenge, critique, and raise awareness of the extensive nature of racism, highlight personal responses, and remind students that racism, and voices highlighting it, are everywhere.

One poem that I have used for years is Chrystos' (1995) "They're Always Telling Me I'm Too Angry." In this passionate poem, Chrystos clarifies the many things that make her angry, justifying both why anger is a natural reaction to oppression, and that voice should be used to identify what these examples of oppression are. The power in the poem is that Chrystos captures racism, sexism, classism, and heterosexism, but also the negative reaction to calling out such oppression from peers, colleagues, and random others. Students read the poem aloud several times, and then respond to one of her final lines: "If you're furious with me because I haven't mentioned something you're angry about get busy & write it yourself" (p. 49).

My intent is to teach writing and expression as a developing skill set that can help students survive the daily violence, racism, and trauma that often reflects urban realities. If students need self-defense, then my role as a writing instructor is to help them develop their words as a way out of dangerous situations. If students need anger management, then I encourage them to develop writing as a way of releasing anger. But I also provide curriculum around how schooling teaches us to silence and deny our anger and emotion. I teach students to write about their addictions, to capture what addictions feel like, in the hopes that they will begin to reflect on their reliance upon drugs. And I provide curriculum around the history of drug use, around plantation labor that provides the drugs so many are addicted to. I provide students forums to capture how those they love may be disrespected by society, and then juxtapose that with historical analyses of legal disrespect of low-income communities of color. In essence, I blend what they tell me they need with curriculum content that deepens their understanding of the issues they write about and ways they can respond to increase their chances at meaningful survival.

Found Poetic Response to Chrystos' They're Always Telling Me I'm Too Angry by Christina

For every person who is quiet
There are dozens of us dying
We bleed their racism
While they tell us This Is Not Blood
Angry that I cannot walk down the street without someone being afraid
Angry that I cannot speak in class without a white student saying I talked over them
Angry that I cannot feel human without some white man saying I am in their way
Angry that welfare line is as big as my hunger
Angry that when I say its always about racism some white person makes me tell him what "it" means when "it" means EVERYTHING!
Angry that health care is a battle because white people don't seem to mind war with me
Angry that my dad is in prison for what white people do on Saturdays, Mondays, and Wednesdays
Angry that everywhere and everyhow and all the time there is racism
Seeping into my pores so that I sometimes think
I should be afraid of Samoans or Laotians or Croatians
So Damn Angry that I sometimes say bitch or ho or whore when I'm referring to my people
So So So So impossibly angry that I sometimes am exactly the problem
Angry that I sometimes believe what they say about me so that I say
What they say about me
Angry Angry Angry but thankfully
I can breathe on Tuesdays, Wednesdays, Thursdays, and Fridays because we have this class the one place where racism is Not Okay
The one place where I am
The one place where my sisters and brothers
Are allowed to be as angry as me.

Assignments to Capture Student Responses

1. Creative freewrites:
   a. Senses of Racism. In this introductory writing, students freewrite responses to my intermittent prompts of "Racism sounds like…, Racism tastes like…, Racism looks like…, Racism smells like…, Racism feels like…."
   b. Another word for Racism is….In this freewrite, I encourage students to come up with a list of words that explain what racism is without using the words "race" or "racism." The key is that this list has to be compelling and clear to someone who lives in the distant future.
   c. Race is What? In this recurring freewrite, students define race as it looks in the room they are currently in. We begin this freewrite in our class, but move to different locations throughout the course, including a grocery store, a homeless shelter, and walking through the neighborhood.
2. Longer assignments:
   a. Capturing Racism. This paper explores what racism looks like from the author's perspective, and encourages the writer to capture, using descriptive analysis, what racism feels like without using the word. Given your capturing, what do you do to not internalize racism?
   b. Racism in the Media. In this paper, students compare and contrast two different sources of media, including, for example, one corporate media source such as CNN, Fox News, MTV, and BET, and one independent media source or locally produced musician or radio broadcast. The purpose is to explore what each media source is saying about racism and what the author does to inform herself about the nature of racism.
   c. Interviewing Racism. This paper combines research with analysis of racism, and is based on students interviewing elders within the community about how they have seen racism changing over the years. Students then compile the interviews into a paper, analyzing themes and providing a comparative perspective of racism today.

Conclusion

This chapter provides a framework for educators to develop, strengthen, and reflect on their own approaches to teaching voice to urban youth. Through capturing stories, experiences, and background context to my personal approaches, I attempt to clarify flexible, responsive, and transparent instructional approaches that encourage students to be themselves, to understand racism and oppression, and begin to develop and find strength in using their voice to challenge what they see as injustice. Because teaching for voice means modeling our voices, demonstrating others who use voice as a profession, and setting up continual writing about the world we live in, assignments allow students the space to write what they need to. Educator techniques that center on freewriting and providing intense feedback and that align classroom management to the purpose of developing voice provide needed structure. The purpose of voice-centered courses is to develop voice through examining personal identity and the larger social context, and then through examining responses to the larger context of racism. This examination is based upon capturing student reality and moving audiences with critical expression. Thus, I try to center student realities, to tap into what motivates students, and to help students express what they would like to change about their immediate world. And in the end, the effectiveness is based entirely upon educator passion; the extent to which students blossom is largely a reflection of the extent to which educators decenter silencing factors that are the norm in most classrooms and schools.

Final Assignment: Letter to my Professor by Shay

Dear Chris:

I feel that this class has helped me express myself better with my words. I've learned how to speak what's on my mind, instead of bottling me all inside. I once thought I used to give too much detail when I spoke. But I've learned that the more I speak with detail others can feel what I feel. This class has helped me get ready for the world's criticism. It has also helped me get a better mindset on how others feel and what they go through. That I'm not the only one struggling in this cold-hearted world.

Chris – Thank you for pushing me when I wanted to just sit back and be lazy. You've seen the words that are stuck in my mind and left on the tip of my tongue. You kept pushing when I couldn't push myself any more, when I wanted class and this school and this world to just be gone. Thanks for helping me express myself. I've always had trouble with that but I feel very confident now that I've been in this class. It was your helping hand that helped me get on that stage to read my poem to all these unknown people. As I clung to the paper and my voice got shaky I remember the love and support from our class and kept on reading. Your voice kept me reading. Thanks for helping me speak out instead of speaking in.

Interlude I

Youth Radio: Celebrating Survival through Developing Voice

Emma Shaw Crane

Writer and activist Arundhati Roy (2004) argued that, "There's really no such thing as the 'voiceless.' There are only the deliberately silenced, or the preferably unheard." Radio is a tool to strengthen and validate those who are deliberately silenced and preferably unheard: youth of color, prisoners, continuation high school students, survivors of abuse, poor people. During the semester-long class at East Bay High, I worked with students to record a CD of their work. My intention in recording E-High students was to honor the stories and affirm the voices of young people kicked out of school, locked up, on welfare, labeled "emotionally disturbed" and shut down by teachers, social workers, and probation officers who treat them as problems to be reformed or disciplined.

My commitment to amplify the voices and stories of marginalized people, and my belief in youth radio as a tool to do that was born when I heard my own voice recorded as a teenager. I realized that despite seven years of daily abuse, I was still alive and able to speak for myself. I was not, as I had been repeatedly told by an abusive coach, stupid or worthless. The experience of listening to my poem, recorded and amplified outside myself in a room full of people, affirmed that I still had my voice, wounded and terrified, but my own. The supportive and empathetic responses of those who listened affirmed my experience: my precious and necessary ability to love and protect myself had been taken from me and that *was not my fault*. That moment deepened my capacity to love and defend myself, and opened up a space for my rage: at my coach, at my parents for their failure to protect me, at myself for lying to protect my abuser, at the teachers who looked away. Listening to my voice, I saw myself: wounded but fiercely and completely alive.

I record stories in the hope that people will listen to their own voices and recognize both their right to anger in the face of tremendous loss and proof of their resilience despite the violence they survived. I choose to work with people who are deliberately silenced because I believe such voices most need space to be carefully listened to. Throughout college, I worked for Prison Radio, a small radio program featuring the voices of incarcerated people. I met Chris a year earlier in a writing seminar at East Bay University, which, like the high school class, was centered on developing critical student voice. There, for the first time in my formal education, I found a space to speak openly about the violence I experienced growing up a girl, a supportive and critical space to heal and recognize my strength, and a framework within which to understand my privilege as a young light-skinned, mixed-heritage woman who identifies and passes white most of the time (my family, like many white American families, includes hidden and often intentionally forgotten histories of people of color; in my case, Arab and African American great-grandparents). I came to E-High the following semester through a second class I took with Chris, titled "Racism and Schooling in the U.S." Instead of staying on campus for the one-hour discussion section in addition to lecture, college students enrolled in "Racism and Schooling" went to local high schools to conduct research, participate in classes or work one-on-one with students.

I arrived at E-High committed to engaging from a place of humility and respect. Growing up in an anti-racist and multicultural family between Southern Mexico and Northern California, I heard stories of predatory university researchers dropping into oppressed communities and taking stories, unaccountable to the people who generously shared their experiences with total strangers. My intention to treat E-High students as experts on the racism, sexism, and classism built into the American schooling system, not as subjects to be studied or observed, meant I had to constantly check myself and be aware of my privilege. Unlike other classes that recruited students to "mentor disadvantaged youth," Chris framed the E-High requirement as a space for exchange, collaboration, and critical engagement.

One of the first times I came to class was the day Sherise read a piece about being raped at a party. After several semesters in college classrooms in which women were silenced, criticized and mocked for speaking openly about sexual violence, I was overwhelmed with fear for Sherise. I expected other students to laugh, talk over her, walk out, or suggest she was responsible for the rape. My fear that Sherise would be blamed (or asked what she was wearing that night at the party) was consistent with my experience of most conversations about sexual violence. As Sherise began speaking, I sat awkwardly on my hands, my throat tight with anxiety. But nobody laughed, or walked out. A young man took his earphones out. The classroom was entirely quiet. The women on either side of Sherise moved closer to her. When she finished speaking, several other women immediately came forward and spoke about their experiences of sexual abuse and incest, followed by two men who spoke about the difficulty of speaking about sexual abuse while trying to conform to narrow definitions of manhood. A young man prefaced his question to Sherise with, "Is it okay if I ask you something…?" This demonstrated his desire not to cross a boundary, and his commitment to making sure she felt respected and safe.

Given the space to speak and write, students in the class were absolutely capable of something most college students I interact with cannot manage: raw and brave writing in a supportive and loving classroom, where each student had the space to break silence and speak about their own experience. That conversation challenged me to bring my own voice to the classroom and engage bravely and honestly. There were several experiences that I had in common with many E-High students, and spoke about in class. As a high school student, I sat through classes completely irrelevant to my life, classes that implied by omission that women, people of color, and queer folks did not exist. As a young woman, I am hollered at, grabbed, followed, expected to care for and clean up after the men around me, and offered twenty bucks for a blowjob while trying to ride the bus, do my job, go for a walk, or cook dinner. As a survivor of abuse, I spent years believing the abuse was my fault and that I was the problem, and that if I only worked harder to be perfect the violence would stop. These common experiences opened up space to trade stories and connect with E-High students inside and outside the classroom.

But there were also key differences, and honest engagement required that I not skim over or minimize those. My father is a physician, and my mother is a community organizer and narrative therapist, a method based in collaborating with people to discover sources of power and resistance within themselves. I grew up upper middle class and rural, rode horses competitively, drove a pick-up truck, went to a private Waldorf school, traveled, and attended an elite university. Despite my initial fear that being honest about where I came from would alienate students, talking about my life with students led to fascinating and challenging questions: What did white people think when they saw images of Hurricane Katrina? What was it like going to a small private high school? How come no one went to jail for smoking pot in my hometown? Students' willingness to listen and ask questions led to conversations that illuminated and allowed us to critically discuss unjust systems.

This kind of engagement breaks down the distance and mistrust common between people with privilege (adults, white people, educators, college students) and the marginalized students of color they "mentor" or teach. Outside of the classroom, however, this distance was reinforced and maintained by upper- and middle-class people who treated me as a hero for merely showing up at the high school. I was repeatedly told, "You're so brave!" and asked if I was "scared" to work with Black and Latino students. This reflects a deeply racist conception of Black and Latino masculinity (that a young white woman would not be safe in a classroom of poor young men of color). Further, these people assumed that the mere presence of an educated, upper-middle-class white woman was beneficial for inner-city youth: "You must teach those kids so much!" I was positioned as an expert on "urban problems" (upon hearing about my engagement at E-High, a wealthy donor to East Bay University asked me, "So, what's the solution to low achieving inner city schools?") East Bay University students frequently asked me if I was Black or Latina, as it was simply too difficult to fathom someone who passes as white taking African American Studies seriously, or choosing to engage with young people of color. While I was heralded as expert, saint, and star activist, the brilliant young people who actually lived the devastating and difficult realities of corner-store-Cheetos-for-breakfast poverty and a school with locked gates and math textbooks from the 1970s were cuffed and slammed to concrete on their way to work, jailed for a pocketful of weed, and labeled "emotionally disturbed" by middle-class teachers who wonder why these students are *so* angry. The expectation that I could or would "speak for" high school students deepened my rage and commitment to creating a space for young people to speak for themselves.

When I arrived in the classroom, I introduced myself and explained that I hoped to record the voices and creative work of the students. I said that I also worked with Prison Radio, and I saw that the students had experiences and histories in common with political prisoners. The process of recording the CD took place over three days, with students leaving Chris' class in pairs to work with me in a separate room. I recorded one student reading her piece, than taught her basic audio recording process, including controlling levels, setting up the microphone, checking microphone cables, prompting and reassuring the reader, and transferring audio from the digital recorder to a laptop. She recorded the next student, then taught him the recording process. He taught the following student, and in this way each student contributed a piece of critical and reflective writing to the disc, recorded and coached another student, and taught a peer basic audio engineering skills.

The CD compilation was given to students, teachers, and family members. It was not sold or broadcast on the radio. For me, the joy wasn't just in a shiny final product, but the process of creating something centered entirely on student voices. Youth radio amplified student voice, built technical literacy, and created something beautiful consistent with critical race theory's principle of storytelling and positioning those who survive racism as experts of their own experience. Instead of relying on an external merit system, or judging student progress based on each individual's ability to outperform their peers, the process of recording, editing, and compiling the CD was a collective project with space for each student's unique and necessary contribution.

The experience of working with students to record their stories pushed me to match their fierce, raw writing and bring my own experience to the classroom. They showed me, in the words of Audre Lorde (1984), that "It is not difference which immobilizes us, but silence" (p. 44) The students in the class gave me space to both reflect on my own privilege as a white student at an elite university and to see the trauma that I have survived as part of a larger, collective experience. This kind of engagement, honest, complicated, and sometimes terrifying, gives me tremendous hope in the possibility of building strong alliances across difference. The process of recording our stories challenged the dominant model of education in which white educators can swoop in and "drop knowledge" on "depraved" Black and Latino students. Instead of "teaching," I was engaging and learning from students, and working with them to create a final product that they were proud of.

One student recorded a devastating piece about community violence in which she wrote "I come from my next door neighbor getting shot on my front steps/hanging out with my cousins/now two of them gone/rest in peace/it's the same sad song." Afterward, listening to her piece to see if she wanted to re-record or make changes, she commented, "I sound hella strong!" Hearing her own voice, recorded just as she wanted, allowed her to reflect on her own strength. This moment exemplifies my belief in youth radio as a tool to honor the voices of the students we work with. It is a way to take back power and claim our stories. As poet professor June Jordan (1989) wrote, "I have been the problem everyone seeks to eliminate…but let this be unmistakable this poem/is not consent I do not consent/to my mother to my father to the teachers/to the F.B.I…to the sneaky creeps in car/I am not wrong: Wrong is not my name/My name is my own my own my own/and I can't tell you who the hell set things up like this/but I can tell you that from now on my resistance/my simple and daily and nightly self-determination/may very well cost you your life" (p. 104).

I cannot think of anything more worthy of celebration than surviving to speak about and back to what has tried to kill us.

Chapter 4

Trauma in the Classroom: Structuring Classrooms to Respond to Urban Students

I aint sposed to talk about being raped at school.
Teachers don't know don't wanna know.
But that shit happened here, at this school.
So I gotta deal with it everyday.
Everyday reminding me of pain tears pain rage pain confused.
How come they aint a class on that.
—From Jacinda's Take Home Journal

Letitia erupted into the class at Central High 20 minutes late, her jet black hair reaching outwards in every direction, unkempt, unlike her typically tight cornrows or occasional small afro-puffs jetting out symmetrically from the back of her head. Typically the most engaged, present student, Letitia would often chide students who came in late, telling them with all seriousness that, "if you don't care about this class, then you don't care about your life." She had missed her first class of the year the previous day, and had not been at school until our class, which met just after lunch. She flopped noisily into her desk, slammed her journal onto the floor, crossed her arms tightly, and slumped backwards, eyes barely visible under her crumpled brow, seething.

The class was already in the midst of dissecting Andre's paper. He was struggling to transpose his being beat by juvenile hall guards with beating his older sister so seriously she ended up going to the hospital. The discussion was intense, and two male students had asked to step out of the room for a "breather" so they could calm themselves down; they later wrote in their journals about how Andre's writing triggered previous experiences with police brutality and violence. When Letitia walked in, several students were debating if Andre needed to be as explicit in showing the story of him beating his sister; they felt the details from his perspective glorified violence against women.

Andre defended his approach, tightening his fists as he argued that "you have to know how upset I was, and I show that real well." Another male student agreed, saying that you can feel what it is like to "be the one punching and kicking her." This made several women in the class even more upset; "But what about how it felt to be kicked?" Shantel asked. Andre jumped in, "but that's why I show how I was beat by the guards in juvey." Christina pushed deeper: "Just 'cause you got beat don't mean I want to hear about how you beat someone like me." Shantel extended the challenge: "It sounds like you're just showing that beating your sister is okay cause you got beat." Andre stood up, shaking. "I fuck up and get fucked with. If you don't want to hear it, then don't give me any fucking feedback."

The class became still, silent. Andre's shoulders slumped in defeat as his eyes began to water. He eeked out a quiet: "I never wanted to hurt my sister." Letitia, who up until this point had remained slumped in her desk, rose up, and stood next to Andre, who stepped back in surprise. The class remained quiet, startled by the obnoxious bell, which rang unasked. Perhaps a dozen options of what I could do skittered through my head, but I froze, unsure of how to wrap this up in the perhaps 20 seconds I had before students from the next class darted into our room. Andre and Letitia stood shoulder to shoulder, facing the class, and no one moved. Letitia spoke: "Everyone can go, but all the guys in the room gotta write about being beat from a black girl's perspective." I jumped in to reinforce, relieved by the solution Letitia offered: "That's your homework for tomorrow: Capture the details and focus on perspective!"

In my head I was already planning the conversation for tomorrow, wondering if this might be the conversation that finally got me fired, finally pushed some students too far. My thoughts were broken by Letitia's presence outside the door as I gathered my belongings and headed to the university where I was teaching educators how to facilitate race-based conversations in high school classrooms. I never made it to that class: instead, Letitia asked me if she could speak to me. Tears pooled up in her eyes, and she asked if we could leave the school. Again in my head were thoughts of my getting fired; I still worried about whether or not I was crossing professional lines I had been taught in educator preparation programs; weren't we told repeatedly to not develop bonds with students, to not be alone with students, especially not off-campus? In hindsight, the lines I was crossing to support my students were exactly what these young adults needed to feel human, and such line crossing reminded me how efforts to support urban students are often professionally and personally risky.

Unsure of where to go, we ended up walking around the grey, rundown, urban neighborhood, circling several blocks for hours. Letitia asked me to listen to her, and she told me stories of her abuse, careful at first not to tell me too much, but when she saw that I was just listening, she opened up. Within twenty minutes, she was telling me about how her father used to molest her, about how her mother beat her until last year, and about how her two cousins raped her the previous weekend. She couldn't get up, couldn't get to school, and saw no reason to. It took all of her strength, she told me, just to come to our class. When she heard what we were talking about, she almost ran out of class. Instead, she told me she decided to live, right then and there, during our class. Because students were talking, engaging in real conversation about what happened to her just two days before. And that, she stressed to me, gave her hope. So much so that she wanted the class to know that she had Andre's back, that he was making great strides by trying to capture the details of the violence and pain he caused. "*He was trying,*" she told me, and wanted the class to realize that was all she ever wanted. Someone to try. Someone to work through the causes of violence, or what Letitia later called "the things that make you get up and smash someone."

I promised her I would not share what she shared with me afterwards, committing myself to ensuring she not get punished for, as she argued, deciding to live. When I spoke, instead of giving her contact information for social workers or psychologists, instead of offering up the partial solutions that my training suggested I provide, against what I have been repeatedly taught to do as a professional, I shared with her my own experiences of being abused. I talked about my father's fists, about regularly getting jumped, and about how I was molested during high school as well. Her tears flowed forth, and we never actually looked directly at each other. I was doing what I could to create some professional distance without really knowing how, so we kept walking around the block, eyes peeled painfully forward. We swapped stories and shared pains, and the barriers of power that keep students separate from teachers, at least for a moment, disappeared. We ended that walk with Letitia laughing and saying, "Man, Chris, you're my fucking teacher! Ha! I didn't think that shit happened to teachers. Or White people! But you're okay. So shit, I gotta be okay. I gotta be."

For the rest of that year, we went on regular walks once a month, helping me to realize that my most effective "teaching" would occasionally be outside the classroom efforts to support students working through trauma. So while I intentionally focused class discussions, exercises, and curriculum on identifying and navigating trauma, Letitia taught me that being myself, being who and how I am is perhaps my greatest strength as an instructor. And my role in helping students develop voice is perhaps the most important thing I can do in schools. Because if schools do not prepare us to deal with our realities, then students will not care about obtuse triangles or grammar or the addition of fractions or which president authorized the treaty of Guadalupe Hidalgo. Without providing space for Andre to work through his rage, in a publically affirming way, school would simply not have worked for him (indeed he was failing all of his classes before enrolling in my class). Without providing space for Letitia to work through the incredibly painful experiences she was still immersed in, she likely would have dropped out of school. She knew that. She knew she needed space to heal and recognize that the pain she felt was not her fault. And she helped me realize that the purpose of schooling is to help people just like her navigate their pain so that they can, eventually, engage in the world. As Letitia argued through her journal: "You have to first survive, and then, you can live."

In this chapter, I demonstrate ways of building trust with students and offer examples of students who were punished for sharing honest voices. I remind educators that this student-focused work cannot happen without concrete efforts to protect students from well-meaning but often woefully unprepared suburban-raised educators and social workers trying to solve urban children's lives with the oppressive tools they have access to. I then capture how students start to view their painful vulnerabilities as strengths, in part through identifying trauma in their lives, and then bearing these personal and societal scars in front of peers in the class. I conclude by capturing my approach to classroom management, and frame rules that students have developed to ensure their classrooms remain safe enough for deep personal challenge.

Recognizing Trauma Is Risky and Rewarding

What I do in classrooms is, in part, focused on developing voice around traumatic experiences. I do not only focus on trauma, and I do not only focus on students who directly speak about the oppressive conditions they grew up in. But my focus on how oppression shapes students, particularly African American students, is at the core of my curriculum and pedagogy. This means that many students take the space I provide to make sense of what they live. And they do this because they can. Thus, my classrooms center student trauma as content and as a way to help students navigate the trauma they share. This intentional framing is exactly what kept Andre from dropping out of school; he wanted to learn to be better and our class was the first and only tool he had access to. Yet I never force a conversation. Students occasionally feel uncomfortable reading aloud and "take a pass," and when students turn in journal entries they do not want me to read, they paperclip those closed, and I honor their request. The point is to foster in students the comfort, willingness, and responsibility to initiate what we talk about; that most often means talking about the traumatic situations they struggle through, but I never require anyone to write about trauma or violence or anything they have faced.

In these classes I am clear that what students and I do is not counseling. I strongly encourage students to seek professional counseling when needed, but I do so aware of the disparities in mental health supports for urban youth. Many youth suffer from post-traumatic stress disorder, and the public school counselors that they are afforded minimal access to often have no specific urban training, but also are systematically overwhelmed. Reporting students to an underprepared, overwhelmed social work system that punishes students for being abused, or reporting students to educators who have no training at all simply continues to exacerbate the educational system's lack of responsiveness to student needs. Several counselors I have worked with have caseloads of up to 1000 students. How a counselor can provide relevant support for so many students is beyond me. School counselors are inadequately supported, unprepared for huge caseloads, and are not trained to respond to so many intensive traumatic experiences (Berton & Stabb, 1996; Brener, Weist, Adelman, Taylor & Vernon-Smiley, 2007; Davis, McIntosh, Phelps & Kehle, 2004; Garland, Lau, McCabe, Hough & Landsverk, 2005; Kassen & Raghavan, 2007; McKay, Lynn & Bannon, 2005). These counselors do not have the time needed to develop trusting relationships, and even in the cases where they reach out to students, they have few viable solutions.

One counselor, at Central High, captured the complexity she faces: "I have 750 students to support. With all the bureaucratic paperwork I am given, that gives me about 10 minutes per student twice a year. And the ones who I spend more time with, what am I supposed to do, call CPS? Have them removed from their homes so they can never see their brothers and sisters or friends again?" Another counselor at the same school was so frustrated that he stopped having drop-in hours: "What for? So that I can tell students where they used to be able to go for help? There's nowhere to send students who need help!" This lack of adequate mental health services to refer students to frustrated these counselors, but also limited the impact they could have. Both counselors were well connected to public health and community-based organizations that, in theory, provide support, but both knew these had waiting lists that would not work for the immediate needs of most students. They also knew what I was doing in my courses, and both had been guest speakers, initiating freewrites and facilitating subsequent dialogues. At East Bay High, a university supervisor asked if he could have his social work students observe my classes as an alternative model to reach a wider range of students, particularly when counselors had to split time between multiple schools. For me, I have always been clear that my coursework is not formal counseling or mental health support, yet this work directly supports overwhelmed school counselors.

Most of the counselors I have worked with intend to create safety with students, and encourage students to share trauma so they can provide guidance and assistance, but there is incentive to not do so. Most counselors are also painfully aware that reporting students to CPS, local police, or a probation officer can exacerbate the issues the student came to the counselor for help with. This can lead students to never again open up to an adult they previously trusted. What compounds the overall lack of support structures is, as a counselor at East Bay High clarified, that if students share their pain then he was legally required to report it. "I don't want to lose my job if I don't follow the law." Because of this threat, that counselor purposefully limits student comfort: "I don't want them sharing details that make me report them, so I make it clear that they shouldn't share with me—mostly by being a bit distant from them."

My voice-centered courses respond to this lack of counseling capacity, yet while I have reported students to CPS, I have never done so without the consent of the student. The students I interact with know that I will not report them without talking to them first, and while I have asked students if I can report them, I have honored the ones who denied my request. Asking for permission reflects my belief that high school students should have more control over their fate than educators allow when we involve those whose options are narrowly confined by the law. The most serious complication of developing voice, for me, is that when students begin to identify their pains, learn to express what those pains do to them, and learn to move more effectively in their immediate context, they face potential punishment from well-intentioned teachers, social workers, and family members.

One example of many students who have written about violence, only to be punished for their writing was James, who I worked with before and after his detainment in a juvenile facility. While still in high school, James was participating in a writing workshop (that I was not teaching) about violence. After a few months, he began to write about the violence he had been part of, and as he wrote, he soon realized how much he needed to escape his gang life. But James was unlucky; he left one of his journals on the lunch counter and another teacher snatched it up, took one look at the contents, and sent him to the principal, who immediately called his probation officer. James was arrested based on the evidence of his writing, and sent to a juvenile facility, despite the protests of the writing instructor, who argued to no avail that James was seeking help to get out of the gang and had made strides in working through the violence that he inflicted on others.

Another example of the negative impact well-intentioned educators can have occurred at Central High. Maricella had written vaguely about being raped. I met with her, asked her f she wanted to talk about her journal entry, and she told me "it's impossible to do anything, so don't tell no one." I referred Maricella to a free counselor, who specialized in sexual assault, and they set up regular appointments; she asked me to drive her so that she could hide the appointments from her family. Meanwhile, a White social work doctoral student from a nearby university began her research project on sexual assault and African American girls. She conducted interviews and focus groups with students; during an interview, in which the students were promised confidentiality, Maricella shared that her aunt and uncle had raped her. The soon-to-be social worker reported the crimes, and within a few weeks, Maricella was forcibly placed into a group foster care home, despite her objections. Within a few months, she stopped going to school and stopped returning my calls to check on her. After not hearing from her for about six months, I saw her at a women's shelter; she was in emergency housing. She shared that she was being beat by her foster parents and raped by her foster brother, but had learned to not share that with anyone that she did not trust with her life. As much as I wanted to report this and get her out of her horrible context, I honored her request not to. Where would she have gone anyway? Maricella is alive today, still struggling through life, and just last year told me: "You were the only adult I could trust. But I was paralyzed. I was afraid to reach out to anyone. I just wanted to hide under a rock 'til I felt okay, but I realized that wont happen under a rock."

These experiences are not rare. I have known dozens of students who, when their traumatic experiences were reported, ended up in worse situations, with even fewer resources. The point for me is that educators are not social workers, but neither set of professionals knows what is in the best interest of each child. We cannot predict what will happen with students if we report them to Child Protective Services or not. And my commitment is to the students, to arming them with skill sets to recognize they can improve personally, and that terrible situations are not their fault. As an educator, I cannot save my students, but I can help them develop tools: their voices, and processes to release pain, rage, frustration, and the fear that growing up with trauma causes. In my experience, voice as a tool helps students learn to navigate their trauma, which can lead to students asking adults for help, but more importantly, provides a foundation to heal.

Turning Pain into Strength: Navigating Trauma

In *Beats, Rhymes, and Classroom Life*, Marc Lamont Hill (2009) clarifies the power of community storytelling through a hip-hop writing class he co-taught. He details how classroom storytelling can be framed as a "practice of 'wounded healing,' where people bearing the scars of suffering shared their stories in ways that provided a form of release and relief for themselves and others" (p. 65). Hill captures how the co-teachers set a foundation for student voice, which in turn "enabled the other students in Hip-Hop Lit to begin imagining the classroom as a potentially safe site for sharing their stories" (p.

69). My classroom intent is similarly focused, as I try to create safe spaces for students to begin sharing their voices, and then deepen what peers have to say. The importance for me is that, as Hill points out within his class, "the process of healing was primarily linked to acts of personal disclosure" (p. 74).

I frame my voice-centered classes as helping students document their realities so they can begin the process of healing through sharing their stories. And I extend this work to provide forums for students to respond in affirming ways, so that they can validate each other's experiences and expand upon what is being shared. What I do not need to do is frame for students the healing power of speaking aloud: this becomes clear to students as soon as they begin to share their stories in front of the class. I balance student voice and expression with a barrage of examples of voice to stimulate student writing, and remind students that people living through what they are living through have survived. Yet I am always humbled by the reality that students choose to write and share aloud traumatic experiences, and then are often amazed at the impact this has; many feel much better after sharing. Their issues are not solved, but they at least voice something they've been taught to silence, often for the first time, and often in public.

Loni's freewrite helped her entire class at Central High begin a collective healing process. Her playful critique of low-quality school lunch "choices" led the class in raucous laughter, but also highlighted the direct impact of poverty on students. She was upset at being forced to eat food chosen by others who may or may not have a commitment to specific dietary needs, cultural norms, or religious considerations (much less what students might want to eat). After Loni's freewrite, which was her most extensive all year, the class erupted into conversation about how difficult getting a tasty meal was. While several students talked about how they wanted more access to fast food, most students talked about the limitation of simply not having a choice. "How come some people get to choose what they eat, but we aint got no choice, just nasty flat ass pizza or some fake-ass burrito?" asked Shantel. Several other classmates visited a well funded, predominantly White and Asian high school about three miles away, and were amazed at their salad bar and full menu. Christina argued they had "damn near 25 things to choose from! And all that shit looked good!"

Though Maricella had been relatively quiet during the food discussion, she extended the conversation the following day by starting her freewrite with Loni's line: "Never did nothing right enough to get peanut butter and jelly." Maricella asked the rest of the class "How come we feel bad cause we poor?" and continued pushing, "but we aint all the same poor. Some of us have more than none, some less than none." After reading, she asked if we could talk about how poor people like her are told they are not good enough. Reminding the class that it was her line, Loni jumped in to say, "You know girl! None of us got much, but some of us aint got shit." Maricella, equally excited, responded, keeping the conversation focused: "but why we made to feel bad cause we aint got shit?" The class spent the next few days talking about internalized oppression, and how being poor makes poor people feel what Hayes argued was: "less than doo doo."

After the week ended, several students asked me what they could do. Anton suggested that he could ask his mother, who worked with some "rich ass White folk" if they would donate "food money or food or something." They came back the following week with an idea they worked out with Anton's mother, whose coworkers agreed to drop off several lunches each day (with Anton). The class had to decide how many to ask for. After weighing if it was asking too much from Anton's mother, and putting her in an awkward place as the only African American woman at her job, the class limited the offer to only

Food freewrite by Loni
I gotta do something with all these y's
I ask y I ask y
you never answer back
I'm in stomach detention-y
Another school lunch 'cause mama aint got a dime
So I eat what these burocrats be sellin
They don't care about Ramadan or diabetes or pork-y
Forcefed the crap my teachers dont give their kids
Mr. Superintendy, would you sit down with me to a bowl of free and reduced lunch-y?
I'm in stomach detention-y
Never did nothing right enough to get peanut butter and jell-y
No bananas no oranges no apples no granoly bars
I get what you give-y
And if I don't like it
Go hungr-y
Go home-y
Stay hungr-y
So I eat and arrest my stomach for free
Aint tryin to eat yo soggy spaghetti, yo kidney bean chil-y
Yo mac-less macncheese, yo wilty lettuces aint got nuthin on me
I'm in stomach detention-y
Going to sleep with flammin hot dreams of homecooked meals
And I cant even eat taco fuckin bell-y!

people in their class. Students went around the room, reporting if they needed the lunch or not; 15 said yes, but only 10 said they'd eat it every day. For the rest of the year, Anton's mother dropped off 12–15 pre-made school lunches, paid for and assembled by a team of her White co-workers the night before.

While these lunches were not seen as a "solution" to poverty, they were appreciated, and they had a more powerful impact upon the class. The class initiated conversation amongst themselves about how to address the immediate issue of hunger, and the larger issue of feeling less worth because of poverty. The class talked about internalized oppression (though they were not familiar with that term until I provided readings on it), and talked about how they cannot blame themselves (or their parents) for having to live in poverty. Later in the year, the class reflected on how these lunches were wonderful, but also helped them take their minds off of the hunger that other students in other classes had. They wrote regular thank you letters, but also talked about how they should not be dependent upon wealthier White people, whom they should not have to rely upon for regular access to food. Shay captured the healing impact of this work on the students in the class through a freewrite written during our conversations, in which she clarified: "It's not my poverty! I don't "have" poverty. Its what this country does to people like me, that's the real poverty. Cause I'm poor, I have to remember that I am not the problem, being poor is."

Having conversations in response to student read-alouds helped deepen student commitment to each other, and provided a foundation for students to examine their responses to poverty. Being able to talk about abuse and poverty also helped students release the rage that both cause. Shay and others in the class wrote about the impact being poor had on them, and their writing was most often about how people treat them, and how they are made to feel. Though writing would not change their poverty, it did get them better fed in the short term, and more importantly, helped students feel better about themselves through recognizing that being poor was not their fault.

This work stands on a curricular foundation of other examples of voice-filled stories. I want students to see that there is a vast body of publicly accessible expression that captures oppression in powerfully concrete ways. Students were joining a conversation, not beginning a new one, and I framed writing responses as often talking directly to a writer, poet, artist, or musician. Thus students were continually responding to poetry, literature, music, and film that captured trauma, oppression, and personal resistance to all of this. Such exposure normalized talking about trauma so that students could see just how widespread living with pain is, and how often others talk about this pain. These exposures allowed them to experiment with emotional topics, but also find creative voices relevant to their lives. Through this work I also learned that the more creative the expression, the more students who were quiet during responses triggered by poems or written stories might tap into their voice, and in turn, share their stories.

For example, that same class read the graphic novel *Blood Song*, which lead several students to finally begin to write. *Blood Song* has no words, and instead is a series of storyboard pictures telling the plight of one young woman, a rural villager who sees her village burned to the ground so that developers could use the land (Drooker, 2002). She eventually makes her way to an urban city, and is lost, hungry, ignored; the pictures are dull, dark, conveying a grey dread. She is lulled by a musician, whose saxophone emits a rainbow of color, offering a creative contrast; they eventually connect, and the man is taken off to jail for continuing to emit this rainbow of color through his music and song. The story ends with the birth of their child, though the man sits locked in jail, the baby's first cries emit the same rainbow of color. After studying the pictures, students broke into groups and wrote collaborative responses to a page of pictures they chose. Over the next week, these writings were expanded into full-length poems.

A group that included Robert and Lou wrote one of these poems. Normally some of the quietest students in the class, Robert and Lou chose a picture of the male character, a Black man with dreads, sitting behind bars. They then wrote about their fathers, whom neither had seen outside of prison. For the first time in class, Robert and Lou took over a small group conversation. They talked about not being able to see their fathers, and when several of the group members suggested they could all write about visiting people in prison, they erupted: "No!" Lou raised his voice from his typical low whisper, "We gonna talk about us not having dads and how everyone tells us we gonna go to jail just like our dads." Robert jumped in, "We the ones behind bars. Moms aint got nuthin cause Dads in lock up. So we supposed to do all these things, take care of folks." The group remained quiet as Robert and Lou talked about the difficulties of being young Black men with incarcerated fathers, and both had followed their father's missteps directly in youth facilities. The group wrote a collaborative poem in two voices: the first and main voice was that of Robert and Lou, who read together and repeated the main line: "Parents Locked Up, We Locked Out, Something Gotta Change Inside." The rest of the group read aloud fears, stereotypes about young Black men, and highlighted how to support friends who are already in the prison system, centering the conversation on those who have family they will never see without chains.

This sharing of stories helped students realize that for every travesty that happened in their life, they were not alone. Almost everyone else in the class had experienced something similar. Conversations about drug abuse, violence, loss, demeaning teachers, angry police officers, family in jails or prisons, evictions, and other serious issues became normalized topics, but also gave students space to sharpen their thoughts about these issues as structural, not personal. And as the class shifted from reading aloud to editing work to ensure points were well heard, the class began to shift away from trauma and its effects and into capturing depth for the audience. That shift was academic; it helped students learn to edit their work, helped them distance themselves from their words, and helped them see that academic work can be useful, if initiated by them. This process of developing voice also helped students become speakers rather than traumatized individuals, and they gained power as they edited their words, tightening their intensity through increased control over their words and emotions. And this is key: students sharing their freewrites helped initiate important conversations that deepened the class, but students editing their work, sharing in their critiques and support of each other is what helped students see that they could do well in school, that they could be okay as people if they built up caring communities. That, students began to argue, was more important than just reading aloud poetry or stories. The act of storytelling is powerful, but sharing in the construction of the stories is what helps students learn to change how they react to that trauma.

Identifying Trauma: Critical Editing

I use two forms of feedback to help students deepen their writing to say what they mean. The first is peer editing, and the second is my own intense feedback. I urge students to help each other with their words and meaning so that they can engage in conversation about their lives while also tightening their writing. I frame feedback as having four goals: (1) Develop writing skills; (2) Help clarify what the author wants to say; (3) Help make sense of what has happened in the author's life and what they see in the world around them; and (4) Help translate personal trauma into a larger, academic conversation, wherein pain is reflective of larger contexts of oppression. June Jordan's peer feedback guidelines shape how I translate these goals into classroom feedback sessions.

Providing critical feedback to peers is initially difficult because students have neither received nor provided close detailed feedback before. While I model my intense feedback to each student, I also provide numerous class-wide feedback sessions where, similar to Jasmine's intro, we collectively break down writing. I also break the class into small groups and facilitate peer feedback teams, and evaluate student feedback to offer constructive criticism (telling someone "this sucks" is not helpful; telling them specifically why you do not like a particular line is). I use feedback I provide as a forum to communicate with each student, responding to their personal writing, while offering criticism that helps students articulate voice that reflects how they want to sound. The feedback cycle reinforces the benefits of editing, and eases students into seeing their work as temporary, as open to improvement, and as attempts to say what we need to. Not surprisingly, students still tend to resist critical feedback from both peers and educators. Students note how rarely their ideas are challenged in useful ways. As they read published poems, I remind them that most poets write dozens of drafts prior to publishing, and that helps ease the burden of equating editing with correcting, which taps into previous negative experiences with teachers who use red ink for grammar, not purpose. This shift from correcting to editing also reminds students that they ultimately have the final say; they can disregard feedback they do not agree with.

Peer Feedback Guidelines
Adapted from June Jordan's Poetry for the People

Ground rules for critical feedback

1. Be supportive, yet critical
2. Be respective, yet challenging
3. Engage
4. Continually ensure writer is open to critical feedback

Feedback Process Guidelines

1. Is the writer open to critical feedback?
2. Is it complete?
   a. Does it have a beginning and a clear end?
3. What is its purpose?
   a. How does this come through?
4. Assess voice
   a. Emotion (Is it there? When? Which emotions? Does it work? Is it Intense?)
   b. Simplicity (Maximum impact with minimal words? Is it precise? Wordy?)
   c. Purpose (Do voice and tone reflect purpose?)
   d. Identity (Do personal perspectives come through? How?
   e. Who is the author?
   f. Does author's identity support the purpose? How so? Does it tell the author's truth?)
5. Is it coherent? Give specific examples of how.
6. Is it sound? Does it flow?
   a. Strong, active verbs (limited passive voice)?
   b. Clarity and directness?
   c. Detailed specifics?
   d. Few abstractions or generalities?
   e. Compelling voice and flow?
7. What are the strengths and weaknesses?
8. How does it fit into or challenge standardized writing?

And such editing ultimately helps students open up to each other while taking their own words more seriously. Tony argued that my feedback taught him "how to teach other students how to say what they want to." Jasmine reflected that "cause you spent so much time on what I wrote, I knew I had to spend at least that much time." And Sherise clarified that all of this time and feedback helped her "trust a teacher, for the first time." She continued, "Without all that feedback from you, I would never have opened up to the rest of the class for more feedback." Thus teaching for voice rests upon a foundation of trust in students, of students trusting each other, and of pushing educators to take our time with student feedback. Receiving feedback means trusting peers with intimate details, with stories that highlight personal vulnerabilities, and helps students learn how to see each other as peers living similar lives, and as students who should show academic interest in each other.

In many classes, I lead a collaborative examination of the word "it" as an entirely vague way of avoiding what the writer actually means. I write "It" on the board, and tell students to freewrite what "it" means. Students usually stumble here, waiting for additional instructions, or freewrite on something entirely unrelated to the word "it." Shantel captures the confusion: "'It' doesn't mean anything, so I'm having a hard time defining it." Christina continues, "Ha! I get it! We use that word all the time but it doesn't mean anything. Like I just said 'I get it,' but no one even knows what I meant by 'it'." The point is that we often use words as placeholders, to complete the structures of sentences, but outside of a structural purpose, these words have no inherent meaning. Rather than use words like "it," I urge students to reframe their sentences to focus on what they are trying to say. Another example from Shantel's journal: "I am so sick of racism; it gets me so mad!" I pushed her immediately: "Capture what you mean by 'it' so that the reader understands exactly what makes you mad." Her response: "I can make a list of things people do that make me mad, like when my teachers tell me not to speak Spanish or when my brother gets pulled over by a cop for walking down the street." The point is to be accountable for every word we use and to get students used to editing each other's words, limiting vagueness. But this leads to students challenging each other over deeper meaning, trying to understand the author's point.

At East Bay High, students were reading over their peers' first draft of a paper, marking any lines they had questions about. Juan was reading Julia's paper, in which she wrote: "…black and latinos fight, but that's not as bad as black on black violence." Juan wanted to know why "it aint as bad?" Julia responded, "that's not my point, my real point is about Black on Black violence." Juan argued that she should focus on Black on Black violence instead of getting the reader stuck on a tangent. But then Juan pushed even further, "What do you mean by Black on

Black violence? What does that look like?" Julia then moved closer to what she was trying to say: "Black men often beat Black women. We walk down the street and they mean mug us, look us up all nasty like a piece of meat." Julia actually wanted to talk about how she felt assaulted when she walks around the neighborhood by Black men, and that was what she meant by Black-on-Black violence. Her focus on gender violence and sexism came out of a conversation based on what she had written, and based on Juan's questioning; her next draft was directly framed around sexism within the Black community. There were traumatic experiences underlying Julia's topic that came out after I asked her to clarify her interest on a later draft, but none of this would have happened without Juan's initial probing.

Intensely Critical Feedback

I provide intense feedback to all students, and provide forums for students to make sense of their interest in what they write, which often becomes a space for students to then clarify their trauma. Like Julia in the above example, my probing is rarely intended to push students to write about traumatic events, but when I ask them why they write what they do, students often respond with personal experience. In reflecting about why students in our class always wrote about "deep topics," Sherise argued that it's because, "We live this shit. And when you give us space to write about whatever we want, we are forced to think. And then knowing that Jasmine and Angela and Jacinda are going to read it, well, it makes me think I should take it seriously. Because they sure as hell will."

Perhaps because I encourage students to write about what makes them angry or what they are most passionate about, many students write about trauma they experienced; sharing close details of the violence, poverty, addiction, and intensity they live (or have lived). There are always a few students who fail to choke back tears as they share pieces of who they are in public for the first time. Students share how they are abused, how they have lost a parent, a brother, a cousin, and dozens of friends. Students talk about their addictions to alcohol, to weed, to crack. Students talk about being unable to put down their video game controllers for fear of having to face the lack of control they have in the "real world." Students talk about the violence they face and the fear of violence they have bestowed upon others. The idea that student work will actually be read brings up all kinds of fear for students, and most talk about not being able to trust others with intimate details. I push on this notion and try to demonstrate that with effort, students can trust each other more than anyone else.

As an additional way to build up trust with students, I take furious notes during student read-alouds, taking down details that I can use to follow up with each student individually. I then turn these notes into written responses to student work, modeling how students can respond to others and push in welcoming ways. These notes become part of the curriculum, where each student reads additional writing that responds directly to issues they initiated. Through such responses, I advocate for students to redirect class dialogues, urging particular students to share their stories, concerns, or critical questioning with the class. My feedback is also designed to help students see how they are being vague, offers suggestions on tightening up their points, and pushes students to ensure their overall purpose is clear. I offer my own poetic responses as examples and to deepen trust, and provide additional reading resources to help stimulate student ideas. Depending on the class, students might get feedback once a week on their out-of-class journals and on their weekly reflections. Students often have up to three pages of typewritten feedback to negotiate per week and are given a similar amount for longer papers.

This amount and intensity of feedback is often initially overwhelming for most students.[1] Since students have rarely received so much feedback throughout their educational experiences, this both adds to the difficulty, and becomes a source of dramatic encouragement. Students eventually look forward to my feedback, and begin to echo (and mock) my terminology: "Push on that" "Dig deeper" and "That is so vague" become commonplace as students accept that I am responding with caring criticism, honesty, and affirmation of their work. While students initially are overwhelmed, they soon recognize that most of their previous educators have not taught or pushed them to clarify what they think and how they feel in their writing. This recognition is often followed by a critical push: Many, like Letitia, ask "Why haven't my teachers cared enough to teach me to write this well? It's as if they didn't really read my papers the past 10 years!" Even graduate students in my courses or observing my teaching remark that they have never received this level of feedback on their work. When students previously received extensive feedback, the content of the feedback was typically limited to grammar and spelling corrections. And my point for students is to find educators who will respond to their ideas with depth and passion equal to that which they put into their ideas. Of the thousands of students I have taught, only a dozen or so have had educators provide such feedback, and this lack of sincere feedback reflects our lack of valuing both educators and students.

Classroom Management for Traumatized Young Adults

Because my classrooms are spaces that require safety for students, and because such safety is an impossible goal because urban students are not actually safe in their lives, my aim is to empower students to create the classroom environments they need. Because students can be more aware than teachers of the emotional state of their peers, because they are often talking with their peers outside of the classroom, and because of their shared youth and cultural context, students notice what a teacher cannot. Thus I aim to empower urban students to facilitate and monitor their own discussions, particularly when the conversations are most intense. This helps students develop trust in each other, but also reinforces the notion that students have the tools for the conversations they need to have already; they just need support in recognizing and then developing the skills. I use my personal feedback to push students in ways I do not do in public, but also am adamant that students hold each other accountable; that means creating classroom rules that enable students the power to do so.

Classroom Rules and Ways to Be
Developed by Students in Period 4 and Dr. Knaus

1. Every class begins with freewriting or guided writing.
2. All members of our class community will be respectful of each other and ourselves. Students and guests not honoring these rules can remove themselves, be removed by Dr. Knaus, or by the entire class.
3. All voices will be heard and everyone must express themselves at least once per day.
4. We will not use profanity or racial slurs (unless appropriate or needed in our writing).
5. Students will help each other say what we want to say and will give each other positive feedback and be critical when needed, but in a positive way.
6. When students think they have nothing to do or need to tune out, students should do what they can to remain present in the classroom, and should write about what is going on.
7. Students are young adults, and can get up and move as needed as long as not distracting other students. Students can leave the classroom when needed as long as we follow school rules.
8. Students should only use cell phones during emergencies and should let Dr. Knaus know ahead of time.
9. Students should only use i-pods while the entire class is writing or when everyone agrees its okay.
10. Students will help break up fights and deal with drugs and alcohol with Dr. Knaus and the entire class.
11. Outside guests are welcome if they follow our classroom rules.
12. Students who cannot focus on school because of personal issues can write or do other work as long as we do not interrupt others and are not interrupted.

In order to create classroom communities that honor students trying to hone their voices, I adapt flexible and concrete classroom management practices. My teaching style is rooted in getting students to talk to each other, and that means decentering power that frames knowledge as held by the instructor. I step back and allow conversation to happen, sometimes after uncomfortable lapses of silence, broken only by a student who feels they should speak because no one else is. I want students to learn to speak on their own, not just when they are called on, and not just when speaking is a prerequisite for a passing grade. And that means I walk around the classroom, rarely sit in the same seat, and urge students to stand up (literally) to speak their mind, to read their words, and to know when to speak, and when to shut up and listen to their peers, or to their mentors, instructors, teachers, elders. Classroom management, in my classrooms, is fluid to allow students to be loud, obnoxious, angry, and at times quiet, tentative, and afraid. I continually remind myself that I am a White man, and that my voice carries particular race and gendered weight. I thus try to challenge my own privilege as a White man and as a teacher—both of which are reinforced in almost every single school-based tradition. Thus I have to continually challenge myself, but also urge students to challenge me (and let them).

As a result, my teaching leads some students to tell me in confidence that I am "too nice" or "too lenient" or that I let "students get away with too much." Yet I also give students what Tony argued is "space to be who we are, and that makes us want to come to class, makes us want to be who we are, but also to fix who we are." Christina argued that I "teach students how to be ourselves." She continued:

> *Some students might take advantage of the space you give, but that is because they are not doing the work. But you let us be loud, silly, stupid. And then we can cry in front of each other. I mean, who cries in school? We posed to be hard. If you made us sit down, yelled at us, or let us think you were made at us, we wouldn't ever trust you enough to talk in class, not about something deep. And when we start talking, then I understood what you mean by we do not know how to be who we want to be.*

Pedro mentioned that "most of the adults we see aint know how to talk through difficult shit." Nique, twenty years old without a high school diploma, argued that "teachers are passive aggressive to each other, so no one shows us right ways to talk—you make us work it out." Jacinda argued that she was initially hesitant to take the class seriously: "When I started actually listening to you and to the rest of us, I realized this class was a lot more work and that you were a lot harder than I thought, 'cause you seem all laid back in class. But not when someone says something racist or sexist or when I turn in a vague paper. Then you are the hardest teacher I've ever had." My creation of the conditions that require students to step up and create the classroom community they want ultimately helps them learn skills that most adults do not have. Students are provided few models of how to talk about racism and sexism, much less violence or rape. And my point is to show that students do not need anything more than their own ideas, their own reflective writing and trust in each other. Yet I also make very clear to students several rules that I will not allow to be broken. Like Christina argued, while I create the space for students to be loud and obnoxious, I also ensure that students respect each other and themselves. Thus, I have four rules that are clarified in the syllabus, in our first few classes, and serve as reminders throughout any class:

Rule #1: Presence is required

The first rule is that each person's presence is required. That means not leaving class while someone is speaking, doing everything possible to be in class, even when there is every reason in the world to not be in school that day, that week, or that month. This rule, and the warmth of our class, has resulted in some students who ditch school all day, only to show up to our class, then leave school again. At several schools, students have snuck onto campus so they could attend our class, and while not ideal, the rule for speaking and listening means being present to understand what we are all living in and through. This is also directly tied to racism: since people of color have long fought for inclusion into educational systems that continue to exclude, if we are to transform schooling, we have to do so in a way that honors all of us, even those who cannot be present because they have fought the system (and been removed from school for so doing).

Rule #2: Students are expected to claim personal space

Because physical and emotional presence is demanded of students, students are expected to recognize when they need to disengage. Students who have experienced trauma may have that trauma triggered purposefully or by chance throughout the day, by teachers, peer students, readings, stray thoughts, or random strangers. Students will develop the capacity to ask for (or demand) personal space needed to be okay in the moment, and the class is expected to respect the space students claim. This may mean leaving the classroom, setting desks to the side, getting up and moving around, sharing emotional outbursts, writing furiously, or just closing down. If students need something in order to be okay, the class expects each other to learn how to claim that space.

Rule #3: Speak and Listen Respect

Just as each student is required to speak their mind and to attempt to develop their thoughts to their fullest, each student is required to listen to their peers. While there are exceptions (students do not need to listen to disrespectful comments), students are required to listen enough to know when something is disrespectful (either to them, or to another peer) and are strongly encouraged to speak out about the injustice or disrespect they hear. A precondition of being in the class is a commitment to speaking aloud, to reading aloud freewrites, introductions, and several larger papers. Another precondition is a commitment to developing capacity to listen intently, respectfully, and to encourage peers to deepen their capacity to speak with clarity, passion, and purpose. This rule helps students recognize the power of talk, but also of listening and empowering others to speak, which is essential if we are to break the silencing norms of racism and sexism.

Rule #4: Confidentiality

Everything we say in our classroom, in our writings, and in our editing or feedback is entirely confidential, limited exclusively to this class. I will not talk about what any of us share to any other person and all students and class visitors are expected to do the same, unless the author/speaker gives us permission. Any student who violates this rule is immediately and permanently removed from the class.[2] Students are not to talk about people in the class, but should discuss the topics we share outside of class. This is essential since we are talking about the impact of living and documenting oppression in school settings that contribute to that oppression.

Students often bring up these rules when peers violate them. The bottom line is that all students must respect others and ensure others are respected. There are examples when students disrespect others, but rather than remove the offender from class, I try to turn each instance into a lesson. I often ask, when a case of disrespect occurs, how we, as a classroom community, should address the student. One example came from East Bay High School: Our class was in the midst of writing when a fight broke out in front of the school. Most of the classrooms emptied as teachers tried in vain to keep students in their rooms. I asked students to remain in the classroom, and most of the students did. When four students who had slipped out to watch the fight came back in, the students who remained dove into a conversation about what it means to leave the community to observe (and participate) in violence. The four apologized, and two of them later helped develop a class-wide plan for responding to school violence. My point was to use the class as a guide to help address violence (as opposed to being passive observers or active participants). Such classroom management strategies urge educators to think less of rules and more of flexibility to enable students to create the structures they need to be safe while still pushing deeply.

Conclusion

I conclude this chapter with a reminder that while not every urban student lives in violent or abusive homes, every student is impacted by trauma that directly shapes their friends, neighbors, and family members, and all of this directly limits capacity to engage in schooling that teaches socially irrelevant, oppressive content. I have tried to clarify how I center such trauma in curricular content, in my feedback, in assignments, freewrites, and in classroom management approaches that provide space to transform educational settings. My point is not that this is easy work: indeed, much of our classroom conversations are spent struggling through what we would like our community to be (and helping to push and support others into sharing and refining their voices). Yet very few educators have had formal training in setting up engaging, culturally responsive, anti-racist classrooms that acknowledge and provide space for the trauma urban children survive. Because of this lack of formal training on sharing voice in school settings that silence students, I expect bumps and bruises. Re-creating such communities in schools is how I teach students to develop their own skill sets as they think about building their own communities. This is how I try to create the conditions for urban students to develop voice. I know no other way than to center the most painful realities we live, and then, in this impossibly uncomfortable public space, students and adults alike can recognize our common pains, struggles, failures, and successes, and become, in a word, human.

INTERLUDE II

So, I Never Speak. I Write.

Rasheedah S. Woodard

I was born with fluid-filled lungs; coughing, choking, no tears, no screams, no voice…silent. I filled notebooks with stories about little girls with no voices, little girls who could make themselves disappear, pretty skinny girls with light skin long hair and light skin boyfriends. My mama bought me my first diary at 10. I wrote that I wanted to be pretty to be light to disappear. At times, I wrote that I wanted to die. I wrote songs of pain and desperation. Black, Brown, white, men, women, and children slashed my tongue each time they told me "you ugly too Black too dark stupid too smart a girl poor too skinny too fat too tall not girly enough too angry too sensitive too quiet talk ghetto talk white dyke faggot homo." I swallowed and absorbed these racist, sexist, classist, and homophobic shards of glass until I was blood stained with self-hatred that kept me quiet and wanting to die. So I never speak. I write.

Surrounded by people who hated me crushed my spirit but made me a fighter. Like a sheep amongst wolves, I walked into my cracked dingy dirty apartment building infested by gangs, guns, drugs, drunks, attackers, abusers, perverts, and murderers; I was always vulnerable, exposed. Hoping and wishing no one offered me drugs, fought me, grabbed me. My mama tried to protect me by never allowing me to play outside until middle school, teaching me how to fist fight, how to use a switchblade, never to talk to strangers, to stay away from parked cars, keep my legs closed, stay away from boys, men, and she forced me to confront anyone who messed with me. Like daggers, "ugly" "Black" "burnt" "ho" stabbed me by vicious tongues of *brothers*, *aunties*, *sisters*, and *friends*. Constantly having to fight venomous tongues, ferocious girls trying to jump me, seeing if I was a "punk," friends talking behind my back, touchy, grabby, boys trying to see if I would fuck, bloods trying to fight me for wearing blue, kept me ready to throw punches and quick to pull out my switchblade. My mama always told me "if anybody ever put they hands on you, fuck 'em up," "don't trip off what people say; only trip if they put they hands on you," "always speak yo' mind," and "be an independent strong Black woman." I fought to prove I wasn't a punk, I said no to prove I wasn't a ho, I acted like nothing bothered me to prove I was a strong independent Black woman but was I ugly? My mama always said I was beautiful but every one else said I was ugly. I wrote that I was unwanted, dirty, dark.

I never felt safe at home. Men and women's assaults carved me with self-hatred so deep I hid under hoody's, baggy sweats, baggy uniforms, and x-large jackets. I figured if everyone said I was ugly then what's the use of trying to be anything more? I stayed to myself. Grinning men called me ugly while grabbing my butt, trying to put their slobbering mouths on me, trapping me in corners and trying to steal my innocence. Light skin men who, when no one was around, pinned my fighting arms down, shoved their tongues in my mouth, and rammed their hands between my legs. The same light skin men who, in public, called me "ugly" "Black" and "burnt." I never asked to be assaulted. Light skin boyfriends told me I was cute, pretended to be my friend, and didn't accept *no*. My ovaries were torn from my womb and breasts ripped off each time a Black man grabbed my wrists, dug their nails into my skin, clasped their hand over my mouth, forced me down, fought my fists and kicks, and rammed their penis inside me because I was a dark Black girl *asking for it*. I wrote: Maybe I *was* ugly? Maybe I *was* stupid? Maybe I *was* trash? Maybe it *was* my fault men kept assaulting me?

My mamas' words and hugs weren't enough to fight against everyone else's words and touches. I started to believe I was ugly, *Black*, stupid, too smart, too dark, too fat, not worthy of living. I stayed in my room with my bad thoughts, my music, and my writing.

IAMblackuglystupiddarkfatunworthy

IAMblackuglystupiddarkfatunworthy

IAMblackuglystupiddarkfatunworthy. I force-fed myself the hatred spewed at me. I never smiled because I knew I was ugly. I suffered in silence; a mixture of hating myself, fearing men, and denying being molested, raped, and abused that imprinted me with an internal sadness and volatile anger never acknowledged but increasingly building. I erupted with each punch thrown, each slice of my wrists, each carve of my thighs, each pill swallowed, and each time I shoved my face in the toilet vomiting out my hate, pain, and insides.

size 13

size 10

size 6

Spitting up blood, I watched my soul swirl away and my curves drop. So I wrote.

School was the only place I felt relatively safe. Mostly Black, much Brown, a few Pacific Islanders and 3 white boys, my inner city school lacked books, adequate teachers, and financial resources, which created low API scores and most of us never graduating. Surrounded by barbed-wire fences and subject to lock-downs, school was an incarcerating assimilatory process of memorizing rich white heterosexual men, chemical equations, mathematical proofs, grammar, a celebration of murderers and regurgitation of information meant to get me into the *best* schools, obtain the *best* careers, and obtain the *best* house, car, and family. But school is where teachers said "you're smart advanced gifted intelligent." I worked hard to be a great scientist, a critical thinker, an excellent writer. School is the only thing I succeeded in; the only place life was kinda ok. Graduating top 1% of my class, I focused on my education to deny life at home. I wrote that I was accepted into the University of California, Berkeley.

At Cal, I was repeatedly reminded of my background being around white, Asian, Latino, and Black students who grew up in one family inhabited houses, with parents who were business owners, professors, doctors, and lawyers. Private school students who drove Mercedes' and BMW's, and made me feel small for being the poor lil' Black girl who had to work, that went to *that* type of school, grew up in *that* type of neighborhood, and had *that* type of family. UC Berkeley is a microcosm of corporate America where Black folks represent less than 3%, white Americans 32.8%, Asian Americans 39.9%, Latinos 13%, and Indigenous Americans less than 1% and is just as divisive (Office of Student Research and Campus Surveys, 2010). White and Asian students constantly assumed I was an idiot athlete incompetent affirmative action charity case. White and Asian students calling me a "nigger affirmative action case" to my face, touching my hair like they were buying me off an auction block, staring at me, the only Black student, to speak for the entire Black community, and always asking if I was an athlete made me cut deeper lacerations into my thighs. I was a diversity token to enhance white students *well-rounded* college experience. I walked around campus with purses clutched at the sight of me, rolled up windows and locked doors from fear of me. I wrote that I cut my arms and legs.

I want to be an OB/Gyn so I was pre-med. General Chemistry had 6 Black students out of over 500 and in Calculus there were 9 of us out of a different 500 students. I was constantly faced with entitled glaring Chinese and white students with stares of rejection "*you're* in this class?" "why would I study with *you*?" "I'd rather study with *anyone else*." Advisors told me I should think about something *other* than medicine. I focused on my stoichiometry and writing to forget the constant attacks. I just wanted to stay under the covers, but sleep was night terrors, lost hair, stomach pains, migraines. I was dying in the sciences. I wrote that I *was* a stupid, unworthy, charity case.

Writing has always been my escape, my outlet, my solace. When I couldn't speak, I wrote. When there was no one to talk to, I wrote. I wrote to bury my thoughts and emotions. I was alone. I couldn't breathe. I needed a space to write. Freshmen year, I forced my way into an African American Studies R1A writing class entitled Social Justice and the Written Word: Developing Personal and Critical Expression because I was in pieces, disconnected, numb, and dying. I was screaming inside. I needed to write to get away. In this class, I sat in a circle, waitlisted. I listened to a white man thank students for sharing this space, ask us how we were doing, and critique his whiteness and privilege as a professor in African American Studies. He asked us to freewrite for 1 min and share. I heard him and fellow students read freewrites on child abuse, violence against women, 1st generation students with undocumented parents, racism at Cal, and so much more. Listening to my colleagues share that much on the first day of class forced me to sit with myself and write, rewrite, and begin to share my truth. My professor pushed me to write seriously and profusely; not to write blindly, vaguely, or passively but with purpose. I started to write about white slave owners raping Black women, Black male headed organizations pushing Black women into kitchens, Black women fighting to be seen as Black AND female, rich white males leaving crumbs for everyone else to share, and a legacy of discriminatory poverty-stricken second-class citizenship stemming from genocide of Indigenous Americans and Western slavery to this day.

Through this class, I began to listen and acknowledge experiences long silenced. This meant admitting that I endured a horrific past and was hurting myself in the present. I beat myself down more and more as I tried to put myself back together. I was numb, detached, and in fragments. Through writing and reflecting, I confronted the internalized hatred and distorted image I had become. I took walks, sat alone in my room, cried, and fought myself to write my thoughts. My classmates listened, snapped, and said "you're such a powerful writer, I'm soooo glad you said that, I wish I could be as brave as you, write like you." Sitting in a circle, facing each other, raw and uncompromised, we listened to each person share their voice. We wrote together, sat in silence together, read Pumla Gobodo-Madikizela, bell hooks, June Jordan, Edwidge Danticat and gave feedback on each other's papers. With my skin inside out, I read my poems and papers aloud to the class. Repeatedly, my classmates and professor critiqued my writings. My professor's voice screamed in my head "Stop being vague!" "Show ME, don't tell me!" "here is where your voice comes in…PUSH on that!" I fought the feedback tooth and nail. How could someone critique my experiences? Critical feedback forced me to reflect on my delivery, thought process, expanded my consciousness and strengthened my voice. By writing, sharing my thoughts, feelings, and experiences, I acknowledged and validated myself. Through my process, I realized how broken I had become. Now, I write to heal my mind, body, and soul.

I write because Black women are dying. I was dying. I am still not completely whole but my process helped me to write, speak, and act. Once I acknowledged and voiced my past and pain, I cut myself less and less, vomited less and less, beat myself less and less; until I stopped. Instead of hurting myself, I mentor women and girls with similar backgrounds as mine; I tell them my story to help them write theirs. I write with them. Constantly sitting with myself, thinking and writing forced me to realize I dropped everything to listen, console, and heal a woman who revealed being raped by a man because I was molested and raped by men. I work with girls and women suffering from suicidal thoughts, eating disorders, depression, low self-esteem, mental disorders, colorism, and any other "ism's" plaguing her existence because our community, collective reflection, writing, and sharing helps me face my own depression, suicidal tendencies, eating disorders, low self-esteem, and internalized isms. I continue to heal myself while I empower and validate the voices of other lil' Black and Brown girls thinking death is a better option, that her curves are disgusting, that food is the enemy, eating a battle, and that vomit has to be a daily part of life. Collective healing, reflecting, and writing are how I transform my silence into action. So I continue to write.

Silence won't help you, save you, or benefit you. I struggled writing this piece because I still struggle with believing my voice is valid. That anybody cares. I can't believe I've revealed so much to you, the reader; but acknowledging, vocalizing and writing, my internalized racism, classism, colorism, and homophobia marked the transformation of my silence into liberation of my mind, body, and spirit through voice. Everything I fought not to say, I fought to keep hidden, I fought to relinquish and/or deny only festered and became the poison that contaminated my mind, body, and spirit. So I write to release and heal other women of color. I write because 1 in 6 women will be sexually assaulted/raped (Tjaden & Thoennes, 1998). I write because 65% of Black women living with AIDS will die. I write that 77% of new HIV/AIDS diagnoses are Black women (Center for Disease Control and Prevention, [CDCP], 2010). I write that over 40,000 women die of breast cancer (CDCP, 2010). I write that only 50% of Brown and Black students graduate from high school (NAACP, 2006; Orfield, Losen, Wald, Swanson, 2004; Stillwell, 2010). I write that 65% of prisoners are Black and Brown men and women (Human Rights Watch Backgrounder, 2003). I write that 52% & 35% of homicides are Black males and females (Bureau of Justice Statistics, 2007). I write because women of color are dying. I write to live.

Chapter 5

Beyond the Classroom: Creating School-wide Structures to Develop Voice

Introduction

I have never been asked by a high school student for help on a standardized test. I have never heard a high school student lament their standardized test scores or the relatively low cumulative scores of the school they are required to attend. All of the urban students I have interacted with have more pressing concerns than being considered "far below" or "below basic." Much of the educational world, however, is focused on getting these students to increase standardized assessments scores. But such scores are not why students go to school; what urban students ask for is often directly related to their daily survival. Thus, while charters, districts, and state departments of education demand that educators increase student test scores, students ask for help navigating violence and oppression. This is a powerful disjoint represented by approximately half of the urban students who leave school before graduation. And yet 50% dropout rates have barely altered district, state, and federal educator conversations about what to do in school. Despite efforts to increase accountability via test scores, reform efforts maintain a course that avoids urban student concerns, needs, and survival.

In this chapter, I clarify how schools can structure curriculum and teaching to develop student voice in ways that address student need. I provide a framework for measuring the academic impact of voice on students, and demonstrate that teacher evaluation and assessment can be tied to student expression in creative ways that simultaneously inform families, educators, and local communities about pressing social issues. Educators must integrate opportunities for student expression into civic decision-making processes, through, in part, regular public forums for student expression, and by structuring student voice into professional development for educators. Ultimately, this requires schools to integrate voice-centered work across the curriculum, and I demonstrate how youth participatory action serves as a foundation for such work. As Duncan-Andrade and Morrell (2008) argued, "One of our goals has to be the transmission of skills that help students to navigate professional and civil life..." and such skills should be demonstrated through meaningful, moving public expression that showcases the capacity to "read, write, and speak at high levels" (p. 29).

Expanding Academic Opportunities to Demonstrate Voice

In an era of standards, measurement becomes the entire conversation, and "high achievement" becomes defined along a standardized continuum that does not allow multiple interpretations of academic success. This is partially because the idea of knowing how well schools are doing on a scale of 1–10 makes life simple. If we can create such numbers, then educators can demand that low-scoring schools do what the high-scoring schools are doing. Thus the notion of direct accountability; ensuring that high scorers remain high and low scorers learn to do what "works." But of course the answer is more complicated. Who gets to define what "works" and what "high levels" are? Who should define that? How well should students do at what? Should we score based on how well students can regurgitate particular facts? If so, what facts should count? What about how well students can do math problems that they will never face in the world outside of school? Or how well students navigate social barriers such as racism and sexism? Or what about how students interact within a global society trained to be in direct competition against each other? Should we score for multiple languages and the capacity to use and program hand-held wireless devices?

Alfie Kohn (2004) argued that, "perhaps the question 'How do we know if education has been successful?' shouldn't be posed until we have asked what it's supposed to be successful *at*" (p. 2). There are a multitude of useful "things" to know, and as a democratic society, we have not yet agreed on which "things" should have most value, much less which "things" schools should be concerned with teaching. Instead of such conversations, schools use standardized assessments to purposefully divide society into those who manage and those who are easily manageable, continuing the legacy of Eugenics, racism, and intentional stratification (Epstein, 2006; *Larry P. and Lucille P. v. Riles*, 1979; Sacks, 2001; Selden, 1999). But this is not a purpose of education that many urban children agree to, and certainly does not reflect democratic values or social justice.

Instead, I argue that schools should help urban students gain more control over their lives, should help students develop skills to navigate the seeming permanence of racism, and should help students develop critical voices that challenge the oppression their lives are shaped by. Thus, measurements of the effectiveness of schools should engage students, educators, community experts, and families. In short, a lot of people should be looking at what is being done in classrooms and schools. A teacher is unable to meaningfully gauge impact on students or the student's impact on others if the teacher only examines within the classroom, and only uses content-based assessment tools (Kohn, 2000; Kornhaber, 2004; Popham, 2001; Shepard et al., 2005). Standards are inadequate for meaningful, inclusive measurement procedures, and schools are not designed to include parents, families, and communities in such conversations (Banks, 2004; Chin, Garcia, Hunter, Araiza & Kim, 2004; Fege & Smith, 2002).

Yet there are creative ways to measure student growth to reflect the cultures, languages, and expectations of parents and families. Because many parents have different goals for schools to educate their children, one direct way to address the multiple definitions of educational success is to ensure educators and parents talk to each other about student learning. Kohn (2000) clarified: "For starters [parents] can be given written descriptions ("narratives") from the teacher—or, better yet, they can participate in conversations *with* the teacher" (p. 41). Parent and family conversations, not limited to formal conversations about punishing disengaging students or bad grades, can determine what a student wants out of school, what the family wants out of the student, and what the school can do to manage both (Henderson, Jacob, Kernan-Schloss & Raimondo, 2004; Price, 2008).

Given the historical reality of urban parental exclusion from schools, first as students, and then later as adults, measurement based on family and student need requires educators to break down barriers in place to protect against the acknowledgment of racism. Lawrence-Lightfoot (2003) captures the continuing legacy of parental exclusion from schools: "[Parents] were not made to feel welcome, and were summoned to the school only when their children were flunking their subjects or behaving badly" (p. xvii). Addressing this exclusion through meaningful conversation with parents about the skills students should leave school with begins to transform this exclusion, but only if there is a corresponding shift to measuring what is useful to families, students, and teachers. It is not enough to ask parents what they want; educators have to respond by changing both what and how we teach to include parents as part of a more expansive notion of success.

Creating Public Forums for Expression

Public forums shift the focus from educators to students and from parent-teacher conferences and open houses to informational, interactive community-based processes. Shantel, frustrated that many of her teachers do not do the work she was required to do in classes, argued for teachers to directly prepare students for such creative work. "If you aint a writer, if you aint a poet, if you don't dance in front of your students, then at least sit down with us. We'll figure it out together." Shantel continued, further challenging educators: "I can move and groove and bust out a powerful paper. But I'm not sure all my teachers can." When asked what she would like from teachers, Shantel clarified that she would "like ya'll to join me on stage. Share how difficult living in this world is. Model how our work is good for the community." Shantel was advocating for educators to join in the conversations students are asked to be in. Shantel's point is that if we are to do this work in public, then we should do it collectively: the lack of educator presence on a stage is obvious, but can be hidden in the classroom. Letitia continued this theme: "If I'm gonna stand up and move people, shouldn't my teacher be with me? Cause then its not about a grade, its about what I'm saying." Letitia saw public forums as a way to have teachers model their support: "And my teacher can show parents that they stand behind me. Make the parents see that they should support our work, too, and then they can all know what we do."

A year after teaching a voice-focused class at Central High, I worked with a social studies teacher to implement a youth participatory action research project that culminated in public performances at one of three student-identified events: the year-end School Board meeting, a multicultural education conference, and a district-wide forum for teachers. Students made their choices and then argued for educator involvement, reinforcing Maricella's demand: "Ya'll gonna hafta share something up there with us." The students wanted us to show that we were in solidarity with them, that we did more than just help prepare them for this public expression, but that we also believed in what they were saying. Their point stuck with me: educators should also perform the work we ask of students. If educators do not model our own voices, if we do not stand by our students as they take huge public risks, then we distance ourselves from their efforts, literally making them stand alone. This reflects Shantel's concern about teachers not doing "the work," but Christina also argued that "[teachers] gotta join us. If you really care about us, then help us fight to make our communities better. If you want me to take my voice seriously, then you betta join me on whatever stage I'mma be on!"

Public expression of student work can be a powerful way to directly center parents and families while expanding notions of academic success; the student audience shifts from the teacher to the community. The purpose of expressing voice is to convey a powerful, passionate, and purposeful message, which can be spoken, painted, displayed, filmed, edited, and packaged as a movie or documentary, turned into song, music, a play, or dance. This creativity requires helping students develop comfort being the center of attention, learning how to hold such attention with responsibility, focused knowledge of an issue, and a capacity to make an audience feel. In order to do this, schools must transform from a limited focus on knowledge demonstrations through tests, papers, and worksheets to public forums that center student voice to directly inform local communities while modeling exactly how much students know and care about specific issues. The ultimate purpose of student-led forums is to: (1) inform and engage the larger community, (2) demonstrate student work in ways that encourage meaningful feedback, (3) increase involvement with school, (4) expand the school day and school work to outside the school grounds, (5) invite broad participation and recognize expertise in a range of non-educators, (6) provide opportunities for students to model the society they advocate for.

While a doctoral student, I co-developed a framework for schools, communities, and colleges to identify, nurture, and showcase student talents. In 2001, I argued, "The development of talent should not be hindered by an absence of showcasing opportunities" (Knaus & Friedman, 2001, p. 10). While opportunities for academic expression are available to a limited number of students across the U.S. (including science fairs, school plays, spelling bees, essay contests, athletic events), these events are often exclusive, and rarely urban (with the exception of sports). When students gain from expressing their voice in public, learning to be comfortable speaking out in a range of ways, schools also become more centrally involved with the communities they are located in (Fisher, 2007; Hill, 2009; Morrell, 2004). Imagine culturally responsive community accessible events that highlight and address social issues of local concern, and include as creative a range of approaches as students can conceive of, from dance, poetry readings, community art gardens, photography exhibits, math Olympics, music performances, public debates on current events or local politics, to student-facilitated ethics fairs with local leaders, documentary film shorts, green designs for urban spaces, and community research presentations. These forums, put on by students who learn to facilitate and host community gatherings, serve as "mini-conferences to promote community, educator, business, and student interest" (Knaus & Friedman, 2001, p. 10).

These forums have implications for the way schools align resources around a shared vision. Particularly in under-resourced urban and rural communities, often where public forums for voice are at a minimum, showcasing voice can provide needed space for community gatherings, and can also provide a forum for collaboration amongst city, county, schools, and community organizations to leverage larger pools of resources.

> *The showcasing of talent must be a product of collaborations between families, schools, communities (including businesses) and universities. The emphasis currently placed on high school athletics is a good example of how collaborative showcases of talent can be powerful community building events that also push students to shine in public, although we would argue that the focus on competition within athletics might not be applicable for all other showcasing events. Again, while there are already numerous programs in place that provide opportunities for showcasing, these opportunities are not supported in strong enough ways, and are often separated from the regular school curriculum. Showcasing talent as a strategy for nurturing talent while building up community-school partnerships requires increased support from communities, businesses, and universities and could easily tap into already established programs such as Gear-Up, MESA, and localized outreach programs. (Knaus & Friedman, 2001, p. 10–11)*

Such public forums create student-led efforts to showcase their work, to directly inform audiences of their choosing, and to solicit critical feedback on the translation of their ideas into academic performance (Fisher, 2007; Muller et al., 1995). One caveat is that because corporate business interests already have direct input into the structure of schools, such interests should be limited to local community-based businesses. Local businesses, identified and invited by students into such exhibitions, join the range of perspectives in participating in student expression. These invited guests use student-developed assessments to provide critical feedback on perceived impact and depth of work. Rather than assign "grades," public forums create opportunities for extensive, real-time feedback from relevant community members, peer students, teachers, administrators, parents, families, practitioners, and content-based experts. Forums could take place weekly, monthly, and annually, with the focus shifting throughout, but with the purpose of providing regular ongoing assessment of the student work (so as to inform and sharpen work).

Inclusive Family and Community Assessments

Within schools, opportunities for such meaningful expression are often primarily limited to a final exam or presentation. These typically occur in project-based schools, where students present their cumulative work for a course, term, or as final chapter of a portfolio of work.[1] Integrating forums for voice requires a more systemic approach to transform notions of academic success and measurement, and compiles feedback for each student, for entire courses, and for teachers to respond, all based on real-time parent and family responses. These developmental portfolios document growth through formative and summative public forums. These forums create a shared context of student work for parents and families to engage with teachers about their children's expressive projects, thereby leveraging family and community knowledge. These cycles of expression become a regularly occurring method of culturally responsive, family-inclusive, student-centered assessment, and feedback directly informs student portfolios. Students can account for (or actively challenge) previous feedback, creating a public discussion of their work. In this form, presentations and performances demonstrate what students think about, how they present issues of concern, how a real public responds to the students' work, and how students in turn respond to this public feedback.

Inclusive, transparent, student-centered forums for voice are a direct expansion of call-and-response, and require a commitment by educators to not limit definitions of voice by controlling who can provide feedback or in what form they provide it. The wider the range of audience members, the less control educators have over feedback, and this is the entire point: standards, assessment, measurement, and academic growth have for far too long been narrowly confined. This expanded notion of academic skill sets urges educators to listen to responses to student performance, and shifts power from educators as solely responsible for student evaluation, to a range of community members. Such feedback, in the form of narrative assessments based on student generated feedback forms (which could include discussion groups, surveys, open-ended questions, and so on), provides forums for educators to talk with students about other people's feedback. Rather than the teacher interpreting feedback for the student, the teacher and entire class sift through feedback, and collectively help each student address (or reject) particular feedback. These feedback cycles promote a dialogue-based analysis of individual student performance based on community input and document the impact teachers have on students over time. In this way, assessment becomes a community-inclusive process, based on individual student expression, teacher support, and community insight.

Youth Participatory Action Research to Improve Teaching

In order for student-led public forums to successfully meet the goals of informing the local community, providing relevant opportunities for authentic feedback, increasing community involvement in schools while expanding school boundaries, and providing students opportunities to model what they want society to be, educators must develop voice in students. In previous chapters, I have demonstrated how courses that focus on developing voice can be structured to prepare urban students for public expression of voice; this work can be integrated across the curriculum or in standalone voice-focused course. Outside of my approaches, numerous examples of voice-focused efforts already exist, though many of these are based in afterschool programming, summer programs, or other outside-the-school-day efforts (Morrell, 2004; Morrell & Rogers, 2006; Rogers, Morrell, & Enyedy, 2007). In this section, I provide a brief overview of youth participatory action research (YPAR), which provides yet another way to integrate voice-framed efforts into school. My purpose here is not to clarify the components of YPAR; that has been done elsewhere with much greater detail (Cammarota & Fine, 2008; Morrell, 2004). Instead, I present several examples and two case studies where students intended to develop and then use their voices to improve their schools. These examples demonstrate that student voice can and should directly shape the institutions that are, in turn, designed to shape them (Freire, 1970).

Public forums are one way to engage a wide range of community members in the day-to-day operation of schools while expanding definitions of student achievement. But schools can also create internal forums for students to engage in research and analysis that directly inform educators about issues at the school. In order to provide the intellectual and academic foundation for urban youth to develop skill sets that support identification of critical local social issues, educators must develop what Duncan-Andrade and Morrell (2008) framed as a "Pan-ethnic Studies" curriculum. The full integration of multidisciplinary curricula directly helps students see how they might need to apply mathematical concepts to the study of social inequality, examining, for example, how income levels correlate to test scores as they might try to determine exactly how much a family of four actually would need to survive on given their local neighborhood's housing prices. Duncan-Andrade and Morrell argue for a centering of critical pedagogy, traditional ethnic studies, social historiography, an anti-colonial and post-colonial discourse, and anti-racist pedagogy. In essence, this correlates to an integration of critical race theory and ethnic studies into each and every classroom, wherein the language of pedagogy reflects an inclusive purpose, and the content responds directly to the students in the classroom. Duncan-Andrade and Morrell clarify: "'Pan-ethnic' implies not merely a question of class but rather a collective multi-ethnic struggle and the centrality of race and ethnicity to transformative work in U.S. education" (p. 138).

Such a curricular foundation helps ensure students have the intellectual foundation to then engage in honest, powerful examination of schools. But educators still need to help students not worry about being evaluated, graded, and ultimately dismissed for expressing what they think (Jocson, 2006; Knaus, 2009). Expression in public forums or in sharing research findings about school inequalities requires safety in dialogue, where students can speak, share, push, take risks, and ultimately learn from each other in what Akom, Cammarota, and Ginwright (2008) framed as "Youthtopias." Youthtopias include: youth-led inquiry, a commitment to understand how race intersects with other forms of social oppression, challenging traditional theories and text; fore-grounding experiential knowledge, the development of critical consciousness; and a commitment to social justice (Akom et al., 2008, p. 13). As Duncan-Andrade and Morrell (2008) argued, "With participatory action research…collective action is a part of the process. This is not just research intended to understand problems; it is a research process designed to intervene in problems, to make them go away" (p. 109). Because of this focus on both learning and doing, on examining inequality for the purpose of addressing it, Youthtopias are based on the creation of student-centered curriculum and educators who tap into, and then respond to the needs of students.

If educators are to value student voice, then space has to be made for students to directly inform educator practice, through identifying problems, studying such problems, proposing concrete solutions, and then working with educators to implement these solutions (Brown, 2010; Delgado & Staples, 2007; Morrell, 2004; Stovall, 2006a). In essence, to develop student voice requires educators to then listen intently to what students argue for, and when educators do not, the process can dramatically backfire, further silencing students (Fielding & Rudduck, 2002; Thomas, 2007). Consider Hayes' frustration when, after presenting research findings to the school board, heard a school board member remark under his breath: "What a waste of time. These kids don't have a clue about the 'real' issues. Most of these kids just don't do the work." Hayes was understandably upset: "Why we gonna do all this work just to have some rich white man punk us?" The class he was in had spent months researching why Black students dropout of high school, and most of the students wanted to confront the board member about his ignorance and stereotype of Black students. Several students led in a discussion about how that ignorance is part of their learning process.

Students recognize, or soon will when they begin to share their expression, that many of the adults they interact with will continue to silence and ignore them. But regardless of whether or not adults will listen to urban youth, developing voice requires structures and opportunities for youth to "study their own social contexts to understand how to improve conditions and bring about greater equity" (Akom et al., 2008, p. 4). In attempting to create Youthtopias within schools, voice operates as a lever to engage students in a "process that develops critical consciousness and builds the capacity for young people to respond and change oppressive conditions in their environment" (Akom et al., 2008, p. 11). Educators must provide the structures for students to identify the problems, develop collaborative teams for solutions, and then work, in tandem with educators and community, to implement solutions (Morrell, 2004).

My approach to youth participatory action research has been from within the framework of critical race theory and undertaken as a necessary component to create Youthtopias. Within a voice-framed approach, YPAR frames student-initiated movements to integrate directly into the scope and function of the daily operation of schools (Morrell, 2006). Youth participatory action research empowers youth to conduct research on social inequality, and while many efforts have been student-centered, efforts also reflect the desires and needs of the adults who collaborate on the research (Fine, Torre, Burns & Payne, 2007). Because of the power relationships surrounding university-led research on urban populations, YPAR offers a collaborative process of identifying problems, developing studies, wrestling with findings, and then presenting outcomes; efforts intentionally acknowledge the oppression urban youth face (Cammarota & Fine, 2008). Because the adults training students are often experts in the field, specific steps must be taken to ensure deep collaboration with youth; this requires humility and presence on the part of educators (Brown, 2010; Morrell, 2006). There are varying levels of student involvement in much that is framed as YPAR, and educators must flatten hierarchies if the intent is to actually empower youth. YPAR is one way in which students can "create products that have an ultimate purpose besides a grade from the teacher," and this beyond-the-classroom mentality extends to serving the community (Morrell, 2004).

Oakland Unified School District's All City Council provides one example of student-initiated YPAR. This citywide high school student group consists of representatives from most district high schools (not including charter schools). Though not formally occupying a seat on the Board, two representatives are provided privileged space to be heard regularly during Board meetings. These representatives in turn lead the All-City Council's research efforts. In 2009–10, the students chose to evaluate teacher effectiveness, and, supported by several adult advocates with expertise in YPAR, developed surveys geared towards teachers and students. Students led data collection, went to the schools they attended, and distributed surveys. Students then tabulated results and presented findings at the end-of-the-year School Board meeting.

While this effort was student led, there was limited room for discussion of the results, and students had little recourse other than to present their findings. Most of the Board members seemed genuinely interested in the findings, but the report was not distributed to all students, teachers, schools, district administrators, or families, and no follow up conversations were scheduled. There were no forums for teachers to challenge or support the results, and there were limited opportunities for students to expand upon the work. One Oakland School Board member remarked after a presentation of All City Council research that, "This was very interesting. The students should be commended for their excellent work" Yet this comment was not followed up with a substantive engagement in the actual findings. In essence, while space was given for the students to conduct research and present findings, there was nowhere to go with those findings. This lack of adult responsiveness is replicated in YPAR efforts across the country, and is echoed by Torre and Fine's (2006) clarification that "…we know that schools, public institutions, and boards of education do typically deflect the critical commentary youth have to offer. And so…adult researchers have a responsibility to find audiences of worth" (p. 281). YPAR efforts must create opportunities to extend meaningful dialogue while working towards the solutions that the research might suggest, otherwise students are set up to not be adequately heard. Fielding and McGregor (2005) clarified this struggle:

> *Current students-as-researchers work tends to underplay and under-explore the later stages of its work. These include making of meaning from the data, agreeing recommendations and suggestions for desirable changes, debating and discussing the validity, desirability, significance and meaning of the report, and taking appropriate action which binds the community together in realising the desired changes. Too often some of these stages are skimped and others ignored; too often, as one very supportive teacher remarked, there is no space, real or metaphorical for, in this case staff, to either register support for the work of students-as-researchers or register disagreement with the findings of their research. There was, in effect, no public space in which young people and adults could, as mutual partners in the development of their school as a learning community, discuss matters of common intention and shared significance. (p. 14)*

YPAR that fails to address each stage of the research process, and that fails to recognize how the schools that frame the research process exclude and silence does not empower youth to advocate for change in their local context (Torre & Fine, 2006).

In documenting a youth research class that directly informed teacher preparation, Tara Brown (2010, p. 6) demonstrated how YPAR can be framed within schools to directly impact student disengagement. This collaborative project, led by a team of university researchers and K–12 students, had three goals:

1. To better understand the schooling experiences of adolescents excluded from mainstream public schools for disciplinary reasons
2. To build on the strengths and address the challenges of students at risk for disciplinary exclusion
3. To develop an action plan to improve the schooling experiences of these students

After guiding students through a personal reflective process of mapping personal educational journeys, and then identifying themes to expand upon (all of which fits directly within efforts to develop voice), youth learned interviewing skills and interview protocol. The students then interviewed peer students and teachers on subtopics based upon the personal mapping, coded the interview data, and collaboratively analyzed findings. The findings were combined to serve as the foundation for action: workshops for pre-service teachers (Brown, 2010). Brown (2010) captured White pre-service teachers unprepared to listen to student voice, but also demonstrated that the students had an impact in raising awareness as to the level of oppression that still occurs. This research process clearly demonstrated the impact students and their research can have, and also gave students a clear, purposeful audience from which to target their findings.

As with many successful YPAR efforts, this example also raised additional important issues relevant to urban schools. In particular, Brown's study highlighted a lack of educator readiness to listen to urban youth voice. YPAR with urban students can identify and address such issues because students of color can teach White educators about the urban communities teachers are often unfamiliar with (Bell, 2002; Gay 2000; Howard, 1999; Loeb & Reininger, 2004). This cultural disjoint is enhanced when educators "neither live nor participate in their students'" communities (Valenzuela, 1999). Educator preparation programs have to prepare teachers for the skills to listen to students and to foster critical voice, and this requires more than one multicultural education course (Delpit, 2006; Horowitz et al., 2005; Nieto, 1996). Educators already on the defensive, already uncomfortable listening to students are going to have a difficult time fostering critical student voice, particularly when that voice might directly challenge their efforts, curricular choices, and pedagogy. As Brown (2010) argues, "Clearly, one such workshop is woefully inadequate for promoting substantive change" (p. 10), just as YPAR without significant support to help educators listen will not ultimately transform schooling.

Student-led Tutor Development

Urban student-led youth action research is not enough to transform the educator preparation process, but should directly inform how teachers are taught. At the school level, urban youth can directly inform specific teachers, develop partnerships and collaborations amongst adults, and can directly shape professional development efforts to support educators. One example of student research led to professional development for tutors at an urban school, demonstrating the power of integrating YPAR into the scope of the school day. At Central High, there was a several-year influx of tutors from a nearby university. Because the university had been increasing its service learning efforts for undergraduates, more and more college students were choosing tutoring of urban students as part of the fieldwork component of several courses. While this led to an immediate increase in the number of tutors available to the school, this also placed a burden on the teachers, who did not know how best to utilize undergraduate tutors with limited previous experience in urban schools. By the second year, student and teacher frustration with tutors was high, and a lead social studies teacher invited me to co-facilitate a research process around this tension.

Within the first week of the six-week unit, students chose to focus on:

1. Measuring the effectiveness of the college tutors
2. Identifying problems that the tutors cause or worsen
3. Developing a process for training tutors to be more useful.

The class split into three groups (each group included an adult member who the students made clear had no more power or voice than anyone else). The first group developed interview questions for every member of the staff, and focused on questions like: "How many tutors come into your classrooms throughout the day?" "How are the tutors helpful" "What would you like tutors to do that they are not able to do?" and "What do you need in order to better take advantage of the tutors?" I was a member of the second group, which developed focus group questions to assess student perspectives on the tutors. Students trained each other on how to facilitate discussions for brevity, to ensure quiet students spoke aloud, and to ensure students would feel comfortable sharing critiques of people (the tutors) they might like a lot. Guiding questions included: "What do you like about the tutors?" "What bugs you about the tutors?" and "How do the tutors help you learn?" The third group convened two sets of tutors, and held a focus group with each group, asking about support they needed, what led them to tutor at this particular school, and what they expected out of their tutoring experience.

The students transcribed the raw data and compiled a ten-page data report (again with students splitting into three teams: a transcription team, a report team, and a solution team). The solution team developed and proposed solutions to the larger class, which resulted in a fascinating discussion of what the tutors needed based on three sets of student-generated data. The class then developed a training protocol, and selected two training teams. The hurried six-week unit ended, with students presenting their proposal for training the tutors to a team of teachers, who were asked for feedback. After being denied funding by the principal, I was asked by the class to advocate for funds to pay student presenters to offer workshops for the tutors. The principal also denied my request, arguing that the tutors were not teaching staff and therefore, could not receive professional development funds. When I came back to the school the following week, the students had asked the entire teaching staff to help convince the principal to reallocate staff professional development funds.

The principal agreed, and for two years, the workshops were required for all new tutors. The first two-hour workshop consisted of students sharing negative educational experiences with tutors, overviews of White privilege, biases that tutors might have, and student expectations of tutors. This workshop was in part designed to push away potential tutors who did not want to confront their own racism, and was effective; there were always fewer tutors in the second workshop. This workshop was based on strategies to work one-on-one with students. The end result of the YPAR effort was a student-run effort to welcome and ensure that potential tutors understood that students only wanted help from people who were committed to their development. Students also trained each other in how to facilitate the trainings. And students were clear that they should be the ones to determine who was committed and who was not; anyone they had questions about was not allowed to tutor at the school. These once-a-quarter workshops cost a fraction of the professional development budget (students were paid at $15 an hour), and put on-boarding procedures for college tutors in the hands of students. When the principal left the school, the effort was immediately cancelled, but several tutors speak about how their interaction with these students helped them commit to becoming teachers.

Student Voice as Professional Development for Teachers

In part as an effort to build upon the success of my previous experience with students educating tutors, I worked with Western High to implement a voice-centered course built upon a YPAR effort to conduct professional development workshops for onsite teachers. I first approached Ms. Johnson, a writing teacher who had participated in a writing workshop I conducted for teachers. She was more than willing to collaborate, and was excited for the additional in-class support I would provide. While we focused on an English class over the course of a semester, students eventually expanded the project to include content-based efforts in Math and Social Studies courses.

Western High is a large urban high school campus, and like many of its peer schools, is split into several smaller schools. The majority African American and Latino students are taught by a majority White teaching staff, and the dropout rate is considerably high (upwards of 40%). Students enrolled in Ms. Johnson's eleventh grade English class were asked if they wanted to improve teaching on the campus. The class voted unanimously to learn how to lead the research process and narrowed down a topic: addressing why students dropout. With guidance from Ms. Johnson and myself, students began with freewriting about why students dropout, and turned these into their first papers, a persuasive paper about why, from a student's perspective, leaving school makes sense. Then students compiled these reasons, and developed a study protocol to determine which teachers were seen as effective by (1) peer teachers, (2) students, and (3) administration. After distributing and collecting these anonymous surveys, students learned to enter data into Excel, and a math teacher taught several lessons guiding data analysis so that students could comfortably tabulate data and present findings.

Students presented these findings to groups of students and teams of Math, English, and Social Studies teachers, sharing concrete statistics about specific efforts teachers make that are seen as effective (or not) by the three different groups. One anonymous student quote that served to start each conversation was "This school makes me need to smoke weed. Teachers be so fucking boring!" Additional findings challenged teacher efforts to develop voice as inauthentic, so that even when teachers were trying to engage students, their efforts often failed to do so. Students critiqued *I Am From* poems in particular as inadequate efforts to tap into voice or keep students engaged. This sparked several conversations about the differences between students and teachers and teachers and administration, and highlighted a larger need expressed by students for a more relevant curriculum. This contrasted with administration identifying standards-based teachers as effective, and with teachers identifying peer teachers who integrated *I Am From* poems into their curriculum as effective.

After these presentations Ms. Johnson asked students to develop their final assignment. The class broke into two groups: those who wanted to write about effective teaching, and those who wanted to design professional development workshops that translated those writings into lessons. Therein became the issue for Ms. Johnson: students were advocating for assignments that did not meet the requirements for an eleventh-grade English class, including not addressing the standards that the school was making a priority. She called me in and we sat down with the students to discuss the dilemma of wanting to empower students to spend time on what they wanted to do, but being beholden to teaching the standards instead. This is precisely the tension of being student centered in a context of high-stakes testing and standards that often appear to be at odds with what urban students see as a relevant curriculum. If educators are going to be student centered and let students guide the curriculum and research process, then standards for a particular subject (in this case, English) might not be met. This was exactly Ms. Johnson's concern and her fears were affirmed by this class; after being empowered to shape the curriculum, going back against the structures they created would have pushed them further away from school. If educators are going to empower students to develop curriculum and engage in voice-centered youth participatory action research, then we have to fully support students, even if that means not meeting standards. This full support is important particularly given that the student research found that students expressed a universal need for relevance.

A poem to My Algebra Teachers, So You Understand Why I Don't Like Math
by Sinque Jackson

I've been trying to tell you why I don't like math
Why I sit in the back of class with my headphones
Listening to Tupac or Iselyfe or someone to take me away from your class
The place that ignores what I know and live and breathe
And how my people die

Its not that I don't understand integers
But how can one be a positive number?
One for Oscar Grant
One Bullet One Shot One Mistake
In a lifetime of police brutality riots and racism
My teachers want only one answer
But the answer cannot be one
Listen: Malcolm X and Dr. King
even our saviors are killed in the streets fighting for equality
There is no way to balance this equation
My people are taught by the worksheets you give to be Less Than
And there are no solutions that will bring Oscar Grant back

So please do not make a word problem out of my life
If Amadou Diallo was shot at 41 times by 4 White Officers
And if 22 of those bullets lodged into his Black Body
The average # of shots fired is not relevant
I do not care about the velocity of each bullet
I do not care about the angles of ricochets or
How many times Officer Sean Carroll fired his gun
We should not care if Officer Richard Murphy shot more than Officer Edward McMellon when
Officer Kenneth Boss shot double that of Officer Carroll
This is not a word problem or an algebraic equation
There are no solutions that will bring Amadou Diallo back

And when you ask me to fill in bubble answers
When you ask me to divide by N or multiply by Y
When you ask me about sine and cosine
Recognize that these are tangents
Mr. Teacher, there is a 50% dropout rate
35% of us go to Juvenile Hall
90% of us are on Free and Reduced Lunch
2% of us will go to a 4 year college
yet 100% of us are Black and Latino
There is a correlation, but its not the answer you are looking for
Mr. Teacher, I know you're trying to get us to learn
But its just that what you are teaching does not reflect
Each day I live and each of us who will die young
So either you change what you teach
Or get used to disappointment
Because it does not matter if the numbers on either side of the equals sign are equal
My people are not
I am a Less Than
I do not have equal rights or an equal chance at life
The numbers just do not add up
And that is why math you teach is not the math we need to learn.

A poem to My English Teachers, So You Understand Why I Sound Like I Do
by Malaysia Smith-Wheaton

I've been trying to tell you why I don't like English
The language and your class
Because both teach me that I am a less than
I did not grow up right I did not grow up white

And each time you assign books that tell me this
Each day I am told I speak not right
Always corrected and rarely respected
I know that like GWBUSH and most teachers ya'll don't like black folk
But I want you to listen so you can teach me
And that means Mr. and Mrs. English teacher
That you have to learn way more than school can teach.

I am not a double negative
No not never
Though understand that with all the violence and poverty I live
I should be
This is not a simile I am not dripping "like blood"
This blood is real, red, and splattered against walls you will not see
Because you do not live here
the pain from bullets inside my brother's dying body is real
not a dangling
modifier
But an untreated hangnail that turned to gangrene because my mother has no health insurance
And the books we read do not never talk about how she sometimes just barely survives

Do not talk again about Shakespeare or Whitman or Emerson or Robert Frost and
Their poetic flow because their distant old English was spoken as my great great grandparents were stolen from their villages while rich white men like those you make me read fawned poetic lines about justice and equality but only for people like them
And my people apparently are not enough
I am not metaphoring the physical not going to read another book by Mark Twain or Jack London or Jack Kerouac these alcoholic drunkards traveling around the world as my great grandparents still couldn't vote these stories menace me and the underlying theme the symbolism the main point is that
Apparently white men can write nicely about trees
while black and brown people are hung from them
you see why perhaps I might not want to learn skills like these.

You see I have a problem with "Great English Literature"
that came out of slavery and imperialism and war
And all these folks are writing in black-face but they don't know black
They wrote or typed or thought at slave-labor made desks while black hands
Washed their feet

Oh the struggle of being a white artist throughout the ages
And you celebrate the colonization of my family each time you ask me to summarize colonial literature to ensure I know how to read or to see if I wasted my time learning the "canon" as if these canons
Were not actually aimed at the necks of my ancestors
You see now that many of my people *choose* to learn to not read
because our death is what you force us to read.

And then and then and then this whole language thing you test me on
Grammar and punctuation and spelling and rules that silence the shrill scream of my rage
Five paragraph essays with standard margins and standard font and standards-based mentalities that do not help me learn to talk to my neighbors or my grandparents or my imprisoned father or my cousins who dropped out of school in 7th and 8th grades because I am trying to learn
I want I need to learn to communicate with a wider range of my peoples
But what you are teaching makes my life harder
More difficult to survive
Blurs the chill from these streets
Obfuscates the death of my people
But you, instead, English Teacher, are proud that I could use that word
Obfuscate
In a sentence.

THAT IS NOT MY POINT and
It shouldn't be yours
My people are dying intellectually starving
We need to read better books by people like us
bookstores go out of business because you teach us that anything worth reading is white
but I need to learn to speak well according to my grandfather
who always thought that white people sounded uptight
Probably because you teach them just like you teach me to obfuscate
The power of our words.

So I demand respect
I speak the language of the streets
My urban slang lingo representin white oppression racism and 500 years of making my people feel stupid F student dropout special education far below basic uneducable ghetto high needs when really
I'm just at risk for recognizing your racist views and choosing to not never again let you in

I think I'm valid so when you tell me I am wrong
I know that you have already lost the battle
Because English is a tool to silence me and what I really need from you
Is to teach me to better use my multiple languages
To code shift and navigate and never ever again obfuscate
And if you can hear me, then let's re-do the curriculum
But if you cannot, then do not never ask me to turn in another
Paper again I will not help you put chains on
Another black neck again
Mr. and Mrs. English Teacher.

A poem to My Social Studies Teachers, So You Understand Why I Do Not Think My Perspective Matters
by Mark Willis

I've been trying to tell you why I don't like your social studies
Why I barely come even when you tell me I'm especially going to like this film, book, story, unit
Because your social studies kinda feels a lot like going to the Doctor's Office
I'm sick I'm ill I'm not feeling too well and everyone's trying to solve me
But no social studies teacher has yet asked me what I think is wrong or what I think we need to do
To fix the problems that I say exist
And you know what Social Studies Teacher?
Today my problem is you.

And I want you to listen. I want you to hear. So since I have already sat in 11 years of classroom chairs
Since I have already sat in approximately 1,980 hours of social studies indoctrination, I think you can sit, take notes, and maybe even ask questions about my 5 minute unaskedforbutyoureallyneedtohearme rant.

Before I begin, I have to ask you a question. Can you hear me? I know you have been trained by 13 years of school, then college, then some training or certification or program or self-help group, and then you became my teacher, told by everyone that you know what I need to know and that you know how to teach me those things that you know that you have been told I need to know. So can you hear me? Can you get past my skin tone, the same beautiful dark hues that make police officers nervous, jumpy around triggers, lots of bullets land in skin tones like mine, and when I walk past you hooded up you clutch your bags tight you walk faster you do not like to stay at our school after dark I think its because of what you think I might do to you, your fear of the same beautiful dark hues we see on tv in the news my people killing and being killed. Can you hear me?

I don't think you can. You know too much social studies, you have too much knowledge of the world and not enough time spent in the shoes I wear. But if you don't know me, how can you know what I need to know? I kinda think this is a social studies question. Something about perspectives and point of view and who gets to write the stories that become his so that he can say its "history" and something about
How national geographic can show black tits somehow that's okay
Because you don't know whose mother that is but I do
That's my mom and you want me to write about her
Or claim some sort of distant bond but you are the one
Showing her naked I think the word you wont use here with my mother but would with yours
Is objectification, right?
And you wonder why those magazines disappear or why we make mustaches on 2002 text books that still tell us Bush is a peace loving baseball owning president? You wonder why we deface books or trash your 1 poster of "Great Black Leaders" you want to know why we do not respect your property is because your property does not respect us.

Yes, we know about Dr. Martin Luther King. Shit, most of us live on MLK Street or went to school at Malcolm X, my cousin went to Carver Elementary and my sister goes to Sankofa and every where are posters of the Black President. Everything is named after "Great Black Leaders" but we don't read them, we read about them. We don't read them, we read what white people think about them.

I kinda think this is a social studies question. Something about perspectives and point of view and who gets to write the stories that become his so that he can say its "history" and something about the real live people who should be studied like my grandfather and why do we do reports on far away countries, regurgitating wikipedia factoids and you should be concerned when we can learn all we need to on our i-phones because my cousin's family is from Zimbabwe and I bet they could have taught us a lot more than some white girl who went there for the peace corps or some CIA report I found online and yet somehow I got an A on the project when all I learned was how easy it is to copy, reword, regurgitate, relay, and never actually learn.

But maybe that's what you are teaching us, social studies is about dates and timelines and pictures of basket-weaving grandmothers who seem nice but I bet when white people were killing them and their buffalo they weren't so nice then but we do not get that story too complicated there is no room for what happened because then I guess we'd have to talk about what still happens and when I have to answer A, B, C, or D (which is always all or none of the above), there is no room for the people who were killed so that we could be here learning false history lessons from teachers who think that teaching that Lincoln freed the slaves because he wanted to preserve the union is liberal progressive or radical but that doesn't get at what we really want to know, which is how the hell do we keep electing people who do not care about black people because we know that Lincoln didn't care we know that none of these people care, but what we do not get much of is who does care and if we care, what can the still-alive-now and in-your-classroom-today students do to help people live and turn this country around and make you all see that this world is not okay.

I kinda think this is a social studies question. Something about perspectives and point of view and who gets to write the stories that become his so that he can say its "history" and something about where are our voices and can I get some teachers who know my community and think I and I are worthy of study but wont do it without my approval and insight and knowledge and voice and heart. I do not think I can save the world alone, Teach. I would like your help. But before I begin, I have to ask you a question. Can you hear me?

These three poems served as a centerpiece for a series of professional development for content-based teachers (in teams of Math, English, and Social Studies teachers). Each group met several times throughout the next few months, revisiting the issues brought up by the poet, in content-based teacher teams, with several students, and the one student poet. Each professional development series began with Sinque, Malaysia, and Mark reading their respective poems aloud to the teacher-student team related to their focus (Mark, for example, shared his poem with the social studies teachers). After reading the poems aloud, two students facilitated the discussion, leading freewrite responses to each poem, and then open discussions. The class had developed additional critical writings, which student authors would then share as related issues came up in the discussions, with the student facilitators deciding which writings should be shared based on the direction and tone of the conversation. These discussions were framed entirely by the students; they were no longer part of a class, and much of the conversations were based on the teachers' questions about the student writing, the initial poet's words, and student experiences.

While I still work with Sinque, Malaysia, and Mark on their writings (the poems presented here are even further revised from when they shared them in the professional development, as they are still trying to teach teachers), it is important to clarify that Ms. Johnson did not work with them on developing their poems. Having extended herself to supporting the students throughout the research process, Ms. Johnson was simply overwhelmed by her teaching load to additionally work one-on-one with the three students. I was able to carve out time to meet with them regularly and co-edit their poems to ensure they conveyed what they wanted to. And in that process, those three students were able to strongly develop their writing, but the rest of the class was not able to focus as much on writing as both Ms. Johnson and I thought should be the case. That is a weakness of this effort that still haunts me, because while we helped the students develop inquiry skills, Excel-based math skills, and a deeper sense of the impact of student voice on teacher effectiveness, as a whole, we did not meet English targets for the grade level, school, or district. This example highlights the potential for this work, but also the need to implement such efforts across the curriculum, integrated within multiple courses, and not reliant upon one overburdened teacher and an outside-the-school volunteer.

What I learned from the process is that professional development efforts should be based upon student research efforts, and can institutionalize student-led evaluations, support, and guidance for urban educators. Such efforts require administrative leadership to develop sustainability and to support teachers, who must adapt their classroom teaching to respond to student interest, experience, and frustration. In this way, schools can empower and develop students to directly inform educator development. YPAR can serve as an intellectually stimulating, academically relevant, multidisciplinary effort to support teacher quality through student-led inquiry. That such efforts rely upon student voice and frame educators to support student critiques and solutions of ineffective teaching based on combinations of student, educator, and administrator insight and upon student teaching efforts also provides a model of school improvement based entirely on local site-based resources. Such a model integrates voice into the function and structure of the school, creates a continual source of student-leaders who can help teachers grow, and taps into the insight of students who are typically silenced and pushed out of schools.

Ultimately, if schools intend to empower students to teach their educators, then schools must develop the structures to support interdisciplinary teaching, and this requires time to collaborate across disciplines and with students. Because the trust for such collaborations, particularly with students, is often lacking in urban schools, students instead opt out of completing high school. If we are to address the dropout crisis, then educators must empower students to develop and showcase their voices, particularly around social issues they identify, and on the very teaching structures that silence their voices around everything that matters to them. It seems educators have tried everything except listening to students.

Conclusion

Transforming schools into voice-centered processes to develop student voice means transforming the structures of schooling; this is difficult work. Students need access to voice-centered curricula, infused with youth participatory action research, based on a multidisciplinary, integrated curriculum that develops student-led cycles of inquiry. This provides a foundation for students to examine problems, then to identify, develop, and implement solutions to local problems. These efforts will significantly engage urban students who have been told they do not matter, but also include their families and local communities. This requires shifting the role of educators and educational leaders who must respond directly to student needs (and this requires knowing what student needs are, from their perspectives). This also requires transforming parent and family involvement and shifting notions of accountability to local communities, through creation of regularly occurring public forums that educate about student insight into local problems. This shifted notion of accountability and student performance to a locally responsive community requires educators to develop student voice, then step out of the way, and in short, shut up and listen to what students have to say.

Always when I work to develop voice in schools, I am reminded of Daniel. A student in my writing class at UC Berkeley, Daniel began his college experience as do most college freshman: unprepared to take himself and his writing seriously. But just a few short weeks into his first year of college, Daniel started taking himself more seriously. He came to my office, shared about how he realized how rare he was; poor Latinos from what he described as the "hood" were not common in his classes. He dove into his coursework from then on, tearing through the books for our class, and asking for additional stories by Latino and Black authors. And after he started reading books that reflected his life, he started writing. His words came alive when writing about his personal experiences, and he started writing stories about growing up in my class. He came to my office hours, encouraged other peers to write and read, and became a leader within a month. He had so much to share, and was continually amazed at how he had "made it" to college, away from the violence, drug addiction, poverty, and racism in his hometown community, in urban Los Angeles. He kept asking me to take him to Oakland schools; he wanted to see what urban Oakland was like, and wanted to help others like him see that there was a way out of the cycles his friends from home hadn't yet gotten out of.

But Daniel didn't make it out. He went home over winter break, never to return. He was shot and killed on New Year's Eve. Daniel never made it back to the second writing class he was to take with me. He left a message just before leaving for home on my office phone: "I can't wait to show you the journal I just got; when I get back it'll be full of my life." Instead, I came to class with an empty chair, placed it in the middle of the room, and asked students to write about the real violence that some of us will not escape, no matter how powerfully we write. Words are not enough. Words may not transform the structures of schooling. Writing may not transform society. We cannot stop the bullets. But we can help students live with purpose. Educators can help students teach us to live more aware of the impact this world has on young people. We can help students navigate the trauma they survive so they do not heap such trauma on others. We can help students step into adulthood more prepared to address the violence that shaped them. We can help students overcome the damage educators too often cause.

This book is my attempt to highlight some of the ways I have learned from students. And the greatest lessons I have learned always come back to the same thing: the older I get, the more I need to shut up to listen.

Excerpt from Daniel's Journal

"Getting jumped is not a joke. I got jumped so much in high school that I too wanted the easy way out. I wanted to get a gun. What else is there to do when 3-5 guys are beating you from every angle? You get up, stand on your feet, keep swinging and swinging until you can't swing no more. The whole world is against you, and no matter what I did, no matter if I stood tall and fought or curled in a ball, I still was going to get beat. This feeling of wanting to give up grows deeper with every punch and kick that I received, until I was left with two swollen and pounding eye sockets and was unable to properly breathe because I was kicked in the stomach so many times I was coughing up blood. I don't blame them. I used to be scared of my father and because I was scared of him, I avoided his presence and even fought with him. I was scared. The guys that beat me were scared. But I still never bought or stole a gun. I fought with my hands. I held onto hope. Even when these guys gave me all the reasons not to. If knowing you have nothing to live for but still fight to survive, if that is not hope, then I don't know what hope is.

The Schools and the Students: *A Brief Guide*

Central High

A large comprehensive public high school in a predominantly Black and Latino urban neighborhood in the East Bay. There is limited public transportation, and the rundown neighborhood experiences some of the highest rates of violence, incarceration, and homicide in the country. During the years reported in the book, the school was approximately 40% African American, 40% Latino, 10% Asian, 5% Filipino, and 5% Pacific Islander.

Christina: A multiracial Black and Latino high school senior at Central High, Christina became the first person in her family to attend college. She took a course from Dr. Knaus in her first term, and is completing her bachelor's degree in English and African American Studies.

Shantel: An African American junior at Central High, who enrolled in Dr. Knaus' writing class. Shantel graduated high school, and has dropped out of a local community college each of the past two years, having instead to work full-time to support her family.

Lupe: A multiracial Black, Latino and White junior at Central High, both of Lupe's parents were killed when she was young, and she was raised (and still lives with) her African American grandmother.

Shay: An African American senior at Central High enrolled in Dr. Knaus' writing class, Shay graduated high school and become a spoken word artist. She works full-time at a local fast food restaurant, and takes night classes at a nearby community college.

Loni: An African American senior at Central High enrolled in Dr. Knaus' writing class, Loni completed her high school requirements at adult school, and received her diploma the year after her senior year. She took classes at a local community college, but without enough funds to pay for her mother's rent, had to quit. She now works several part-time jobs, and applies for scholarships each year, hoping to get enough to pay for her mother's rent and go back to college.

Maricella: An African American junior enrolled in Dr. Knaus' writing class at Central High, Maricella now attends a historically black college in the south, and writes for the school newspaper.

Andre: An African American junior at Central High enrolled in Dr. Knaus' writing class, Andre dropped out of school his senior year. He was arrested just after graduation, served six months in jail, and is trying to earn his G.E.D. through adult school.

David: A Latino junior just released from a juvenile facility at the time of Dr. Knaus' writing class, David was placed in Dr. Knaus' class at Central High as a condition of the school letting him re-enroll. His father is serving a life sentence for gang-related violence. After the class, he went missing; most students assumed he was living with his gang-affiliated cousins. He resurfaced several years later, and at the counseling of Robert, relocated out-of-state to escape gang-life.

Robert: An African American junior at Central High, Robert had never met his incarcerated father. He spent six months in a juvenile facility and now attends community college, where he is working on expunging his record so that he can become a prison guard.

Letitia: An African American junior at Central High, Letitia relocated to the south to live with her aunt, and is completing her bachelor's degree. She plans on enrolling in a teacher certification program so that she can teach Social Studies in urban high schools. While in college, she began to speak in public about sexual assault and violence against women.

Lou: An African American junior at Central High, Lou struggled through high school, but graduated with his class. He was very close with his father, who was incarcerated when Lou was ten. Several years after the writing class, Lou's father was released, and Lou works several jobs to support his father.

Hayes: An African American senior at Central High, Hayes did not pass the California High School Exit Exam, and graduated with a certificate of completion. He earned his G.E.D. in adult school, and works temporary construction jobs.

Anton: An African American senior at Central High, Anton graduated and attended community college for several years. His mother worked as a secretary in a high-profile corporate office, and had spoken to several classes about professional attire and demeanor. Through her role, she was able to secure a scholarship for Anton, and he is excited about transferring to a four-year university.

East Bay High (E-High)

A small public high school set in a racially mixed neighborhood in the East Bay, the school is just down the road from a major university. There is close access to public transportation, and the neighborhood is a mix of wealthy White and Asian families, public housing that provide's low-income residences to mostly African American and Latino families, and middle-income apartments. During the years reported in the book, the school was approximately 55% African American, 40% Latino, and a combined 5% Asian, Pacific Islander, and White.

Pedro: A Latino junior at East Bay High, Pedro had been kicked out of two previous high schools. He graduated from E-High, and began taking courses at a local community college, but stopped taking courses after his first year, deciding instead to work full-time at his father's landscaping business.

Julia: An African American and Mexican American senior at East Bay High, Julia grew up speaking Spanish and English. She completed her high school at a local community college, and earned her Associates Degree. She now works several part-time jobs while trying to save money to transfer to a four-year university.

Juan: A Latino junior enrolled in Dr. Knaus' writing class at East Bay High, Juan came from a violent family context, and faced family violence from his brother, who was actively involved in a local gang. Juan's family lived with the constant threat of homelessness, and Juan lived on friends' couches for most of his sophomore year.

Angela: An African American senior enrolled in Dr. Knaus' writing class at East Bay High, Angela did not earn enough credits to graduate high school. She enrolled in adult school, but dropped out, and has since worked several part-time jobs.

Jasmine: An African American junior at East Bay High, Jasmine became a writer after Dr. Knaus' class. She always has a journal with her, and has read her poems aloud at a number of local spoken word events. She completed her G.E.D. through adult school, and is now trying to figure out how to afford college.

Marco: An African American junior enrolled in Dr. Knaus' writing class at East Bay High, Marco dropped out of school the following year. He continues to write in the hopes that he can record a hip hop album.

Sherise: An African American senior enrolled in Dr. Knaus' writing class at East Bay High, Sherise has struggled to earn her G.E.D. She had several internships after leaving high school without a diploma, but none paid enough for her to enroll in community college. She stopped going to adult school after not passing the G.E.D. test, and has been working part-time jobs and trying to save money to complete her G.E.D. in community college.

Jacinda: An African American and Native American senior enrolled in Dr. Knaus' writing class, Jacinda did not graduate high school. She enrolled in a workforce development program, completed her G.E.D., and plans to attend a four-year university as soon as she can save the needed funds.

Nique: An African American junior enrolled in Dr. Knaus' writing class at East Bay High, Nique left school when she found out she was pregnant. Now a young mother of two, Nique has been unable to complete her G.E.D. or hold down a job.

Enrique: A Latino junior enrolled in Dr. Knaus' writing class at East Bay High, Enrique left school at the end of the semester to work full-time as a day laborer.

Western High

This large comprehensive public high school is in an urban neighborhood in the East Bay. With some access to public transportation, the community is predominantly low-income Latino families, with decreasing African American and Filipino populations. During the years reported in the book, the school was approximately 30% African American, 45% Latino, 10% Pacific Islander, 5% Asian, and 10% Filipino.

Sinque Jackson: An African American junior at Western High during the project, Sinque graduated valedictorian, and is now attending a four-year university. She has published several poems, and writes for the school newspaper.

Malaysia Smith-Wheaton: An African American junior at Western High during the project, Malaysia completed her Associates Degree with a 4.0 GPA, and earned a full scholarship to a local four-year university. With her ultimate goal of obtaining a Ph.D., Malaysia is planning on double majoring in African American Studies and Social Work.

Mark Willis: An African American junior at Western High during the project, Mark graduated high school and completed a year of community college. Frustrated by the lack of relevance in his courses, he has taken several years off from school, works several part-time jobs, and writes regularly in his journals.

Various Schools

Tony: A multiracial African American and Latino student who left high school barely able to read and without a diploma, Tony eventually went to community college, learned how to read and write, and after three years, transferred to a four-year university. After completing his undergraduate degree Tony began working as a coordinator of an afterschool program, and is now in his second year of graduate school.

Dave: A multiracial Filipino and African American junior who attended predominantly White schools, Dave earned his G.E.D., enrolled in community college, and then attended an elite university, where he went on to earn his Master's degree.

James: A seventeen-year-old African American student who was placed in a juvenile facility for repeated violence in schools and for selling marijuana on campus, James has spent much of his life in youth and adult facilities. At last contact, he was living in a group home for young adults with extensive police records.

Taisha: An African American undergraduate student at East Bay University, Taisha had attended urban schools and was the first student in her family (and the only student from her high school) to attend a four-year university the year after graduating high school.

Daniel Ramirez: A first-year Latino undergraduate student at UC Berkeley, Daniel enrolled in Dr. Knaus' writing course in his first semester. He was killed during winter break, when he went home to visit his family.

Notes

Introduction

1. These high schools are represented as Central High, East Bay High, and Western High School; additional information about each school and each student who provides quotes, dialogue, or writing samples can be found under the final section of the book.

Chapter 1

1. I have since changed my middle name to Bodenheimer, my maternal grandmother's maiden name.

Chapter 2

1. See, for example, Bob Marley, Oliver Mtukudzi, and Nneka, but U.S. artists also include Blue Scholars, Immortal Technique, and Ise Lyfe, to name but a few.
2. At the time of writing, Dave was completing his doctorate in history. He was a senior in a high school writing class I co-taught five years prior to his successful navigation of college; he is still the only person in his extended family to have attended college.
3. Tony wrote me this note in 1999, several years before online chatting and text messaging became a short writing norm for many youth.
4. While a first-year college student at the time of this writing, Christina was also a high school student in my writing course the previous year (the only student from her high school to enroll directly into a four-year college).

Chapter 3

1. While Maricella identified as Mexicana, and both of her parents were from Mexico, her father is seen as African American, at least until people hear his accent.
2. Poets included Ai, Sherman Alexie, Chrystos, Ana Castillo, Sonia Sanchez, Sapphire, and June Jordan.
3. One powerful example of how educators pass on students of color without bothering to educate them is from my experience with collegiate athletes. I have tutored and worked with a half dozen athletes at two Division I universities who had not yet learned to read, had not been diagnosed by any special education testing, and all of whom expressed continual interest in trying to be taught. Instead, because of their athleticism, their lack of being taught was tolerated system-wide, and they were promoted through K–12 and college despite not being able to read.

Chapter 4

1. This level of feedback is unreasonable to expect from full-time teachers in our current educational system, since I spend upwards of an hour per student per week providing feedback, in addition to grading, curriculum planning, home visits, coordinating outside speakers, and my own writing related to the class.

2. In 12 years of teaching, only one student did not honor this in a public forum and the class voted to kick him out of class. I am not naïve: students will share the details of what they hear, and I encourage them to talk through lessons we wrestle with in class. Yet incidents of publicizing another student's trauma have been very rare and typically were shared in meaningful ways, with prior permission.

Chapter 5

1. See, for example, project-focused schools like Envision Schools in California and New York-based Quest to Learn, and the Buck Institute for Education: *http://www.bie.org/*.

References

Akom, A. A., Cammarota, J., & Ginwright, S. (2008). Youthtopias: Towards a New Paradigm of Critical Youth Studies. *Youth Media Reporter*, August 15.

Alexie, S. (Writer/Director), Bond, B. C. (Producer), & Benear, J. (Producer). (2003).*The Business of Fancydancing* [Motion picture]. New York: Wellspring Media.

Allen, Q. (2010). Racial Microaggressions: The Schooling Experiences of Black Middle-Class Males in Arizona's Secondary Schools. *Journal of African American Males in Education, 1*(2), 125–143.

Allen, R. L. (1990). *Black Awakening in Capitalistic America: An Analytic History.* Trenton, NJ: Africa World Press.

Alliance for Excellent Education (2009). *Understanding High School Graduation Rates in the United States.* Washington, DC: Alliance for Excellent Education.

Allison, D. (2002). Deciding to Live: Preface to the First Edition. In D. Allison, *Trash.* New York: Plume.

Alonso, A. (1998). Urban Graffiti on the City Landscape. Paper presented to the Western Geography Graduate Conference, San Diego State University. February 14, 1998.

Anderson, J. D. (1988). *The Education of Blacks in the South, 1860–1935.* Chapel Hill, NC: University of North Carolina Press.

Antibalas (2004). *Big Man. Who is This America?* New York: Artemis Records.

Apple, M. W. (1993). *Official Knowledge: Democratic Education in a Conservative Age.* New York: Routledge.

Archuleta, M. L., Child, B. J., & Lomawaima, K. T. (2000). *Away from Home: American Indian Boarding School Experiences.* Heard Museum.

Asante, M. K. (1998). *The Afrocentric Idea.* Philadelphia, PA: Temple University Press.

Aud, S., Fox, M. A., & KewalRamani, A. (2010). *Status and Trends in the Education of Racial and Ethnic Groups.* Washington, DC: National Center for Educational Statistics (NCES 2010015).

Aud, S., Hussar, W., Planty, M., Snyder, T., Bianco, K., Fox, M. A., Frohlich, L., Kemp, J., & Drake, L. (2010). *The Condition of Education, 2010.* Washington, DC: National Center for Educational Statistics (NCES 2010028).

Baldwin, J. (1962). *The Fire Next Time.* New York: Vintage.

Baldwin, J. (1972). *No Name in the Street.* New York: Laurel.

Baldwin, J. (1985a) *The Evidence of Things Not Seen.* New York: Holt.

Baldwin, J. (1985b). A Talk to Teachers. In J. Baldwin. *The Price of the Ticket: Collected Nonfiction.* New York: St. Martin's Press.

Banks, J. A. (1995). Multicultural Education: Historical Development, Dimensions, and Practice. In J. A. Banks & C. A. M. Banks (Eds.), *Handbook of Research on Multicultural Education*, 3–24. New York: Macmillan.

Banks, J. A. (1996). *Multicultural Education, Transformative Knowledge, and Action: Historical and Contemporary Perspectives.* New York: Teachers College Press.

Banks, J. A. (2004). Multicultural Education: Historical Development, Dimensions, and Practice. In J. A. Banks & C. A. M. Banks (Eds.), *Handbook of Research on Multicultural Education,* 2nd ed., 3–29. San Francisco: Jossey Bass.

Banks, J. A., & McGee Banks, C. (2009). *Multicultural Education: Issues and Perspectives.* New York: Wiley.

Banks, J. A. (1993). The Canon Debate: Knowledge Construction and Multicultural Education. *Educational Researcher, 22*(5), 4–14.

Barber, B. R. (1992). *An Aristocracy of Everyone: The Politics of Education and the Future of America*. New York: Oxford.

Barone, T. (2006). Making Educational History: Qualitative Inquiry, Artistry, and the Public Interest. In G. Ladson-Billings and W. F. Tate (Eds.), *Education Research in the Public Interest: Social Justice, Action, and Policy*, 213–230. New York: Teachers College Press.

Behn, R. (1992). *The Practice of Poetry: Writing Exercises from Poets who Teach.* New York: Harper Paperbacks.

Bell, D. (2004). *Silent Covenants: Brown V. Board of Education and the Unfulfilled Hopes for Racial Reform.* New York: Oxford University Press.

Bell, L. A. (2002). Sincere Fiction: The Pedagogical Challenge of Preparing White Teachers for Multicultural Classrooms. *Equity and Excellence in Education, 35*(3), 236–244.

Berdan, K., Boulton, I., Eidman-Aadahl, E., Fleming, J., Gardner, L., Rogers, I., & Solomon, A. (2006). *Writing for a Change: Boosting Literacy and Learning through Social Action.* National Writing Project. San Francisco, CA: Jossey-Bass.

Berton, M. W., & Stabb, S. D. (1996). Exposure to Violence and Post-traumatic Stress Disorder in Urban Adolescents. *Adolescence, 31*(122), 489–98.

Bigelow, B. (1995). Discovering Columbus: Rereading the Past. In D. Levine, R. Lowe, B. Peterson, & R. Tenorio (Eds.), *Rethinking Schools: An Agenda for Change*, 61–68. New York: New Press.

Black, S. (Director/Producer), & Kincaid, J. (Writer). (2001). *Life and Debt.* New York: Tuff Gong Pictures.

Bowen, W. G., & Bok, D. (1998). *The Shape of the River: Long-Term Consequences of Considering Race in College and University Admissions.* Princeton, NJ: Princeton University Press.

Brant, B. (1994). *Writing as Witness: Essay and Talk.* Toronto: Women's Press.

Brener, N. D., Weist, M., Adelman, H., Taylor, L., & Vernon-Smiley, M. (2007). Mental Health and Social Services: Results From the School Health Policies and Programs Study. *Journal of School Health, 77*(8), 486–499.

Brewer, D. D. (1992). Hip Hop Writers' Evaluations of Strategies to Control Illegal Graffiti. *Human Organization, 51*, 188–196.

Brock, R. (2005). *Sista Talk: The Personal and the Pedagogical.* New York: Peter Lang.

Brown, T. (2010). ARISE to the Challenge: Partnering with Urban Youth to Improve Educational Research and Learning. *Perspectives on Urban Education*, Summer.

Bureau of Justice Statistics. (2007). Black Victims of Violent Crimes. Available online at: <bjs.ojp.usdoj.gov/content/pub/pdf/bvvc.pdf>.

Cammarota, J., & Fine, M. (2008). *Revolutionizing Education: Youth Participatory Action Research in Motion.* New York: Routledge.

Campbell, M. S. (1994). Harlem Renaissance: Art of Black America. New York: Abrams.

Carr, F. (1997) *Wicked Words: Poisoned Minds—Racism in the Dictionary*. Lakewood, CA: Scholar Technological.

Centers for Disease Control and Prevention. (2010). U.S. Cancer Statistics Working Group. *United States Cancer Statistics: 1999–2007 Incidence and Mortality Web-based Report*. Atlanta, GA: Department of Health and Human Services, Centers for Disease Control and Prevention, and National Cancer Institute; 2010. Available at: http://www.cdc.gov/uscs.

Children's Defense Fund (2006). *State of America's Children 2006*. Washington DC: Children's Defense Fund.

Chin, M., Garcia, T., Hunter, C., Araiza, O. E., & Kim, S. (2004). *We Interrupt this Crisis—with Our Side of the Story: Relationships Between South Los Angeles Parents and Schools*. Los Angeles: Community Asset Development Re-Defining Education (CADRE).

Chrystos (1995). They Are Always Telling Me I'm Too Angry. In *Fugitive Colors*. Cleveland, OH: Cleveland State University Poetry Center.

Clark, K. B., & Clark, M. (1947). Racial Identification and Preference in Negro Children. In T. M. Newcomb & E. L. Hartley (Eds.), *Readings in Social Psychology*, 169–178. New York: Holt.

Clark, W. A. V. (1987). School Desegregation and White Flight: A Reexamination and Case Study. *Social Science Research, 16*(3), 211–228.

Coker, N. (2004). *A Study of the Music and Social Criticism of African Musician Fela Anikulapo-Kuti*. New York: Edwin Mellon Press.

Conchas, G. Q. (2006). *The Color of Success: Race and High Achieving Urban Youth*, New York: Teachers College Press.

Darling-Hammond, L., Rustique-Forrester, E., & Pecheone, R. L. (2005). *Multiple Measures Approaches to High School Graduation*. Stanford, CA: Stanford University School Re-design Network.

Davis, A. S., McIntosh, D. E., Phelps, L., & Kehle, T. J. (2004). Addressing the Shortage of School Psychologists: A Summative Overview. *Psychology in the Schools, 41*, 489–495.

Davis, D. B. (1966). *The Problem of Slavery in Western Culture*. Ithaca, NY: Cornell University Press.

Davis, K. (2007). *A Girl Like Me*. Reel Works Teen Filmmaking. Available at http://mediathatmatters.org.

De Fina, A. (2007). Code Switching and the Construction of Ethnic Identity in a Community of Practice. *Language in Society, 36*, 371–392.

Delgado, M., & Staples, L. (2007). *Youth-Led Community Organizing: Theory and Action*. New York: Oxford University Press.

Delgado, R. (Ed.). (1995). *Critical Race Theory: The Cutting Edge*. Philadelphia: Temple University Press.

Delpit, L. (2006). *Other People's Children: Cultural Conflict in the Classroom*. New York: New Press.

DeMeulenaere, E. (2009). Fluid Identities: Black Students Negotiating the Transformation of Their Academic Identities and School Performances. *International Journal of Critical Pedagogy, 2*(1), 30–48.

Dewey, J. (1916). *Democracy and Education: An Introduction to the Philosophy of Education*. New York: Free Press.

Drooker, E. (2002). *Blood Song: A Silent Ballad*. New York: Harcourt.

Duncan-Andrade, J. M. R., & Morrell, E. (2008). *The Art of Critical Pedagogy: Possibilities for Moving from Theory to Practice in Urban Schools*. New York: Peter Lang.

Dunning, S., & Stafford, W. (1992). *Found and Headline Poems. Getting the Knack: 20 Poetry Writing Exercises*. Urbana, IL: NCTE.

Epstein, K. K. (2006). *A Different View of Urban Schools: Civil Rights, Critical Race Theory, and Unexplored Realities*. New York: Peter Lang.

Ethnic Studies Now. (2007). *A 2007 Student Report on the State of Ethnic Studies at Columbia University*. http://socialjustice.ccnmtl.columbia.edu/index.php/Ethnic_Studies.

Fege, A. F., & Smith, A. J. (2002). *Using NCLB to Improve Student Achievement: An Action Guide for Community and Parent Leaders*. Washington, DC: Public Education Network.

Fegley, S. G., Spencer, M. B., Gross, T. N., Harpalani, V., & Charles, N. (2008). Bodily Self-awareness: Skin Color and Psychosocial Well-being in Adolescence. In W. Overton & U. Mueller (Eds.), *Body in mind, mind in body: Developmental perspectives on embodiment and consciousness,* 281–312. Mahwah, NJ: LEA Inc.

Feiner, J., & Klein, S. (1982) Graffiti Talks. *Social Policy, 12*, 47–53.

Ferguson, A. A. (2001). *Bad Boys: Public Schools in the Making of Black Masculinity*. Ann Arbor: University of Michigan Press.

Fielding, M., & McGregor, J. (2005). Deconstructing Student Voice: New Spaces for Dialogue or New Opportunities for Surveillance? Paper Presented to the American Educational Research Association, Montreal, Canada.

Fielding, M., & Rudduck, J. (2002). The Transformative Potential of Student Voice: Confronting the Power Issues. Paper presented at the Annual Conference of the British Educational Research Association, University of Exeter, England.

Fine, M. (1991). *Framing Dropouts: Notes on the Politics of an Urban Public High School*. Albany: SUNY Press.

Fine, M., Torre, M. E., Burns, A., & Payne, Y. A. (2007). Youth Research/Participatory Methods for Reform. In D. Thiessen & A. Cook-Sather (Eds.), *International Handbook of Student Experience in Elementary and Secondary Schools,* 805–828. New York: Springer.

Fisher, M. (2008). *Black Literate Lives: Historical and Contemporary Perspectives*. New York: Routledge.

Fisher, M. T. (2007). *Writing in Rhythm: Spoken Word Poetry in Urban Classrooms*. New York: Teachers College Press.

Forbes, J. D. (2008). Ethnic or World Studies: A Historian's Path of Discovery. In T. P. Fong (Ed.), *Ethnic Studies Research: Approaches and Perspectives*, 58–91. Lanham, MD: Altamira Press.

Fordham, S., & Ogbu, J. (1986). Black Students' School Success: Coping with the Burden of "Acting White." *Urban Review, 18*, 176–206.

Freire, P. (1970). *Pedagogy of the Oppressed.* New York: Continuum.

Freire, P. (1973). *Education for Critical Consciousness.* New York: Continuum.

Freire, P. (2004). *Pedagogy of Indignation.* Boulder, CO: Paradigm Publishers.

Futrell, M. H. (2004). The Impact of the Brown Decision on African American Educators. In J. Anderson, Byrne, D. N., & T. Smiley (Eds.), *The Unfinished Agenda of Brown v. Board of Education*, 79–96. New York: Wiley.

Garland, A. F., Lau, A. S., Yeh, M., McCabe, K. M., Hough, R. L., & Landsverk, J. A. (2005). Racial and Ethnic Differences in Utilization of Mental Health Services Among High-Risk Youths. *American Journal of Psychiatry, 162*, 1336–1343,

Garrison, M. J. (2009). *A Measure of Failure: The Political Origins of Standardized Testing.* New York: SUNY Press.

Gay, G. (2000). *Culturally Responsive Teaching: Theory, Research, and Practice.* New York: Teachers College Press.

Gay, G. (2007). The Rhetoric and Reality of NCLB. *Race Ethnicity and Education, 10*(3), 279–93.

Gibson, M. A., & Ogbu, J. U. (1991). *Minority Status and Schooling: A Comparative Study of Immigrant and Involuntary Minorities.* New York: Garland.

Ginwright, S., Noguera, P., & Cammarota, J. (2006). *Beyond Resistance! Youth Activism and Community Change.* New York: Routledge.

Giroux, H. A. (2001). *Theory and Resistance in Education: A Pedagogy for the Opposition.* Westport, CT: Praeger.

Goldberg, N. (1986). *Writing Down the Bones: Freeing the Writer Within.* Boston, MA: Shambhala.

Goldstein, R. A. (2007). Who You Think I Am Is Not Necessarily Who I Think I Am: The Multiple Positionalities of Urban Student Identities. In J. L. Kincheloe & K. Hayes (Eds.), *Teaching City Kids: Understanding and Appreciating Them,* 97–107. New York: Peter Lang.

Goodell, W. (2009). *The American Slave Code in Theory and Practice: Its Distinctive Features Shown by Its Statutes.* N.P.: Bibliolife.

Gordon, B. M. (1995). Knowledge Construction: Competing Critical Theories and Education. In J.A. Banks & C. McGee Banks (Eds.), *Handbook of Research on Multicultural Education*, 184–199. New Work: Macmillan.

Greene, M. (2001). *Variations on a Blue Guitar: The Lincoln Center Institute Lectures on Aesthetic Education.* New York: Teachers College Press.

Guangxi Film Studio (Producer), & Yimou, Z. (Director/Producer). (1999). *Not One Less* [Motion picture]. China: China Film Group Corporation.

Gutmann, A. (1999). Democratic Education. Princeton, NJ: Princeton University Press;

Hauser, R. M., Simmons, S. J., & Pager, D. I. (2004). High School Dropout, Race/Ethnicity, and Social Background from the 1970s to the 1990s. In G. Orfield (Ed.), *Dropouts in America: Confronting the Graduation Rate Crisis*, 85–106. Cambridge, MA: Harvard University Press.

Henderson, A., Jacob, B., Kernan-Schloss, A., & Raimondo, B. (2004). *The Case for Parent Leadership.* Lexington, KY: Pritchard Committee for Academic Excellence.

Hill, M. L. (2009). *Beats, Rhymes, and Classroom Life: Hip Hop Pedagogy and the Politics of Identity.* New York: Teachers College Press.

Holzman, M. (2006). *Public Education and Black Male Students: The 2006 State Report Card.* Schott Educational Inequality Index, Cambridge, MA: The Schott Foundation for Public Education.

Hooks, b. (1994). *Teaching to Transgress*. New York: Routledge.

Horowitz, F. D., Darling-Hammond, L., Bransford, J., Comer, J., Rosebrock, K., Austin, K., & Rust, F. (2005). Educating Teachers for Developmentally Appropriate Practice. In L. Darling-Hammond & J. Bransford (Eds.), *Preparing Teachers for a Changing World: What Teachers Should Learn and Be Able to Do*. 88–125. San Francisco: Jossey Bass.

Howard, G. R. (1999). *We Can't Teach What We Don't Know: White Teachers, Multiracial Schools*. New York: Teachers College Press.

Howard, T. C. (2008). Who Really Cares? The Disenfranchisement of African American Males in Pre K–12 Schools: A Critical Race Theory Perspective. *Teachers College Record, 110*(5), 954–985.

Howerton D., & Thomas, C. (2004). Help for High School Students Who Still Can't Read. *English Journal, 93*(5), 77–82.

Human Rights Watch Backgrounder. (2003). Incarcerated America. Available online at: <http://www.hrw.org/legacy/backgrounder/usa/incarceration/ >.

Jacobson, J., Olsen, C., Rice, J. K., Sweetland, S., & Ralph, J. (2001). *Educational Achievement and Black-White Inequality.* Washington, DC: National Center for Educational Statistics (NCES 2001061).

Jimerson, S. R., & Kaufman, A. M. (2003). Reading, Writing, and Retention: A Primer on Grade Retention Research. *The Reading Teacher, 56* (7), 622–635.

Jocson, K. M. (2006). "The Best of Both Worlds": Youth Poetry as Social Critique and Form of Empowerment. In Ginwright, S., Noguera, P., & Cammarota, J. (Eds.), *Beyond Resistance! Youth Activism and Community Change*, 129–147. New York: Routledge.

Jones, L., & Newman, L. (1996). *Our America: Life and Death on the South Side of Chicago*. New York: Pocket Books.

Jordan, J (1989). *Naming Our Destiny: New and Selected Poems*. New York: Thunder's Mouth Press.

Jordan, J. (2000). *Soldier: A Poet's Childhood*. New York: Basic Books

Kassen, M., & Raghavan, C. (2007). Exposure to Urban Violence and Contributory Factors to Posttraumatic Stress in a Diverse College Sample. Paper presented at the annual meeting of the American Society of Criminology, Atlanta, Georgia.

Kincaid, J. (1988). *A Small Place*. New York: Farrar, Straus, and Giroux.

Knaus, C. B. (2006). *Race, Racism, and Multiraciality in American Education*. Bethesda, MD: Academica Press.

Knaus, C. B. (2007). Still Segregated, Still Unequal: Analyzing the Impact of No Child Left Behind on African American Students. In *The State of Black America: Portrait of the Black Male,* 105-121. Washington, DC: National Urban League.

Knaus, C. B. (2009). Shut Up and Listen: Applied Critical Race Theory in the Classroom. *Race, Ethnicity, and Education, 12*(2), 133–154.

Knaus, C., & Friedman, D. (2001). Affirmative Reaction: Towards Developmental Equity in Education. Paper presented to the Annual Meeting of the Association for the Study of Higher Education, Richmond, VA.

Kohn, A. (2000). *The Case Against Standardized Testing: Raising the Scores, Ruining the Schools*. Portsmouth, NH: Heinemann.

Kohn, A. (2004). *What Does It Mean to Be Well Educated? And More Essays on Standards, Grading, and Other Follies*. Boston, MA: Beacon.

Kornhaber, M. L. (2004). Assessment, Standards, Equity. In J. A. Banks & C. A. M. Banks (Eds.), *Handbook of Research on Multicultural Education*, 2nd ed., 91–109. San Francisco: Jossey Bass.

Krishnamurti, J. (1953). *Education and the Significance of Life*. Ojai, CA: Krishnamurti Foundation.

Kruse, K. M. (2005). *White Flight: Atlanta and the Making of Modern Conservatism*. Princeton, NJ: Princeton University Press.

Ladson-Billings, G. (1994). *The Dreamkeepers: Successful Teachers of African American Children*. San Francisco: Jossey-Bass.

Ladson-Billings, G. (1999). Just What is Critical Race Theory, and What's It Doing in a Nice Field Like Education? In L. Parker, D. Deyhele, S. Villenas (Eds.) *Race Is…Race Isn't: Critical Race Theory and Qualitative Studies in Education*, 7–30. Boulder, CO: Westview Press.

Larry P. and Lucille P., v. Riles, C-71-2270. 495 F. Supp. 926; 1979 U.S. Dist.

Lawrence-Lightfoot, S. (2003). *The Essential Conversation: What Parents and Teachers Can Learn from Each Other*. New York: Ballantine Books.

Loeb, S., & Reininger, M. (2004). *Public Policy and Teacher Labor Markets: What We Know and Why It Matters*. Lansing: The Education Policy Center at Michigan State University.

Loewen, J. (1996). *Lies My Teacher Told Me: Everything Your American History Textbook Got Wrong*. New York: Touchstone.

Lorde, A. (1984). The Transformation of Silence into Language and Action. In *Sister Outsider: Essays and Speeches by Audre Lorde*, 43–44. Berkeley, CA: The Crossing Press.

Lynch, M. (2006). *Closing the Racial Academic Achievement Gap*. Chicago, IL: African American Images.

Lyon, G. E. (1999). *Where I Am From: Where Poems Come From. Young Writers Series #2*. Spring, TX: Absey & Co.

Macedo, D. (2006). *Literacies of Power: What Americans Are Not Allowed to Know*. Boston, MA: Westview Press.

Macedo, D., & Bartolomé, L. I. (1999). *Dancing with Bigotry: Beyond the Politics of Tolerance*. New York: Palgrave.

Martin, T. (1983). *Literary Garveyism: Garvey, Black Arts, and the Harlem Renaissance*. Dover, MA: Majority.

Martínez, E. (1995). Distorting Latino History: The California Textbook Controversy. In D. Levine, R. Lowe, B. Peterson, & R. Tenorio (Eds.), *Rethinking Schools: An Agenda for Change*, 100–108. New York: New Press.

Matlwa, K. (2007). *Coconut*. South Africa: Jacana Media.

Mauer, M., & King, R. S. (2004). *Schools and Prisons: Fifty Years after Brown v. Board of Education*. Washington, DC: The Sentencing Project.

McCombs, B. L. (2007). Balancing Accountability Demands with Research-Validated, Learner-Centered Teaching and Learning Practices. In C. E. Sleeter (Ed.), *Facing Accountability in Education: Democracy and Equity at Risk*, 41–60. New York: Teachers College Press.

McIntyre, A. (1997). *Making Meaning of Whiteness: Exploring Racial Identity with White Teachers*. New York: SUNY Press.

McKay, C. (1930). *Harlem: Negro Metropolis*. New York: Dutton.

McKay, M. M., Lynn, C. J., & Bannon, W. M. (2005). Understanding Inner City Child Mental Health Need and Trauma Exposure: Implications for Preparing Urban Service Providers. *American Journal of Orthopsychiatry, 75*(2), 201–210.

Morgan, H. (1995). *Historical Perspectives on the Education of Black Children.* Westport, CT: Praeger.

Morrell, E. (2004). *Becoming Critical Researchers: Literacy and Empowerment for Urban Youth*. New York: Peter Lang.

Morrell, E. (2006). Youth-Initiated Research as a Tool for Advocacy and Change in Urban Schools. In Ginwright, S., Noguera, P., & Cammarota, J. (Eds.), *Beyond Resistance! Youth Activism and Community Change*, 111–128. New York: Routledge.

Morrell, E., & Rogers, J. (2006). Becoming Critical Public Historians: Students Study Diversity and Access in Post *Brown v. Board* Los Angeles. *Social Education, 70*(6), 366–369.

Mtukudzi, O. (2004). *Tozeza. Nhava*. Tuku Music/Sheer Sound: Zimbabwe.

Mtukudzi, O. (2006). *Tozeza. Wonai*. Tuku Music/Sheer Sound: Zimbabwe.

Muller, L., Bright., S., Changler, G., Esteva, A., Lewis, S., Rose, S., Smith, S., Teves, S., Villalobos, R. A., & Wilson, P. (1995). *June Jordan's Poetry for the People: A Revolutionary Blueprint*. New York: Routledge.

National Association for the Advancement of Colored People (2006). *Equity Matters: Ensuring Access to Quality Education for Minority Students*. Baltimore, MD: Author.

Nieto, S. (1996). *Affirming Diversity: The Sociopolitical Context of Multicultural Education*, 2nd Edition. White Plains, NY: Longman.

Oakes, J. (1985). *Keeping Track: How Schools Structure Inequality*. New Haven, CT: Yale University Press.

Office of Student Research and Campus Surveys. (2010). Undergraduate Statistics. Available online at: <osr2.berkeley.edu/twiki/bin/view/Main/UgStatF2010#table%205>.

Ogbu, J. U. (1991). Low School Performance as an Adaptation: The Case of Blacks in Stockton, California. In M. A. Gibson & J. U. Ogbu (Eds.), *Minority Status and Schooling: A Comparative Study of Immigrant and Involuntary Minorities,* 249–285. New York: Garland Publishing.

Orfield, G., Losen, D., Wald, J., & Swanson, C. (2004). *Losing Our Future: How Minority Youth Are Being Left Behind by the Graduation Rate Crisis.* Cambridge, MA: The Civil Rights Project at Harvard University. Contributors: Urban Institute, Advocates for Children of New York and The Civil Society Institute.

Perry, T., & Delpit, L. (1998). *The Real Ebonics Debate: Power, Language, and the Education of African-American Children*. Boston, MA: Beacon Press.

Pierce, C. (1974). Psychiatric Problems of the Black Minority. In S. Arieti (Ed.), *American Handbook of Psychiatry,* 512–523. New York: Basic Books.

Pihama, L. (1985). Are Films Dangerous? A Maori Woman's Perspective on The Piano. *Hecate, 20*(2), 239–242.

Popham, W. J. (2001). *The Truth about Testing: An Educator's Call to Action*. Alexandria, VA: Association for Supervision and Curriculum Development.

Power, F. C., Higgins, A., & Kohlberg, L. (1989). *Lawrence Kohlber's Approach to Moral Education*. New York: Columbia University Press.

Price, H. B. (2008). *Mobilizing the Community to Help Students Succeed*. Alexandria, VA: Association for Supervision and Curriculum Development.

Rampey, B. D., Dion, G. S., & Donahue, P. L. (2009). *The Nation's Report Card: Long-Term Trend 2008*. Washington, DC: National Center for Educational Statistics (NCES 2009479).

Rees, J. (2003). A Crisis Over Consensus: Standardized Testing in American History and Student Learning. *Radical Pedogogy, 5*(2). Available online at http://radicalpedagogy.icaap.org/content/issue5_2/03_rees.html.

Rogers, J., Morrell, E., & Enyedy, N. (2007). Studying the Struggle: Contexts for Learning and Identity Development for Urban Youth. American Behavioral Scientist, 51(3), 419–443.

Roy, A. (2004). Speech given upon receiving the Sydney Peace Prize at the University of Sydney, November 4. Available online: www.smh.com.au/articles/2004/11/04/1099362264349.html.

Rumberger, R. W., & Thomas, S. L. (2000). The distribution of dropouts and turnover rates among urban and suburban high schools. *Sociology of Education, 73*, 39–67.

Sacks, P. (2001). Standardized Minds: *The High Price of America's Testing Culture and What We Can Do to Change It.* New York: Da Capo Press.

Santa Cruz, N. (2010). Arizona Bill Targeting Ethnic Studies Signed into Law. *Los Angeles Times*, May 12.

Sapphire (1996). *Push*. New York: Vintage.

Selden, S. (1999). *Inheriting Shame: The Story of Eugenics and Racism in America*. New York: Teachers College Press.

Shepard, L., Hammerness, K., Darling-Hammond, L., Rust, F., Snowden, J. B., Gordon, E., Guitierrez, C., & Pacheco, A. (2005). Assessment. In L. Darling-Hammond & J. Bransford (Eds.), *Preparing Teachers for a Changing World: What Teachers Should Learn and Be Able to Do*, 275–326. San Francisco: Jossey Bass.

Shields, C. M., Bishop, R., & Mazawi, A. E. (2005). *Pathologizing Practices: The Impact of Deficit Thinking on Education.* New York: Peter Lang.

Shor, I. (1992). *Culture Wars: School and Society in the Conservative Restoration*. Chicago: University of Chicago Press.

Silver, J. (Producer), Wachowski, A. (Writer/Director), & Wachowski, L. (Writer/Director). (1999). *The Matrix* [Motion picture]. Burbank, CA: Warner Bros.

Silvera, M. (1983). *Silenced.* Toronto: Sister Vision.

Singleton, G. E., & Linton, C. W. (2005). *Courageous Conversations about Race: A Field Guide for Achieving Equity in Schools*. Thousand Oaks, CA: Corwin Press.

Smith, L. T. (1999). *Decolonizing Methodologies; Research and Indigenous Peoples*. New York: Zed.

Solorzano, D., Ceja, M., & Yosso, T. (2000). Critical Race Theory, Racial Microaggressions, and Campus Racial Climate. *Journal of Negro Education, 69*(1), 60–73.

Steiner, D. (1999). Searching for Educational Coherence in a Democratic State. In S. L. Elkin & K. E. Soltan (Eds.), *Citizen Competence and Democratic Institutions*, 225–257. University Park: Pennsylvania State University Press.

Steele, C. M., & Aronson, J. (1995). Stereotype Threat and the Intellectual Test Performance of African Americans. *Journal of Personality and Social Psychology, 69*(5), 797–811.

Stillwell, R. (2010). *Public School Graduates and Dropouts from the Common Core of Data: School Year 2007–08*. National Council on Education Statistics, NCES 2010341. Washington, DC: Department of Education.

Stovall, D. (2006a). Where the Rubber Hits the Road: CRT Goes to High School. In A. Dixson & C. Rousseau (Eds.), *Critical Race Theory in Education: All God's Children Got a Song*, 233–239. New York: Routledge Press.

Stovall, D. (2006b). From Hunger Strike to High School: Youth Development, Social Justice, and School Formation. In S. Ginwright, P. Noguera, & J. Cammarota (Eds.), *Beyond Resistance! Youth Activism and Community Change*, 97–109. New York: Routledge.

Swanson, C. B. (2006). Diplomas Count: An Essential Guide to Graduation Policy and Rates. *Education Week*, June 22.

Tannenbaum, J., & Bush, V. C. (2005). *Jump Write In! Creative Writing Exercises for Diverse Communities, Grades 6–12.* San Francisco: Jossey-Bass.

Thiong'o, N. W. (1986). *Decolonising the Mind: The Politics of Language in African Literature*. Portsmouth, NH: Heinemann.

Thomas, D. (2007). Breaking Through the Sound Barrier: Difficulties of Voiced Research in Schools Uncommitted to Pupil Voice. Paper presented at the British Educational Research Association Annual Conference, Institute of Education, University of London.

Tjaden, P., & Thoennes, N. (1998). *Prevalence, Incidence and Consequences of Violence Against Women Survey*. Washington DC: National Institute of Justice & Centers for Disease Control & Prevention.

Torre, M., & Fine, M. (2006). Researching and Resisting: Democratic Policy Research by and for Youth. In S. Ginwright, P. Noguera, & J. Cammarota (Eds.), *Beyond Resistance! Youth Activism and Community Change*, 269–285. New York: Routledge.

Trafzer, C. E., & Keller, J. A. (2006). *Boarding School Blues: Revisiting American Indian Educational Experiences*. Lincoln: University of Nebraska Press.

Ture, K., & Hamilton, C. V. (1967). *Black Power: The Politics of Liberation*. New York: Random House.

Valdes, G. (1996). *Con Respeto: Bridging the Distances Between Culturally Diverse Families and Schools*. New York: Teachers College Press.

Valenzuela, A. (1999). *Subtractive Schooling: U.S.-Mexican Youth and the Politics of Caring*, New York: SUNY Press.

Walker, V. S. (1996). *Their Highest Potential: An African American School Community in the Segregated South*. Chapel Hill: University of North Carolina Press.

Watkins, W. H. (2001). *The White Architects of Black Education: Ideology and Power in America, 1865–1954*. New York: Teachers College Press.

Webber, T. (1978). *Deep Like the Rivers: Education in the Slave Quarter Community, 1831–1865*. WW Norton.

Weis, L., & Fine, M. (2005). *Beyond Silenced Voices: Class, Race, and Gender in United States Schools*. New York: University of New York Press.

Western, B., & Pettit, B. (2005). Black-White Wage Inequality, Employment Rates, and Incarceration. *American Journal of Sociology, 111*(2), 553–578.

Wheeler, R., & Swords, R. (2006). Code-Switching: Teaching Standard English in Urban Classrooms. National Council of Teachers of English.

Williams, H. A. (2005). *Self-Taught: African American Education in Slavery and Freedom*. Chapel Hill, NC: University of North Carolina Press.

Woodson, C. G. (1933). *The Mis-education of the Negro*. Trenton: NJ: First Africa World Press.

Woodson, C. G. (2004). *The Education of the Negro Prior to 1861: A History of the Education of the Colored People of the United States from the Beginning of Slavery to the Civil War*. Whitefish, MT: Kessinger Publishing.

Wright, R. (1957). *White Man Listen*. New York: HarperCollins.

Wyngaard, M. V. (2007). Culturally Responsive Pedagogies: African American High School Students' Perspectives. In J. L. Kincheloe & K. Hayes (Eds.), *Teaching City Kids: Understanding and Appreciating Them*, 121–129. New York: Peter Lang.

Yosso, T. (2005). *Critical Race Counterstories Along the Chicana/Chicano Educational Pipeline*. New York: Routledge.

INDEX

X

Y

ROCHELLE BROCK &
RICHARD GREGGORY JOHNSON III,
Executive Editors

Black Studies and Critical Thinking is an interdisciplinary series which examines the intellectual traditions of and cultural contributions made by people of African descent throughout the world. Whether it is in literature, art, music, science, or academics, these contributions are vast and far-reaching. As we work to stretch the boundaries of knowledge and understanding of issues critical to the Black experience, this series offers a unique opportunity to study the social, economic, and political forces that have shaped the historic experience of Black America, and that continue to determine our future. Black Studies and Critical Thinking is positioned at the forefront of research on the Black experience, and is the source for dynamic, innovative, and creative exploration of the most vital issues facing African Americans. The series invites contributions from all disciplines but is specially suited for cultural studies, anthropology, history, sociology, literature, art, and music.

Subjects of interest include (but are not limited to):

- EDUCATION
- SOCIOLOGY
- HISTORY
- MEDIA/COMMUNICATION
- RELIGION/THEOLOGY
- WOMEN'S STUDIES
- POLICY STUDIES
- ADVERTISING
- AFRICAN AMERICAN STUDIES
- POLITICAL SCIENCE
- LGBT STUDIES

For additional information about this series or for the submission of manuscripts, please contact Dr. Brock (Indiana University Northwest) at brock2@iun.edu or Dr. Johnson (University of Vermont) at richard.johnson-III@uvm.edu.

To order other books in this series, please contact our Customer Service Department:

(800) 770-LANG (within the U.S.)
(212) 647-7706 (outside the U.S.)
(212) 647-7707 FAX

Or browse online by series at www.peterlang.com.